PRESENTED BY THE JUNIOR LEAGUE OF ATLANTA, INC.

PUBLISHED BY
THE JUNIOR LEAGUE OF ATLANTA, INC.

PHOTOGRAPHY
Steve Pelosi

FOOD STYLING
Terry Colby, Andrea Frank

PROP STYLING
Beverly Beard

ART DIRECTION & DESIGN
Melia Design Group

TYPOGRAPHY & COMPOSITION
Barbara Teeslink

BOOK MARKETING & CONSULTING
Faith Brunson

This book is dedicated to the people of Atlanta.

There is no truer grit than yours.

Title page: Rack of Lamb with Georgia Pecan Crust, page 183;
Green Beans with Peppers and Leeks, page 78; Creamy Polenta
with Mint and Chervil, page 128; Winfield's Fruit Tart, page 243.

First Edition
First Printing, June 1995
50,000

Copyright ©1995 The Junior League of Atlanta, Inc.
3154 Northside Parkway, NW
Atlanta, Georgia 30327

Library of Congress Number: 95-60310
ISBN: 0-87197-425-8

Manufactured in the United States of America by
Favorite Recipes® Press
2451 Atrium Way
Nashville, Tennessee 37214

Photographs copyright © 1995 by Steve Pelosi
Book design by Melia Design Group
Dust Jacket, Introduction and Junior League articles
written by Dianna Edwards Thorington
True Grits logo illustration by Kent Barton
Typography and composition by Barbara Teeslink

All proceeds from the sale of
True Grits: Tall Tales and Recipes from the New South
will benefit the community and the charitable activities of
The Junior League of Atlanta, Inc.

INTRODUCTION

True Grits: Tall Tales and Recipes from the New South is a celebration of contemporary Atlanta and her people. Through their diversity and humanity and dogged determination, we see the true Atlanta. A small town dressed up in skyscrapers. An international city where the common currency is a smile. A place where you don't have to speak the language to understand the meaning of "Southern Hospitality."

Thus True Grits: Tall Tales and Recipes from the New South seemed an appropriate metaphor/title for a cookbook that was determined to be more than a cookbook. Part love-letter; part testimony; as much a feast for the heart as for the senses, True Grits is New Southern to its core.

Which means it contains some of the best efforts—literary, culinary, and artistic—of the many different people and cultures who have shown the great good sense to call this melting pot of a city home.

The Junior League of Atlanta is proud to bring you True Grits: Tall Tales and Recipes from the New South. Proceeds from its sale will be reinvested in the community.

BY DIANNA EDWARDS THORINGTON

CONTENTS

The Junior League of Atlanta, Inc. is an organization of women committed to promoting voluntarism and to improving the community through the effective action and leadership of trained volunteers. Its purpose is exclusively educational and charitable.

TRUE GRITS

EXECUTIVE COMMITTEE

EDITOR
Melissa Davis Hinchman

CO-EDITOR
Beth Bishop Touzet

CREATIVE/PRODUCTION MANAGER
Theresa Maiuri Dean

RECIPE DEVELOPMENT
Ansley Merritt Conner
Kirsten Smith Berney
Allan McAdams Thrasher

TESTING COORDINATOR
Carey Mills Poole

EDITORIAL COORDINATOR
Laurie McBrayer Coleman

Chicken Wings

By Carmen Deedy
Illustration by 'Lindy Burnett

In 1963, during our last months in Cuba, it became increasingly difficult to obtain food. Milk and bread were tightly rationed; meat was a luxury rarely procured. *La bolsa negra*, the black market, however, flourished. It was through a murky character with Machiavellian connections that my father secured for us...a chicken.

It was delivered to our home like a neonate: born from my father's coat, wrapped in newspaper and dripping blood. Our mother called on her finest

▶

culinary wizardry, as well as every household saint she could remember, to aid her in the preparations. My sister and I feasted on the unfamiliar aromas escaping the kitchen and filling every room.

When the young fowl was finally drawn from the oven we heard our mother cry out in dismay, "Ay, no!" We all gathered around the stove: Lilliputian to begin with, this poor underfed revolutionary bird was now no larger than a quail.

My sister and I couldn't hide our disappointment anymore than our hunger and we were surprised when, as my mother began to carve the tiny bird, Papi, our father, insisted on the chicken wings.

"Everybody know it is the tastiest part of the chicken, I hope you don't mind," he added in his gentle, apologetic manner. I didn't mind at all. At three years of age I was as frail and thin as that poor chicken myself. The swinging of my skinny legs from the dining room chair best expressed my delight as Mami placed both a drumstick and thigh on my plate.

We remembered that splendid meal for months to come and when we

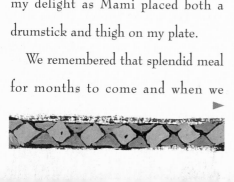

A SOUTHERN SOIREE

Southern Pickled Shrimp, page 31

———

Country Ham and Shrimp on Toast, page 22

———

Sweet & Spicy Pecans, page 18

———

Peachy Lime Guacamole with Blue Corn Chips, page 21

———

Warmed Cranberry Brie with Granny Smith Apples, page 17

———

Assorted Sparkling Waters and Champagne

APPETIZERS

received our visas and emigrated to Decatur, Georgia, our first dinner was an American chicken. No scrawny bird this, it filled the center of our modest kitchen table. As my mother began to carve a generous portion of the breast for my father I cried, "No, Mami! Papi likes the chicken wings—remember Papi, it is the best part of the chicken!"

My mother and father exchanged a glance I couldn't fathom and without missing a beat my mother said, "That is the Cuban chicken, honey. Unfortunately the American chicken, she is not so lucky to have such delicious wings."

She must have been telling the truth because in the thirty years that he has spent in exile in this country I have never seen my father touch a chicken wing. ■

Black Bean Cakes

JERRY NAGLER, VICKERY'S CRESCENT AVENUE BAR & GRILL

INGREDIENTS

[
SERVES 8
PREPARATION TIME:
2 3/4 HOURS, PLUS
CHILLING TIME
]

2 cups dried black beans
2 tablespoons white pepper
2 tablespoons chopped garlic
2 cups Mojo criollo (see Note)
2 tablespoons salt
6 cups water
1 large green bell pepper, chopped
1 large red bell pepper, chopped
1 medium red onion, chopped
2 tablespoons ground cumin
2 tablespoons chili powder
1 tablespoon salt
2 cups plain bread crumbs
Clarified butter for sautéing
8 ounces spinach, rinsed, trimmed
3 thin slices red onion
2 tablespoons balsamic vinegar

DIRECTIONS

• Sort and rinse the black beans. Combine the black beans, white pepper, garlic, Mojo criollo, 2 tablespoons salt and water in a medium saucepan. Bring to a boil; reduce heat. Simmer for 2 hours or until the black beans are tender, adding additional water as needed. Drain the black beans, reserving 1 cup liquid.

• Combine the black beans, green pepper, red pepper, chopped onion, cumin, chili powder, 1 tablespoon salt, bread crumbs and reserved liquid in a large bowl; mix just until moist but firm.

• Shape the bean mixture into a log 2 to 3 inches in diameter on a large sheet of waxed paper. Wrap the log in waxed paper and twist the ends to seal. Chill until firm.

• Cut the log into 1/2-inch slices. Cook the cakes in a small amount of clarified butter in a skillet for 1 1/2 minutes or until crisp on each side. Set the cakes aside.

- Add the spinach, onion slices and balsamic vinegar to the skillet. Cook until the spinach is wilted and soft. Arrange on a serving platter. Top with the black bean cakes. Garnish with sour cream, salsa and lime wedges.
- *Note: Mojo criollo is a Spanish marinating sauce found in the ethnic section of most major grocery stores.*

White Bean Dip

INGREDIENTS

SERVES 32
PREPARATION TIME:
30 MINUTES, PLUS
CHILLING TIME

1 large clove of garlic
1 medium jalapeño, seeded
2 (15-ounce) cans cannellini beans, drained
3/4 cup plain low-fat yogurt
4 teaspoons fresh lime juice
3/4 teaspoon ground cumin
1/4 teaspoon salt
1/8 teaspoon cayenne
1 medium tomato, seeded, chopped
2 teaspoons fresh parsley

DIRECTIONS

- Process the garlic and jalapeño in a food processor until finely chopped. Rinse the beans and drain. Add the beans to the food processor. Process until a paste forms. Scrape down side of the processor bowl. Add the yogurt, lime juice, cumin, salt and cayenne. Process until smooth. Spoon into a bowl.
- Reserve a small amount of the tomato and parsley. Stir the remaining tomato and parsley into processed bean mixture.
- Chill, covered, in the refrigerator.
- Heat in a double boiler over hot water at serving time. Spoon into a serving bowl. Sprinkle with the reserved tomato and parsley. Serve with corn chips.

Clarified Butter

Clarifying butter refers to removing the milk solids which cause overbrowning. Melt butter over low heat and skim off any foam. Let stand until the solids settle to the bottom and gently strain off the clear portion.

Blue Corn Blini with Salmon

FOR THE BLINI SAUCE

[
SERVES 4
PREPARATION TIME:
1 HOUR, PLUS
CHILLING TIME
]

3/4 cup sour cream or light sour cream
1/4 cup crumbled mild goat cheese
Juice of 1/2 lime
1 jalapeño, roasted, peeled, seeded, minced
1/4 teaspoon white pepper

FOR THE BLINI BATTER

6 tablespoons milk
1 tablespoon dry yeast
2 teaspoons sugar
1/4 cup flour
1/4 cup blue cornmeal
1 egg yolk
2 tablespoons unsalted butter or margarine, softened
2 egg whites
1/4 teaspoon cream of tartar
1/4 cup unsalted butter or margarine

FOR THE BLINI FILLING AND ASSEMBLY

1/4 cup finely chopped roasted red bell pepper
1/4 cup finely chopped roasted yellow bell pepper
1/4 cup chopped onion
2 tablespoons chopped cilantro
8 ounces smoked salmon, in 4 thin slices

TO PREPARE THE BLINI SAUCE

- Combine the sour cream, goat cheese, lime juice, jalapeño and white pepper in a small bowl; mix well. Chill for up to 24 hours.

TO PREPARE THE BLINI

- Heat the milk in a saucepan just to a simmer.
- Combine the milk with the yeast and sugar in a medium bowl; mix well. Let stand for 10 to 15 minutes. Whisk in the flour and blue cornmeal.
- Mix the egg yolk and 2 tablespoons butter in a mixer bowl until light and fluffy. Add the yeast mixture; beat for 10 minutes or until the batter no longer clings to the beaters.
- Beat the egg whites in a mixer bowl until foamy. Add the cream of tartar; beat at high speed until stiff peaks form. Fold gently into the batter.
- Melt 1 tablespoon of the remaining butter at a time in a 6-inch skillet over medium-high heat; heat until the foam begins to subside. Add the batter ¼ at a time. Bake for 2 minutes on each side.
- Remove to a warm plate with a spatula; keep warm in a 150-degree oven while making the remaining blini.

TO ASSEMBLE THE BLINI

- Sprinkle the blini with the roasted red and yellow peppers, onion and cilantro; roll to enclose the filling.
- Form each salmon slice into a rose-shaped cup; place 1 in the center of each blini. Spoon the blini sauce over the salmon. Serve immediately.
- *Variation: Substitute yellow cornmeal for the blue cornmeal.*
- *Note: The blini batter can be made a few hours in advance, but should be filled just prior to serving.*

ASIAN CHICKEN FINGERS

FOR THE CHICKEN FINGERS

SERVES 6
PREPARATION TIME:
45 MINUTES, PLUS
MARINATING TIME

2 large whole chicken breasts, boned, skinned
3 tablespoons chopped fresh cilantro
2 tablespoons minced garlic
2 tablespoons fish sauce (see note)
2 tablespoons sugar
1 teaspoon five-spice powder
$1/8$ teaspoon ground white pepper
$2/3$ cup water
2 tablespoons light soy sauce
2 teaspoons dark soy sauce

FOR THE PLUM SAUCE

1 (16-ounce) can purple plums (about 9 plums), drained, seeded
$1/2$ cup drained canned apricots
3 tablespoons white vinegar
$1/8$ teaspoon salt
$1/8$ teaspoon sugar
Cayenne to taste

TO PREPARE THE CHICKEN FINGERS

- Rinse the chicken and pat dry.
- Cut each chicken breast into 6 to 8 strips. Place between 2 sheets of waxed paper; pound with a meat mallet until thin. Place in a glass baking dish.
- Combine the cilantro and garlic in a bowl; mix well. Add the fish sauce, stirring to make a smooth paste. Add the sugar, five-spice powder, white pepper and water; mix well. Add the light soy sauce and dark soy sauce; mix well. Pour the marinade over the chicken, coating well. Marinate, covered, in the refrigerator for 2 hours or longer.
- Place the chicken on a baking sheet. Broil for 5 minutes on each side or until the chicken is tender. Do not overcook. Let stand until cool.

- Combine the plums, apricots, vinegar, salt, sugar and cayenne in a blender container. Process until smooth.

- Serve the chicken fingers at room temperature with plum sauce for dipping.
- *Note: The fish sauce, also called nam pla, can be found in the Oriental section of the grocery store.*

WARMED CRANBERRY BRIE

INGREDIENTS

1/3 cup crushed cranberry sauce
2 tablespoons brown sugar
1/4 teaspoon rum extract
1/8 teaspoon ground nutmeg
1 (8-ounce) round Brie cheese
2 tablespoons chopped pecans

[
SERVES 4
PREPARATION TIME:
15 MINUTES
]

DIRECTIONS

- Combine the cranberry sauce, brown sugar, rum extract and nutmeg in a bowl; mix well.
- Peel off the top of the Brie cheese round, leaving 1/4 inch rim.
- Top the Brie cheese with the cranberry mixture. Sprinkle with the chopped pecans.
- Bake at 500 degrees for 4 to 5 minutes.
- Serve with crackers or sliced green apples.
- *Variation: Substitute orange extract for the rum extract.*

Holiday Cheer

Serve Holiday Cheer at your next holiday open house or winter party. Combine 2 quarts hot apple cider with 1/4 cup maple syrup and 1/4 cup sugar. Stir in 1 cup lemon juice and 1 quart golden rum. Float apples studded with cloves in the punch bowl. Garnish with cinnamon sticks.

BRIE TART

INGREDIENTS

1 (8-inch) unbaked pie shell
1 pound chilled Brie cheese with rind
6 egg yolks
$^1/_4$ teaspoon ginger
1 teaspoon brown sugar
$^1/_8$ teaspoon saffron
$^1/_4$ teaspoon salt
1 teaspoon sugar
$^1/_2$ teaspoon cinnamon

[
SERVES 8
PREPARATION TIME:
1 HOUR
]

DIRECTIONS

- Bake the pie shell at 425 degrees for 10 minutes. Let stand until cool. Reduce the oven temperature to 375 degrees.
- Remove the rind from the chilled Brie cheese. Cut the rind into small pieces with a moistened knife; set aside.
- Beat the softened Brie cheese, egg yolks, ginger, brown sugar, saffron and salt in a mixer bowl until smooth. Spoon into the baked pie shell. Sprinkle the cheese rind pieces over the top. Sprinkle a mixture of sugar and cinnamon around the edge of the pie shell.
- Bake for 30 minutes or until set and golden brown.
- Serve warm or cool with crackers.
- *Variation: Substitute 12 individual baked 1-inch tart shells for the pie shell and bake the filled tart shells for 10 to 12 minutes. Omit the saffron.*

Sweet and Spicy Pecans

Sweet and Spicy Pecans are delicious and easy to prepare. Toss 2 cups Georgia pecan halves with 2 tablespoons melted butter or margarine. Sprinkle with mixture of 1 tablespoon sugar, $^1/_2$ teaspoon ground cumin, $^1/_2$ teaspoon chili powder, $^1/_4$ teaspoon ground red pepper and $^1/_8$ teaspoon garlic salt, tossing to coat. Spread pecans on a baking sheet. Bake at 325 degrees for 15 minutes, stirring occasionally.

REFRESHING ENDIVE APPETIZER

THE COMBINATION OF ENDIVE AND LEMON IN THE APPETIZER IS VERY
REFRESHING ON A HOT DAY; IT IS ALSO A GOOD PALATE CLEANSER.

INGREDIENTS

[SERVES 10
PREPARATION TIME:
15 TO 20 MINUTES]

5 tablespoons sour cream, light sour cream
   or nonfat sour cream
8 ounces cream cheese, Neufchâtel cheese
   or nonfat cream cheese
Juice of 1 lemon
Grated rind of 2 lemons
2 or 3 heads endive
Paprika to taste
Fresh parsley sprigs
1 lemon, sliced

DIRECTIONS

- Combine the sour cream and cream cheese in a bowl; mix until
  smooth. Add the lemon juice and lemon rind; mix well.
- Trim the bottoms from the heads of endive, discarding the outer leaves.
  Fan out the leaves on a serving platter.
- Spoon the cream cheese mixture onto the endive leaves. Sprinkle with
  the paprika.
- Arrange the parsley and lemon slices on the platter.

SAVORY FETA CHEESECAKE

FOR THE CRUST

1 cup fine toasted bread crumbs
1 cup finely ground pecans
1 1/2 cups melted butter or margarine

[
SERVES 18
PREPARATION TIME:
1 1/2 HOURS
]

FOR THE FILLING AND THE ASSEMBLY

32 ounces cream cheese, softened
16 ounces feta cheese, crumbled
4 ounces goat cheese, crumbled
4 eggs
1/2 cup milk
1/4 teaspoon hot pepper sauce
1 cup marinara sauce

TO PREPARE THE CRUST

• Combine the bread crumbs, pecans and butter in a bowl; mix well. Sprinkle the mixture into the bottom of a 9-inch springform pan. Set aside.

TO PREPARE THE FILLING

• Beat the cream cheese in a mixer bowl until light and fluffy. Add the feta cheese, goat cheese and eggs; beat well. Stir in the milk and hot pepper sauce. Spoon into the prepared springform pan. Place in a larger pan containing 2 inches boiling water.
• Bake at 350 degrees for 20 minutes. Reduce the oven temperature to 300 degrees. Bake for 1 hour longer. Cool to room temperature.

TO ASSEMBLE THE CHEESECAKE

• Remove the side of the pan. Top the cheesecake with marinara sauce. Serve with pita chips or crackers.

Helpful Hint
———
Cover the outside of a springform pan with aluminum foil before baking in a boiling water bath.

PEACHY LIME GUACAMOLE

INGREDIENTS

1 medium Georgia peach
5 medium ripe avocados
1 cup chopped fresh cilantro
Salt and black pepper to taste
Garlic salt to taste
Red pepper powder to taste
Juice of 1 lime

[
SERVES 6
PREPARATION TIME:
30 MINUTES,
PLUS 1 HOUR
CHILLING TIME
]

DIRECTIONS

• Peel the peach and slice into halves, removing the pit. Chop into very small pieces. Peel the avocados and cut into halves, removing the pits. Place the avocado halves cut side down and slice thinly; rotate and slice into small pieces.
• Combine the chopped peach, chopped avocados, cilantro and seasonings in a large glass bowl. Add the lime juice gradually, tossing gently.
• Chill for 1 hour or longer. Toss before serving.
• Serve with blue corn tortilla chips or your favorite chips.

Helpful Hint

The ripening of an avocado can be hurried by placing the avocado in a paper bag. When the fruit is softened, it can be refrigerated for up to ten days.

COUNTRY HAM AND SHRIMP ON TOAST

INGREDIENTS

[
SERVES 8
PREPARATION TIME:
1 1/4 HOURS
]

1/2 cup butter or margarine
12 ounces chopped cooked country ham
3 cloves of garlic, finely chopped
1 leek bulb, finely chopped
1/2 cup brandy
2 cups whipping cream
1/4 teaspoon cayenne
1 teaspoon chopped fresh sage
1 1/2 pounds fresh small shrimp, peeled, deveined
3 tablespoons chopped fresh Italian parsley
8 slices bread, trimmed, cut into points, toasted

DIRECTIONS

- Melt the butter in a large heavy skillet over high heat. Add the country ham. Sauté quickly. Add the garlic and leek.
- Sauté until the leek begins to wilt; remove from heat. Stir in the brandy. Return to heat. Stir in the whipping cream, cayenne and sage.
- Cook until thickened, stirring constantly. Add the shrimp. Simmer for 2 minutes or until the shrimp turn light pink. Stir in the parsley.
- Serve on the toast points.

ITALIAN TORTE

INGREDIENTS

SERVES 15

PREPARATION TIME:

30 MINUTES, PLUS

CHILLING TIME

16 ounces cream cheese or Neufchâtel cheese,
  softened
8 ounces mild goat cheese
2 cloves of garlic, minced
4 teaspoons minced fresh oregano
1/8 teaspoon ground pepper
1/2 cup chopped, drained, oil-pack sun-dried tomatoes
1/2 cup chopped, drained, marinated artichoke hearts
1/2 cup finely chopped hearts of palm
3/4 cup pesto
1 whole sun-dried tomato
2 tablespoons toasted slivered almonds
Several sprigs of fresh oregano
Several sprigs of fresh parsley

DIRECTIONS

- Line a soufflé dish with plastic wrap.
- Beat the cream cheese, goat cheese, garlic, minced oregano and
  pepper in a mixer bowl until smooth. Combine the chopped sun-dried
  tomatoes, artichoke hearts and hearts of palm in a bowl; mix well.
- Spread 1/3 of the cheese mixture evenly in the prepared dish.
- Spread the pesto evenly over the cheese mixture. Layer half the
  remaining cheese mixture, sun-dried tomato mixture and remaining
  cheese mixture over layers.
- Chill, wrapped in plastic wrap, for several hours.
- Uncover the torte. Invert the torte onto a serving dish. Slice and fan
  the whole sun-dried tomato. Arrange on top of the torte.
- Cover sides of the torte with toasted almonds. Arrange sprigs of
  oregano and parsley around the edge.
- Serve with melba toast, pita toasts, crackers or fruit.
- *Variation: Substitute 1 teaspoon dried oregano for the fresh minced oregano.*

Mushroom and Ricotta Cheese Pate

INGREDIENTS

1 pound mushrooms
1/4 cup chopped celery
1 cup toasted pecans
1/2 cup ricotta cheese
1/2 cup grated Parmesan cheese
1/2 cup minced fresh parsley
1/4 cup unsalted butter or margarine
1/2 cup minced shallots
1 cup freshly toasted bread crumbs
2 tablespoons chopped fresh basil
3 sprigs of fresh oregano
1 teaspoon salt
Cayenne to taste

[
SERVES 10
PREPARATION TIME:
2 HOURS
]

DIRECTIONS

- Butter an 8-cup loaf pan and line with waxed paper or parchment paper.
- Process the mushrooms, celery, pecans, ricotta cheese, Parmesan cheese and parsley in a food processor until a coarse mixture forms.
- Melt the butter in a skillet over medium heat. Add the shallots.
- Sauté the shallots until pale. Add the mushroom mixture, bread crumbs, basil, oregano, salt and cayenne; mix well. Pack the mixture into the prepared pan. Cover with additional buttered waxed paper.
- Bake at 400 degrees for 1 to 1 1/2 hours or until tester comes out clean. Let stand until cool. Invert onto a serving platter.
- Note: Pâté is best served cool, but not cold.

STUFFED MUSHROOMS TARRAGON

INGREDIENTS

[
SERVES 6
PREPARATION TIME:
45 MINUTES
]

1 pound large mushrooms
2 tablespoons olive oil
1/2 cup bread crumbs
2 tablespoons grated onion
1/2 teaspoon dried tarragon
1/2 teaspoon pepper
1/2 cup shredded Swiss cheese
2 tablespoons (about) milk
2 tablespoons grated Parmesan cheese

DIRECTIONS

• Clean the mushrooms. Remove the stems from the mushroom caps; chop the stems and set aside.
• Rub the mushroom caps lightly with the olive oil.
• Combine the chopped mushroom stems, bread crumbs, onion, tarragon and pepper in a medium bowl; toss well. Add the Swiss cheese; toss gently. Stir in just enough milk to moisten.
• Stuff the mushroom caps with the mixture. Sprinkle with the Parmesan cheese. Arrange on a baking sheet.
• Bake at 375 degrees for 15 minutes.
• *Variation:* Substitute cream or stock for the milk.
• *Note:* The bread crumb mixture may be prepared in advance. Stuff the mushroom caps when ready to bake.

Rillettes of Fresh and Smoked Salmon
Brasserie LeCoze Restaurant

Prepare Rillettes of Fresh and Smoked Salmon like those from the Brasserie LeCoze Restaurant for your next dinner party. Bring 2 cups white wine and 1 tablespoon minced shallot to a boil. Add 6 ounces fresh salmon. Cook until the salmon is partially cooked through. Remove the salmon to a platter, reserving the cooking liquid; flake the salmon. Combine 4 ounces finely chopped or ground smoked salmon with 3 ounces homemade mayonnaise (page 147, made with half olive oil and half vegetable oil) and the flaked salmon. Stir in 1 teaspoon minced chives and grated rind of 1/4 lemon. Add enough reserved cooking liquid until of the desired consistency. Stir in salt, pepper and juice of 1/4 lemon. Chill in the refrigerator. Serve with sliced French bread.

NEAPOLITAN TERRINE

FOR THE BASIL TOMATO SAUCE

[
SERVES 16
PREPARATION TIME:
45 MINUTES,
PLUS 11 HOURS
CHILLING TIME
]

1 (15-ounce) can cut peeled tomatoes
2 tablespoons olive oil
3/4 cup chopped onion
1 tablespoon minced garlic
2 bay leaves
1/2 teaspoon sugar
1 tablespoon chopped fresh basil
1 (7-ounce) jar chopped, drained, oil-pack sun-dried tomatoes

FOR THE CHEESE LAYER AND ASSEMBLY

8 ounces cream cheese or Neufchâtel cheese, softened
2 tablespoons margarine, softened
1 tablespoon chopped fresh basil
1 tablespoon minced garlic
1 tablespoon olive oil
1/2 cup grated Parmesan cheese
9 to 10 slices mozzarella cheese

TO PREPARE THE BASIL TOMATO SAUCE

- Drain the tomatoes, reserving 1/4 cup juice. Heat the olive oil in a large skillet over medium heat. Add the onion and garlic.
- Sauté until translucent. Stir in the tomatoes, reserved juice, bay leaves, sugar and basil.
- Bring to a boil; reduce heat. Simmer for 6 to 10 minutes or until thickened, stirring occasionally. Remove from heat. Remove the bay leaves. Stir in the sun-dried tomatoes. Spoon into a covered container.
- Chill, covered, for 3 hours or until ready to use.

TO PREPARE THE CHEESE LAYER

- Beat the cream cheese and margarine at medium speed in a mixer bowl until creamy. Add the basil, garlic, olive oil and Parmesan cheese; beat until smooth. Set aside.

- Line a 3- to 4-cup bowl with plastic wrap, leaving a 6- to 7-inch overhang on all sides.
- Cut 5 to 6 slices of the mozzarella cheese into halves diagonally to form triangles. Arrange triangles in pinwheel fashion in the prepared bowl, making sure lower points meet in center bottom of the bowl. Spread 1/2 of the cheese mixture over cheese triangles.
- Spread 1/2 of the basil tomato sauce over layers.
- Cut 2 slices of the mozzarella cheese into halves to form rectangles. Cover sauce layer with rectangles. Layer remaining cheese mixture and remaining basil tomato sauce over rectangles.
- Cover the top of the terrine with the remaining mozzarella cheese slices.
- Fold overhanging plastic wrap over the top of the terrine; seal well. Place a weight on the top of the terrine. Chill for 8 hours or for up to 3 days. Remove the weight and unwrap the terrine. Invert the terrine on a serving platter. Serve with crackers or bread.

SUN-DRIED TOMATO SPREAD

INGREDIENTS

8 ounces cream cheese or Neufchâtel cheese, softened
1/4 cup chopped, drained, oil-pack sun-dried tomatoes
4 green onions, chopped
1/4 cup chopped pecans
Hot pepper sauce to taste
Worcestershire sauce to taste

[
SERVES 4
PREPARATION TIME:
20 MINUTES
]

DIRECTIONS

- Beat the cream cheese in a mixer bowl until smooth. Add the tomatoes, green onions, pecans and seasonings; mix well.
- Serve with sliced French baguettes or plain crackers.
- *Variation: Substitute 1/4 cup drained, diced, seeded, oil-pack roasted red pepper for the tomatoes and substitute walnuts for the pecans.*

MONTRACHET CHEESE AND SALMON QUESADILLAS

INGREDIENTS

SERVES 4

PREPARATION TIME:

45 MINUTES

4 ounces Montrachet cheese
1 tablespoon drained prepared horseradish
2 tablespoons nonfat sour cream
2 tablespoons chopped fresh dill
Salt and pepper to taste
4 (8-inch) flour tortillas
4 ounces thinly sliced smoked salmon
Chopped fresh dill to taste
2 teaspoons capers
Fresh dill sprigs
1 lemon, sliced into very thin wedges

DIRECTIONS

- Combine the cheese, horseradish, sour cream, 2 tablespoons dill, salt and pepper in a bowl; mix well.
- Heat a large skillet over medium-high heat. Cook 1 tortilla at a time in the preheated skillet for 1 minute on each side or until brown spots appear.
- Spread each tortilla with 1 tablespoon of the cheese mixture. Top each with 1 ounce of the salmon. Sprinkle with dill to taste and capers.
- Cut the quesadillas into wedges. Top with dill sprigs and lemon wedges.
- *Note: The cheese mixture may be prepared 24 hours in advance.*

WILD MUSHROOM QUESADILLAS

THE ATLANTA CATERING COMPANY

INGREDIENTS

[
SERVES 5
PREPARATION TIME:
40 MINUTES
]

8 ounces dried ancho chiles
1/4 cup red currant jelly
1 1/2 teaspoons chopped shallot
1/4 teaspoon chopped garlic
1 tablespoon honey
2 1/4 teaspoons white wine vinegar
1 1/2 cups sour cream
8 ounces mixed wild mushrooms, sliced
2 tablespoons olive oil
1 teaspoon chopped garlic
7 ounces goat cheese, crumbled
10 (8-inch) flour tortillas

DIRECTIONS

- Rinse the chiles. Soak the chiles in hot water until soft. Remove the stems and discard. Purée the chiles, jelly, shallot, garlic, honey and vinegar in a food processor or blender. Add the sour cream; process well. Set aside.
- Sauté the mushrooms in the olive oil in a skillet for 5 minutes. Add the garlic. Sauté for 2 minutes longer. Remove from heat. Stir in the goat cheese.
- Spread 2 heaping tablespoonfuls of the mushroom mixture on 1 flour tortilla. Top with another tortilla. Grill the quesadilla on a flat griddle on both sides until golden brown. Repeat with the remaining mushroom mixture and flour tortillas.
- Cut each quesadilla into 4 pieces. Serve with the ancho chile sauce.
- *Note: Ancho chile sauce may be stored in the refrigerator for up to 2 weeks.*

ULTIMATE SALSA

INGREDIENTS

SERVES 32
PREPARATION TIME:
30 MINUTES, PLUS
CHILLING TIME

2 cups chopped, peeled fresh tomatoes
2 cups chopped, seeded, peeled fresh tomatoes
4 green onions, chopped
2 teaspoons crushed garlic
1 fresh jalapeño, seeded, deveined, minced
1 Anaheim pepper, seeded, chopped
1/2 cup chopped fresh cilantro leaves
1 (4-ounce) can chopped green chiles
2 tablespoons tomato paste
1 tablespoon lemon pepper
2/3 cup coarsely chopped black olives
2 teaspoons hot pepper sauce
3 tablespoons distilled vinegar
1/4 cup extra-virgin olive oil

DIRECTIONS

- Combine the tomatoes, green onions, garlic, peppers, cilantro, green chiles, tomato paste, lemon pepper, black olives, hot pepper sauce, vinegar and olive oil in a bowl; mix well.
- Chill, covered, in the refrigerator until serving time.
- Serve with corn tortilla chips.
- *Note: May store in the refrigerator for several weeks. May also serve atop tacos or with grilled foods.*

Helpful Hint

To peel and seed tomatoes, immerse tomatoes into boiling water for about twenty seconds. Remove tomatoes with a slotted spoon and immediately plunge into ice water. Core each tomato with a paring knife. Slip remaining skin off tomato. Cut off both ends of tomato. Push seeds out of the middle sections with thumbs; remove seeds from end pieces.

SOUTHERN PICKLED SHRIMP

FOR THE MARINADE

SERVES 12
PREPARATION TIME:
15 MINUTES,
PLUS 2 HOURS
MARINATING TIME

1/4 cup fresh lemon juice
1 1/2 teaspoons salt
Hot pepper sauce to taste
1 teaspoon sugar
3/4 cup olive oil
3/4 cup red wine vinegar
3/4 cup water
2 bay leaves
2 1/2 teaspoons celery seeds

FOR THE SHRIMP MIXTURE

2 pounds deveined, peeled, cooked shrimp
2 cups sliced onions
1 (2-ounce) bottle capers

TO PREPARE THE MARINADE

- Combine the lemon juice, salt, pepper sauce, sugar, olive oil, vinegar, water, bay leaves and celery seeds in a bowl; mix well.

TO PREPARE THE SHRIMP MIXTURE

- Layer the shrimp, onions and undrained capers in a large bowl. Pour the marinade over the layers.
- Marinate, covered, in the refrigerator for 2 hours or longer. Drain; discard the bay leaves.
- Serve with wooden picks.
- *Note: May add more salt and lemon juice to marinade if needed.*

SPICY SPINACH PINWHEELS

INGREDIENTS

SERVES 48
PREPARATION TIME:
30 MINUTES, PLUS
CHILLING TIME

2 (10-ounce) packages frozen chopped
  spinach, thawed
1 cup sour cream or light sour cream
8 ounces cream cheese or Neufchâtel cheese,
  softened
1 cup mayonnaise
1 teaspoon minced fresh jalapeño
1 teaspoon minced fresh garlic
6 green onions, chopped
1/2 cup chopped black olives
1 (4-ounce) can chopped green chiles
1/4 teaspoon hot pepper sauce
1 envelope ranch salad dressing mix
1 (8-ounce) can chopped water chestnuts, drained
2 teaspoons chili powder
10 large flour tortillas

Helpful Hint
———
Toss fresh black olives in a few
tablespoons of vodka to keep
them fresh longer.

DIRECTIONS

- Squeeze the excess moisture from the spinach. Combine the spinach, sour cream, cream cheese, mayonnaise, jalapeño, garlic, green onions, olives, green chiles, hot pepper sauce, salad dressing mix, water chestnuts and chili powder in a large bowl; mix well.
- Spread the spinach mixture on each of the flour tortillas; roll to enclose filling. Wrap each tortilla tightly in waxed paper. Place in a sealable plastic food storage bag or in an airtight container.
- Chill overnight.
- Unwrap and cut the tortillas into slices before serving.

To Dance with the White Dog

EXCERPT FROM
TO DANCE WITH THE WHITE DOG
BY TERRY KAY
ILLUSTRATION BY DON MORRIS

Kate called before sundown and, minutes later, Carrie called. Both wanted to know if he would have dinner with them. He refused both offers, telling them he was not hungry, but he was, and he decided he would bake fresh biscuits and have biscuits and molasses.

It would not be hard to bake biscuits, he thought. He had sat at the kitchen table hundreds of times and watched her at the cabinet, her hands flashing over the dough, and it did not seem a hard thing to do. He knew the ingredients she used.

He stood at the cabinet and took the wood mixing bowl and scooped three cups of flour from the flour bin, and then he measured out two teaspoons of baking powder and a teaspoon of baking soda and a teaspoon of salt and he mixed it together with his hands. Then he took up a palmful of shortening from the can and dropped it into the middle of the flour mixture, but it did not seem enough and he added another palmful and he began to knead the shortening and flour mixture together, but it was greasy and stuck to his hands.

The dog watched him from the doorway leading into the middle room. "Don't think I know what I'm doing, do you?" he said to the dog. "Think I forgot about the buttermilk, don't you?" He had forgotten, and talking to the dog reminded him. He pulled across the room on his walker and took the buttermilk from the refrigerator and returned to the cabinet and began to pour the buttermilk over the wad of dough. "Ought to be enough," he judged aloud. "Can't

▶

CASUAL AUTUMN
SUPPER

Grilled Corn & Roasted Red Pepper Chowder, page 44

———

Grilled Salmon BLT, page 136

———

Assorted Fruits & Cheeses

———

Apple Pie, page 208

———

Beer

SOUPS

be that hard to make biscuits."
He kneaded the buttermilk into
the shortening-and-flour mixture and the dough became like
glue, sticking to his fingers.
"Need some more flour," he
said profoundly to the dog. The
dog tilted her head curiously.

He worked for another
thirty minutes with the dough,
adding flour and buttermilk
and shortening until it caked
on his fingers, and then he
decided the dough was firm
enough and he rolled it out on
waxed paper and cut it with
the cutter. He had fifty-two
biscuits. "Great God," he said
in amazement. "I just wanted
two or three."

The biscuits were not
eatable. They were flat and
hard and were colored a murky
yellow. He put one in front of
the dog and the dog sniffed
and looked up at him sadly and
trotted away. "Don't know
what's good, do you?" he said.
He wiped butter across the top
of two of the biscuits and
poured molasses over them and
cut one with his knife and
tasted it. He spit the biscuit
from his mouth and sat at the
table and laughed silently.

She would be laughing,
too, he thought. Or scowling.
Thinking him an old fool for
trying to do something that
she had done with ease. Got to
get one of the girls to show
me how to cook biscuits, he
decided. Can't be that hard. ∎

CHILLED BACON LETTUCE AND TOMATO SOUP

CHEF BRUCE BARTZ, THE GEORGIAN CLUB

> SERVES 8
> PREPARATION TIME:
> 15 MINUTES, PLUS
> CHILLING TIME

INGREDIENTS

1 pound tomatoes, peeled, seeded, chopped
1 small cucumber, peeled, seeded, chopped
4 shallots, trimmed
2 1/2 tablespoons extra-virgin olive oil
2 1/2 tablespoons red wine vinegar
4 cups tomato juice
1/2 cup whipping cream
Salt to taste
Cayenne to taste
1 cup shredded lettuce
4 slices crisp-fried bacon, crumbled

DIRECTIONS

- Place the tomatoes, cucumber and shallots in a food processor container. Process just until coarsely chopped.
- Add the olive oil, wine vinegar and tomato juice. Process until puréed. Add the cream, salt and cayenne. Process until blended.
- Chill, covered, in the refrigerator. Ladle into soup bowls. Top with the lettuce and bacon.
- *Variation: For a more healthful version, substitute plain yogurt for the cream.*

COLD CURRY CARROT SOUP

INGREDIENTS

SERVES 8
PREPARATION TIME:
1 HOUR,
PLUS 6 HOURS
CHILLING TIME

2 cups chopped onions
1/4 cup olive oil
3 large cloves of garlic, minced
2 tablespoons chopped fresh gingerroot
2 pounds carrots, peeled, chopped
2 teaspoons curry powder
1/2 teaspoon pepper
2 teaspoons salt
8 cups chicken stock
1/4 cup chopped fresh chives

DIRECTIONS

- Sauté the onions in the olive oil in a saucepan for 10 minutes. Add the garlic, gingerroot, carrots, curry powder, pepper, salt and chicken stock; mix well.
- Bring the carrot mixture to a boil; reduce heat. Simmer for 30 minutes or until the carrots are tender, stirring occasionally. Remove from heat. Let stand until cool.
- Purée the carrot mixture a small amount at a time in a food processor. Pour into a bowl.
- Chill, covered, for 6 hours or longer. Ladle into soup bowls.
- Sprinkle with chopped fresh chives.

FRESH FRUIT SOUP

INGREDIENTS

6 cups sliced strawberries
3 cups plain yogurt
1 teaspoon sugar or to taste
1 1/2 teaspoons lemon juice
Chopped fresh mint to taste

[
SERVES 6
PREPARATION TIME:
30 MINUTES,
PLUS 1 HOUR
CHILLING TIME
]

DIRECTIONS

• Process the strawberries in a food processor until puréed.
• Add the yogurt, sugar and lemon juice. Process just until blended.
• Chill, covered, for 1 hour. Ladle into soup bowls. Sprinkle with the mint.
• *Variation: Substitute blueberries or peaches for the strawberries.*

PEACH AND RASPBERRY SOUP

INGREDIENTS

1/2 cup white wine
1 cup orange juice
2 tablespoons sugar
3 1/2 cups chopped peeled Georgia peaches
2 cups plain yogurt
2 cups fresh raspberries

[
SERVES 6
PREPARATION TIME:
45 MINUTES,
PLUS 1 HOUR
CHILLING TIME
]

DIRECTIONS

• Combine the white wine, orange juice and sugar in a saucepan; mix well.
• Cook over medium heat until the sugar dissolves, stirring constantly. Stir in the peaches.
• Cook for 5 minutes or until the peaches have released their juices, stirring frequently. Let stand until cool.
• Purée the peach mixture in a food processor. Add the yogurt. Process just until blended. Chill, covered, for 1 hour or longer.
• Purée the raspberries in a food processor; strain into a bowl. Ladle the peach soup into soup bowls. Top with the raspberry purée.

TOMATO AND RED PEPPER SOUP

INGREDIENTS

2 pounds red bell peppers, roasted
2 tablespoons olive oil
1 1/2 cups coarsely chopped onions
1 clove of garlic, chopped
3 pounds tomatoes, chopped
1 tablespoon minced fresh basil
1 teaspoon salt
1/8 teaspoon pepper

SERVES 6
PREPARATION TIME:
1 1/2 HOURS,
PLUS CHILLING TIME

DIRECTIONS

• Cut 1 of the red peppers into 1/2 x 1 1/2-inch strips; reserve. Cut the remaining red peppers into quarters, reserving the juices.
• Heat the olive oil in a saucepan over low heat. Add the onions; mix well.
• Cook, covered, over low heat for 10 minutes or until tender, stirring occasionally. Add the garlic; mix well.
• Cook, covered, for 5 minutes, stirring occasionally. Stir in the tomatoes, basil, salt and pepper. Bring to a simmer; reduce heat to low.
• Cook, covered, for 15 minutes, stirring occasionally. Add the red pepper quarters and reserved juices; mix well. Process the mixture a small amount at a time in a food processor until smooth.
• Strain through a fine sieve into a bowl, pressing with the back of a spoon. Stir in the reserved red pepper strips.
• Chill, covered, in the refrigerator. Ladle into soup bowls. Serve with sour cream and corn salsa.

Corn Salsa

Corn Salsa is delicious served with Tomato and Red Pepper Soup. Combine 1 cup fresh corn kernels, 1 medium chopped tomato, 1/4 cup finely chopped red bell pepper, 1/4 cup finely chopped green bell pepper, 1/4 cup chopped red onion, 1/4 cup peeled seeded chopped cucumber, 2 tablespoons olive oil, 1 tablespoon fresh lime juice, 1 tablespoon julienned fresh basil, 1 teaspoon seeded and chopped jalapeño, 1/2 teaspoon salt and 1/4 teaspoon pepper.

ZUCCHINI WATERCRESS SOUP

INGREDIENTS

1/4 cup butter or margarine
2 cups chopped onions
3 cups chicken stock
2 pounds zucchini, coarsely chopped
1 bunch watercress
Salt and pepper to taste
Lemon juice to taste
1 cup whipping cream

> SERVES 6
> PREPARATION TIME:
> 45 MINUTES,
> PLUS 1 HOUR
> CHILLING TIME

DIRECTIONS

- Melt the butter in a saucepan. Add the onions; mix well.
- Cook, covered, over low heat until tender. Stir in the chicken stock. Bring to a boil. Add the zucchini; mix well.
- Cook for 20 minutes or until the zucchini is tender, stirring frequently. Remove from heat. Stir in the watercress. Let stand for 5 minutes.
- Process the soup a small amount at a time in a food processor until smooth. Pour into a bowl. Season with salt, pepper and lemon juice. Stir in the cream.
- Chill, covered, for 1 hour or longer. Ladle into soup bowls.
- Garnish with additional watercress and croutons.
- *Variation: Omit the cream and decrease your daily intake of fat.*

Helpful Hint

Turn an ordinary soup into something distinctive with a sprinkling of finely minced parsley or chives, sliced cauliflowerets, julienned carrots or celery, finely chopped hard-cooked eggs or thin slices of lemon.

For variety, swirl whipped cream, sour cream or plain yogurt across the surface of each serving bowl of soup. Serve croutons, shredded cheese, toasted almonds or bacon bits in separate bowls to be added as desired.

BAKED POTATO SOUP

THE PEASANT RESTAURANTS

INGREDIENTS

SERVES 8
PREPARATION TIME:
1 HOUR

^{1}/2 cup chopped onion
^{1}/2 cup chopped celery
1 tablespoon margarine
4 cups half-and-half
1 ^{1}/2 teaspoons salt
1 ^{1}/2 teaspoons pepper
2 tablespoons margarine
3 tablespoons flour
2 large potatoes, baked, peeled, cut into ^{3}/4-inch cubes
1 cup shredded Cheddar cheese
^{1}/2 cup bacon bits
^{1}/2 cup sour cream
Chopped fresh chives to taste

DIRECTIONS

- Sauté the onion and celery in 1 tablespoon margarine in a sauté pan until tender.
- Combine the onion mixture, half-and-half, salt and pepper in a large saucepan; mix well. Heat to the boiling point, stirring occasionally.
- Heat 2 tablespoons margarine in a saucepan until melted. Whisk in the flour. Cook for 3 minutes or until of roux consistency, whisking constantly. Whisk into the half-and-half mixture. Cook until thickened, stirring constantly. Add the potatoes; mix well. Cook just until the potatoes are heated through, stirring frequently.
- Ladle into soup bowls. Top each serving with Cheddar cheese, bacon bits, sour cream and chives.

SHRIMP, CLAMS AND MUSSELS IN MISO BROTH

CHEF TOM CATHERELL, TOM TOM

SERVES 8
PREPARATION TIME:
1 HOUR

INGREDIENTS

4 cups fish stock
Pinch of saffron
2 tablespoons olive oil
2 teaspoons sesame oil
2 teaspoons chile oil
2 shallots, finely chopped
2 cloves of garlic, finely chopped
1 teaspoon chopped gingerroot
2 red chiles, seeded, chopped
2 ounces miso
8 small leeks, finely chopped
1 carrot, finely chopped, blanched
2 ounces snow peas
4 spring onions, sliced
1 small zucchini, sliced
1 ounce bean sprouts
6 basil leaves, shredded
16 shrimp, peeled, deveined
16 Manila clams
16 mussels

Miso

Miso, a basic Japanese seasoning, is prepared by grinding a mixture of cooked soybeans, steamed rice and salt and fermenting it in brine. Miso is available in Japanese markets.

DIRECTIONS

• Bring the fish stock, saffron, olive oil, sesame oil, chile oil, shallots, garlic, gingerroot, chiles and miso to a boil in a stockpot; reduce heat. Simmer over low heat until the flavors are blended, stirring occasionally. Stir in the leeks, carrot, snow peas, spring onions, zucchini, bean sprouts and basil.

• Simmer for 20 minutes, stirring occasionally. Add the shrimp, clams and mussels; mix well.

• Cook for 5 minutes, stirring occasionally. Ladle into soup bowls.

Espresso Black Bean Chili with Grits

FOR THE GRITS

> 5 cups water
> 1/2 teaspoon salt
> 1 1/2 cups grits

[
SERVES 6
PREPARATION TIME:
1 1/2 HOURS
]

FOR THE CHILI

> 2 medium onions, chopped
> 4 cloves of garlic, minced
> 1/4 cup olive oil
> 1 1/2 tablespoons instant espresso powder
> 1 1/2 tablespoons chili powder
> 1 tablespoon ground cumin
> 1 tablespoon dried oregano
> 1 (28-ounce) can crushed tomatoes
> 1 (8-ounce) can tomato sauce
> 2 bay leaves
> 2 (14-ounce) cans black beans, drained, rinsed

TO PREPARE THE GRITS

- Bring the water and salt to a boil in a saucepan. Stir in the grits.
- Cook over low to medium heat for 25 minutes or until the grits are of the desired consistency, stirring occasionally. Remove from heat. Cover to keep warm.

TO PREPARE THE CHILI

- Sauté the onions and garlic in the olive oil in a stockpot over medium heat until soft. Add the espresso powder, chili powder, cumin and oregano; mix well.
- Cook for 5 minutes, stirring occasionally. Stir in the tomatoes, tomato sauce and bay leaves. Simmer for 15 minutes, stirring occasionally. Stir in the black beans. Simmer for 15 to 30 minutes or until the chili is of the desired consistency. Discard the bay leaves.
- Spoon the chili over the grits on individual plates. Garnish with shredded Monterey Jack cheese and chopped fresh cilantro.
- *Note: If espresso powder is not available, use 3 tablespoons instant coffee granules.*

Grilled Corn and Roasted Pepper Chowder

Chef Bruce Bartz, The Georgian Club

[
SERVES 10
PREPARATION TIME:
2 HOURS
]

INGREDIENTS

8 ears of fresh corn, shucked
8 slices bacon
2 medium onions, finely chopped
3 stalks celery, finely chopped
1/2 cup flour
8 cups chicken stock
3 red bell peppers, roasted, peeled, seeded, chopped
3 medium potatoes, peeled, chopped
1 1/2 cups whipping cream
1/2 cup Southern Comfort liqueur
2 tablespoons chopped fresh thyme
Salt and pepper to taste

Roasted Peppers

To prepare roasted red peppers, rub the red peppers on all sides with oil. Place on the grill rack. Grill over hot coals until the skin is blistered and charred on all sides, turning frequently; do not burn. Place the red peppers in a sealable plastic bag immediately; seal tightly. Allow to steam in the bag until cool. Peel, seed and chop the red peppers when cool.

DIRECTIONS

• Grill the corn over medium-hot coals until slightly charred but not burned, turning occasionally. Remove the corn to a wire rack.
• Let stand until cool. Cut the tops of the corn kernels with a sharp knife into a bowl. Scrape the ears with a knife to remove the juice.
• Fry the bacon in a stockpot until crisp; crumble and set aside. Add the onions and celery to the stock pot with the bacon drippings. Cook over medium heat for 10 minutes or until the vegetables are tender. Stir in the flour.
• Cook over low heat for 10 minutes, stirring constantly. Add the chicken stock, stirring until mixed. Bring to a simmer.
• Simmer for 20 minutes, skimming as necessary. Add the corn, red peppers and potatoes. Simmer for 30 minutes, stirring occasionally. Stir in the cream, liqueur, thyme, crumbled bacon, salt and pepper.
• Simmer for 10 minutes, stirring frequently. Ladle into soup bowls.

TORTILLA SOUP

SERVES 8

PREPARATION TIME:

1 1/2 HOURS

INGREDIENTS

1 1/2 pounds boneless skinless
  chicken breast halves
1 large onion, chopped
2 fresh jalapeños, seeded, chopped
4 cloves of garlic, minced
2 large carrots, chopped
4 teaspoons vegetable oil
1 teaspoon ground cumin
1 teaspoon chili powder
1 teaspoon lemon pepper
1 teaspoon salt
1 tablespoon hot pepper sauce
1/2 cup flour
1 (14-ounce) can whole tomatoes
4 (14-ounce) cans chicken broth
8 corn tortillas, cut into thin strips
Vegetable oil for frying
1/2 cup sour cream
1 avocado, chopped
1 cup shredded Cheddar cheese
Chopped fresh cilantro to taste

DIRECTIONS

- Rinse the chicken and pat dry; chop.
- Sauté the onion, jalapeños, garlic, carrots and chicken in 4 teaspoons oil in a stockpot for 5 minutes. Stir in the cumin, chili powder, lemon pepper, salt, hot pepper sauce and flour until mixed. Add the tomatoes and chicken broth; mix well.
- Simmer for 1 hour, stirring frequently.
- Fry the tortilla strips in 1/4 inch oil in a skillet until crisp; drain.
- Arrange several tortilla strips in each soup bowl. Spoon 1 tablespoon each of the sour cream and chopped avocado over the tortilla strips. Ladle the soup over the layers; sprinkle with the cheese and cilantro.
- Note: To decrease the caloric value of the tortilla strips, spray the tortilla strips with nonstick cooking spray and arrange on a baking sheet. Bake at 350 degrees for 5 minutes or until brown.

HEARTY VEGETABLE SOUP

TULLIE SMITH HOUSE

*The flavor of this soup is enhanced by the use of fresh herbs.
It is a wonderful addition to the low-fat diet when made with
vegetable broth and without the addition of meat.*

SERVES 10
PREPARATION TIME:
1 1/2 HOURS

Tullie Smith Farm

A plantation-plain house built in the 1840s, the Tullie Smith House is listed on the National Register of Historic Places. Because the house was originally located east of Atlanta outside the city limits, it survived the near-total destruction of Atlanta in 1864. The house, detached kitchen, and related outbuildings were moved to the Atlanta History Center beginning in 1969. The farm complex serves as tangible evidence of the rural past in a metropolitan area where agriculture has essentially disappeared. Everyday activities typical of 19th-century rural Georgia are performed at the site, including open-hearth cooking, animal care, black-smithing, basket weaving, candle making, quilting, spinning, weaving, and other craft demonstrations. This is one of the few places in Atlanta where visitors can see cotton growing and the herbs that were so essential to both cooking and medicine. Costumed interpreters lead tours of the house, which is furnished with simple pieces of the furnishings and household objects typical of the period. The farm is the setting for the Folklife Festival and for Civil War Encampment, each of which attracts more than 4,000 students, tourists, and families each year.

INGREDIENTS

4 ears of fresh corn
1 (28-ounce) can whole peeled tomatoes
4 cups water
1 large onion, chopped
4 large carrots, chopped
4 to 6 cloves of garlic, minced
4 to 6 stalks celery with tops, chopped
1 ham hock
8 ounces fresh snap beans
4 medium potatoes, peeled, chopped
1/2 small head cabbage, shredded
1 (10-ounce) package frozen lima beans
1 (28-ounce) can crushed tomatoes
1 (14-ounce) can beef broth
1/4 cup chopped fresh parsley
1 tablespoon chopped fresh basil or 1 teaspoon dried basil
1 1/2 teaspoons chopped fresh marjoram or 1/2 teaspoon dried marjoram
1 1/2 teaspoons chopped fresh thyme or 1/2 teaspoon dried thyme
1 1/2 teaspoons chopped fresh rosemary or 1/2 teaspoon dried rosemary
1 large bay leaf
1 teaspoon salt
1 teaspoon pepper

DIRECTIONS

• Cut the tops of the corn kernels with a sharp knife into a bowl. Scrape the ears with a knife to remove the juice. Chop the whole peeled tomatoes, reserving the juice.
• Bring the water, onion, carrots, garlic, celery and ham hock to a boil in a stockpot over medium-high heat. Add the undrained corn, snap beans, potatoes, cabbage and lima beans; mix well. Bring to a boil, stirring occasionally. Add the undrained chopped peeled tomatoes, undrained crushed tomatoes, beef broth, herbs, salt and pepper; mix well. Bring to a boil; reduce heat.

- Simmer, partially covered, for 1 hour or until of the desired consistency, stirring occasionally. Discard the bay leaf. Remove the ham hock; chop the ham, discarding bone. Return the chopped ham to the stockpot; mix well.
- Ladle into soup bowls. Serve with crusty French bread or corn bread for a good Southern comfort meal.
- *Variation: Substitute one 10-ounce package frozen snap beans for fresh snap beans and 2 cups frozen corn for fresh corn. For variety, use chicken or vegetable stock in place of beef stock. Substitute 2 chicken breast halves for the ham hock or omit both for a vegetarian soup.*
- *Note: Store in the refrigerator for up to 1 week or freeze for future use.*

GEORGIA PEANUT SOUP

INGREDIENTS

[SERVES 4
PREPARATION TIME:
25 MINUTES]

1 shallot, chopped
2 stalks celery, chopped
2 teaspoons butter or margarine
1 tablespoon flour
1 cup chicken stock
3 tablespoons smooth salt-free peanut butter,
  made from freshly ground peanuts
1/2 cup low-fat milk
1/2 cup water
2 tablespoons crushed salt-free Georgia peanuts

DIRECTIONS

- Sauté the shallot and celery in the melted butter in a medium skillet for 5 minutes. Add the flour, tossing to coat well.
- Stir in half the chicken stock. Simmer for 5 minutes. Add the remaining chicken stock. Simmer for 5 minutes longer. Strain, reserving the liquid and vegetables.
- Blend the peanut butter into the reserved liquid in a saucepan. Stir in the milk.
- Combine 3/4 cup of the peanut butter and stock mixture with the reserved vegetables in a blender or food processor container; process until smooth. Stir into the saucepan.
- Cook until heated through, adding the water as needed for the desired consistency. Serve hot or cold, topped with the crushed peanuts.

Southern Corn Bread

Serve Southern Corn Bread with your favorite soup. Combine a mixture of 1 beaten egg and 2 cups buttermilk with 2 cups stone-ground white or yellow cornmeal, 2 teaspoons baking powder, 1 teaspoon baking soda, 1 teaspoon salt and 1 tablespoon sugar (optional). Stir in 1/4 cup oil or melted shortening. Spoon into greased 8x8-inch baking pan or iron skillet. Bake at 400 degrees for 20 minutes or until corn bread tests done.

WILD MUSHROOM SOUP

INGREDIENTS

SERVES 4
PREPARATION TIME:
1 HOUR

2 medium shallots, minced
1 tablespoon olive oil
1 tablespoon butter or margarine
8 ounces fresh shiitake mushrooms, sliced
8 ounces fresh cremini mushrooms, sliced
8 ounces fresh button mushrooms, sliced
1 tablespoon flour
1/3 cup vermouth
2 cups beef stock
1/2 cup water
Salt and pepper to taste
1/4 teaspoon minced fresh rosemary
1/4 cup sour cream
1/4 cup chopped fresh parsley
2 tablespoons sliced almonds, toasted

Helpful Hint

Store leftover mushrooms in a non-recycled brown paper bag in the refrigerator to prevent the mushrooms from turning brown.

DIRECTIONS

- Sauté the shallots in the olive oil and butter in a saucepan until tender. Add the mushrooms; mix well.
- Sauté until the mushrooms are tender and most of the liquid has been absorbed. Sprinkle with the flour. Cook for 2 to 3 minutes or until mixed, stirring constantly. Stir in the vermouth. Add the beef stock, water, salt and pepper; mix well.
- Simmer for 30 minutes. Stir in the rosemary.
- Ladle into soup bowls. Top each serving with sour cream, parsley and almonds.
- *Variation: Dry white wine may be substituted for the vermouth.*

A Tale of Three Teas

BY MICHAEL LEE WEST
ILLUSTRATION BY CHERYL COOPER

My grandmother used to say that iced tea runs through the veins of any native Southerner. I believed her. As a Louisiana baby, I was served coffee and tea in a glass Evenflo bottle (with a cross-cut nipple, of course). Even now, forty years later, I have a profound weakness for the brew. My back porch is a famous drinking spot, but it also doubles as a dining/family room, while the summer night gently darkens around us, like tea that has steeped too long.

Add a couple of eccentric relatives, preferably Southern, and start telling stories.

Growing up in a region where appetites and thirsts are legendary, I have come to believe that sweet tea is the basis of Southern living. To make a perfect jug of tea, you need more than boiling water and a tin of leaves. First, supply the background. A large wooden porch, preferable screened, is a nice beginning. Add wicker chairs and at least one glider. A mild breeze, especially if it carries the scent of charcoal or freshly cut grass, is especially welcome. Flowers lend an exotic touch (if you find yourself inclined in that direction), such as nasturtiums and violets, either floating in the glass or anchored in a lemon round. Add one Southern orchestra—crickets, June bugs, and bullfrogs—and you are well on your way to perfection.

There is nothing more comforting than the sound of warm tea poured into thin, ice-filled glasses. Understand that tea making isn't complete until you own a small collection of pitchers. Clear, simple jugs are always lovely, but on special occasions bring out your cobalt and cranberry

►

LIGHT GARDEN
LUNCHEON

Peach & Raspberry Soup, page 38

Spinach & Strawberry Salad, page 66

Summer Style Chicken Cutlets, page 160

*Cream Cheese Scones with
Raisins,* page 286

La-Di-Da-Tea, page 50

SALADS

glass. As you pour, remind yourself that antique glassware enhances the depth and beauty of tea, not to mention your afternoon, especially when you add lemon, mint and a lace-edged napkin. On especially muggy nights, press the cold wet glass to your forehead. Hold a glass to the light, admiring its rich colors of citrine and topaz. Expound upon the virtues of iced tea—cold and tart, warm and plain, sweet and tangy, spiced and spiked. It's versatile, generous, eager to please, the perfect beverage for any meal. (Also, it's non-denominational.)

In the Deep South, tea drinking commences immediately after breakfast (length: the time it takes to drink 3 cups of coffee). Walk barefoot into your kitchen, letting the screen door slam behind you, and measure 2 cups cold water. Pour into an enamel pan and turn up the flame. When the water begins to smile (as the French say), remove the pan. Add 2 family-sized tea bags and cover for ten minutes. Purists will stick to plain tea—unsweetened and unadorned, but I myself crave a bit of sweetness. And no matter how it's served, tea fits into any menu or season. It's the back-bone of summer, especially when served with pecan chicken salad and garden tomatoes. In the fall or winter you can add warmth and spices. I have a tattered book of recipes for "Russian Tea," but I prefer a steamy cup, laced with sugar and a splash of Cointreau.

ALMOND SALAD WITH ORANGE VINAIGRETTE

FOR THE VINAIGRETTE

$^3/_4$ cup olive oil
$^1/_4$ cup red wine vinegar
1 tablespoon orange juice
1 teaspoon grated orange rind
$^1/_2$ teaspoon poppy seeds
$^1/_8$ teaspoon salt
$^1/_8$ teaspoon pepper

FOR THE SALAD

1 head Bibb lettuce, torn into bite-size pieces
1 head leaf lettuce, torn into bite-size pieces
1 (11-ounce) can mandarin oranges, drained
10 fresh strawberries, sliced
1 green onion, chopped
$^1/_2$ cup almonds, toasted

TO PREPARE THE VINAIGRETTE

• Whisk the olive oil, wine vinegar, orange juice, orange rind, poppy seeds, salt and pepper in a small bowl.

TO PREPARE THE SALAD

• Toss the lettuce, mandarin oranges, strawberries and green onion in a salad bowl. Add the vinaigrette, tossing to coat.
• Sprinkle with the almonds.

[
SERVES 6
PREPARATION TIME:
20 MINUTES
]

GRILLED LETTUCE WITH STILTON CHEESE

CHEF BRUCE BARTZ, THE GEORGIAN CLUB

SERVES 8
PREPARATION TIME:
30 MINUTES

FOR THE DRESSING

1/2 cup balsamic vinegar
1 1/2 cups olive oil
1 teaspoon dry mustard
Salt and pepper to taste

FOR THE SALAD

1 head romaine
1 head radicchio
2 spears Belgian endive, cut into quarters
1 red bell pepper, sliced into 8 rings
1 green bell pepper, sliced into 8 rings
1 yellow bell pepper, sliced into 8 rings
1 red onion, sliced into 8 rings
8 ounces Stilton cheese, crumbled

TO PREPARE THE DRESSING

• Whisk the balsamic vinegar, olive oil, dry mustard, salt and pepper in a bowl until blended.

TO PREPARE THE SALAD

• Cut the romaine and radicchio into 8 wedges, leaving the cores intact.
• Dip the lettuce wedges, endive, bell pepper rings and onion rings into the dressing just until moistened.
• Place the pepper and onion rings on the grill rack. Grill over medium-hot coals for 5 minutes on each side or until tender-crisp.
• Grill the romaine, radicchio and endive on both sides over medium-hot coals for 2 to 3 minutes or just until wilted.
• Arrange the romaine, radicchio and endive on a serving platter.
• Top with the bell pepper rings and onion. Sprinkle with the Stilton cheese.

Most people make iced tea without thinking—indeed, they're puzzled when you ask them for a recipe. Nevertheless, the perfect brew eluded me for years. In a world of complicated beverages, tea making is utterly fundamental. Even a child can make it. Most cooks don't measure—they just draw up a pan of cold water, bring it to a boil, drop in a few tea bags, and steep. Maybe they'll shake in sugar, straight from the bag (certainly they won't use a measuring cup, with its increments marked off to the Nth degree).

My grandmother did not have a cookbook-lined kitchen; her cuisine was a product of instinct and memory (she was the biscuit-making daughter in a family of ten children—the second-oldest sister was the hair-braider, and she went to her grave without learning how to make a decent pot of tea). I remember shopping with my grandmother at Central Grocery in New Orleans, across the street from the French Market. She explained that tea fell into three basic groups: green, oolong, and black. Her favorite was Earl Grey ("Elegant, sweet, and fruity"), with Darjeeling's mild taste a close second. Pekoe, she explained, referred to the size of the leaf, not the flavor. As she bought Lapsang souchong, garlic braids, and Tabasco, she observed that men liked robust flavors. She was speaking of the Mississippi "chaps" from her youth—men who

▶

accompanied their women to the Amite River Baptist Church, but in their mind they were hunting quail from Thanksgiving Day until Christmas. In her generation, Southern women worshipped their menfolks. Indeed, I remember my great-grandmother's house, where the men ate in the dining room, circled and coddled by women bearing platters of fried chicken and biscuits.

Perhaps the world has changed—or perhaps my grandmother didn't understand that men are as variable as tea leaves. Some are gentle, subtle; others are bland like weak coffee. They can be cloudy and mysterious, too hot or too cold. Now and then you find one who is acidic—a bitter lemon ruining the flavor of your whole brew. You have no choice but to throw it out and start over. And some men, bless their hearts, are downright sweet.

My grandmother also believed in the excellence of tea leaves; she eschewed prepackaged bags. "Would you dream of using instant coffee?" she'd scold when I'd reach for a plastic-wrapped box in Piggly Wiggly. "Tea leaves are to tea what fresh perked is to coffee." Well that made sense. Even though it seemed troublesome to strain her brews, she never used a tubage in her life.

After my grandmother passed away, my mother became the "tea maker" in our

▶

WHITE BEAN SALAD

INGREDIENTS

2 cups cooked white beans
1/2 cup chopped onion
3 tablespoons chopped fresh Italian parsley
1/4 cup chopped yellow bell pepper
1/4 cup chopped red bell pepper
1/2 teaspoon white pepper
1/8 teaspoon salt
2 tablespoons balsamic vinegar
1 tablespoon white wine vinegar
2 tablespoons olive oil
1 head romaine, separated into leaves

[SERVES 6
PREPARATION TIME:
15 MINUTES,
PLUS 30 MINUTES
CHILLING TIME]

DIRECTIONS

• Combine the white beans, onion, parsley, yellow pepper, red pepper, white pepper, salt, balsamic vinegar, wine vinegar and olive oil in a bowl; mix well.
• Chill, covered, for 30 minutes to 3 hours; drain.
• Spoon onto a romaine-lined serving platter.

Beet and Feta Salad

INGREDIENTS

4 large beets
6 tablespoons olive oil
2 tablespoons honey
2 tablespoons red wine vinegar
2 large cloves of garlic
2 tablespoons chopped fresh oregano or 2 teaspoons dried oregano
1 1/2 teaspoons Dijon mustard
Salt and pepper to taste
1 small red onion, chopped
3/4 cup feta cheese, crumbled
1/3 cup walnuts, toasted

SERVES 4
PREPARATION TIME:
1 1/2 HOURS

DIRECTIONS

- Wrap the beets in foil. Roast in a 400-degree oven for 1 1/4 hours or until tender. Let stand until cool. Peel and slice the beets.
- Process the olive oil, honey, wine vinegar, garlic, oregano and Dijon mustard in a blender until thickened. Pour into a bowl.
- Stir in the salt, pepper and onion.
- Arrange the beets on a serving platter; sprinkle with the feta cheese and walnuts. Drizzle with the olive oil mixture.
- *Note: Use rubber gloves when handling beets to prevent staining.*

family. While she confessed to using tea bags (still, she always uses black tea), she also conceded certain secret techniques—part science, part hocus-pocus. Although tea water must be boiled in order to bring out the flavor, she never lets her water boil very long (she claims it causes the water to taste metallic). She never boils tea water in aluminum and she never reboils water. Also, she recommends stainless steel, glass, or enamel (although I remember when she served tea in those wide-lipped aluminum tumblers, the kind that came in jewel-toned colors and made me shiver when my teeth touched the cold metal rim). Recently she has taken to serving all beverages in lovely etched goblets made of the thinnest crystal, and it seems as if we are drinking liquid jewels. While cranberry glass and crystal provide a certain atmosphere, the true secret to my mother's tea is a sugar syrup.

How To Make A Sugar Syrup
(Stolen From Michael Lee's Mother)

1 1/2 cups cold water
1/2 cup sugar

Place in a saucepan and stir over low heat until sugar is dissolved. Increase heat and bring to a boil. Boil ten minutes or until mixture is reduced to a thick syrup (about 1 cup). Cool. Pour into steeped tea. Add lemons, if desired.

▶

Basic Sweet Tea

1 family-sized tea bag
2 cups water
1 to 1½ cups sugar
Juice of two lemons
(or 1 scoop instant
lemonade, if you are that
sort of person)
3 cups cold water
sliced lemons

Bring water to just a hint of a boil. Add tea bags, remove from heat, and cover pan. Wait five minutes. Add sugar to your favorite pitcher. Pour steamed tea over sugar and stir. Add 3 cups cold water. My mother adds 1 small can of limeade and 1 small can lemonade, reducing her sugar to ¼ cup (or less—sugar is a very personal thing, she says). Next, she adds lemons, limes, oranges, and fresh mint. She has been known to pour the whole brew into a silver punch bowl, adding champagne, thus creating her famous tipsy tea.

Another family favorite is La-Di-Da Tea.

La-Di-Da Tea
(Also Stolen From Michael Lee's Mother)

1. Make a sugar syrup; cool.
2. Pour into a cut-glass punch bowl.
3. Stir in the juice of 6 lemons, 6 oranges, 3 cups plain, brewed tea, and ½ bottle gin.
4. Stand 1 hour.
5. Stir in 2½ quarts chilled carbonated water.

In my mind's eye, food and love and writing are inexorably linked. Their destines collide

CALYPSO SALAD

INGREDIENTS

²/3 cup water
¹/3 cup long grain rice
¹/2 teaspoon salt
1 teaspoon olive oil
¹/2 cup chopped onion
¹/2 cup chopped green bell pepper
1 cup chopped seeded tomato
¹/4 cup chopped fresh cilantro
1 (15-ounce) can black beans, rinsed, drained
1 tablespoon red wine vinegar
1 tablespoon lime juice
2 tablespoons olive oil
1 avocado, sliced

[SERVES 6
PREPARATION TIME:
30 MINUTES,
PLUS CHILLING TIME]

DIRECTIONS

• Bring the water to a boil in a saucepan. Stir in the rice, salt and 1 teaspoon olive oil; reduce heat to low.
• Cook, covered, for 20 minutes or until the rice is tender and the water is absorbed. Rinse the rice with cold water; drain.
• Combine the rice, onion, green pepper, tomato, cilantro and black beans in a bowl; mix well. Stir in a mixture of the wine vinegar, lime juice and 2 tablespoons olive oil.
• Chill, covered, for several hours. Top with the avocado slices.

ORIENTAL COLESLAW

SERVES 8
PREPARATION TIME:
30 MINUTES

INGREDIENTS

1 package any flavor ramen noodles with
  seasoning packet
1/2 cup slivered almonds, toasted
2 tablespoons sesame seeds, toasted
1/3 cup olive oil
3 tablespoons vinegar
2 tablespoons sugar
3 cups shredded red and green cabbage
1 cup shredded carrots
6 green onions, thinly sliced
Salt and pepper to taste

DIRECTIONS

- Crumble the ramen noodles, reserving the seasoning packet.
- Combine the ramen noodles, almonds and sesame seeds in a bowl; mix well.
- Whisk the reserved seasonings, olive oil, vinegar and sugar in a bowl until mixed.
- Combine the cabbage, carrots and green onions in a bowl; mix well.
- Toss the cabbage mixture and ramen noodle mixture with the dressing in a salad bowl just before serving. Season with salt and pepper.
- *Note: To save time and energy, substitute 1 package of the coleslaw mix available in the produce department of your grocery store for the cabbage and carrots.*
- *Variation: Add chopped grilled chicken and serve as an entrée.*

daily in my kitchen. As a young tea maker, my brews were too strong, sweet, bitter, cloudy. Only in middle age have I learned the art of tea making. Like everything else in life, whether it's love, writing novels, or raising children, you need to relax. Throw away those measuring cups and reach for your child's yellow cat mug, the one that holds exactly 1 1/4 cups sugar. Understand that a less than perfect glass of tea isn't the end of the world—more than likely, it's drinkable. Remember the words of a famous Southern heroine—tomorrow is always another day, especially when it comes to perfecting recipes. ▪

LENTIL AND MUSHROOM SALAD

FOR THE DRESSING

¹/2 teaspoon salt
2 tablespoons olive oil
2 tablespoons vegetable oil
¹/4 cup red wine vinegar
2 tablespoons Dijon mustard
1 teaspoon chopped fresh cilantro
¹/2 teaspoon dried oregano
¹/4 teaspoon Worcestershire sauce
3 to 5 drops of hot sauce

Helpful Hint

When cooking dried beans, always add the salt at the end of the cooking process. Salt added at the beginning will slow the cooking process.

FOR THE SALAD

1 cup dried lentils   *¹/4 cup chopped fresh parsley*
3 cups water   *1 green bell pepper, chopped*
1 teaspoon salt   *1 large tomato, chopped*
2 cups fresh mushrooms, sliced *1 clove of garlic, minced*
¹/3 cup chopped green onions

TO PREPARE THE DRESSING

• Combine the salt, olive oil, vegetable oil, wine vinegar, Dijon mustard, cilantro, oregano, Worcestershire sauce and hot sauce in a jar with a tight-fitting lid, shaking to blend.

TO PREPARE THE SALAD

• Sort the lentils; rinse. Bring the water and salt to a boil in a saucepan. Add the lentils.
• Cook for 20 to 25 minutes or until the lentils are tender, stirring occasionally; drain.
• Combine the lentils, mushrooms, green onions, parsley, green pepper, tomato and garlic in a large salad bowl. Add the dressing, tossing to coat.
• Chill, covered, for 3 to 12 hours or longer.
• *Variation: Omit the cilantro.*
• *Note: The flavor of the salad is enhanced if prepared several days in advance.*

GREEK PASTA SALAD

SERVES 8
PREPARATION TIME:
30 MINUTES,
PLUS 1 HOUR
CHILLING TIME

FOR THE DRESSING

1 tablespoon chopped fresh parsley
1 clove of garlic, minced
1 tablespoon dried oregano
1/2 teaspoon salt
1/2 teaspoon pepper
1/4 cup white vinegar

FOR THE SALAD

8 ounces orzo pasta
1 medium cucumber, chopped
4 ounces feta cheese, crumbled
1/2 cup chopped black olives
1/2 cup chopped green olives
2 large tomatoes, chopped
1/4 cup olive oil

TO PREPARE THE DRESSING

• Combine the parsley, garlic, oregano, salt, pepper and white vinegar in a jar with a tight-fitting lid, shaking until mixed.

TO PREPARE THE SALAD

• Cook the orzo pasta using package directions until al dente.
• Combine the orzo, cucumber, feta cheese, olives, tomatoes and olive oil in a large bowl; mix well. Add the dressing, tossing to coat.
• Chill, covered, for 1 to 24 hours.
• *Variation: Add 2 cups chopped cooked chicken, turkey or shrimp and serve as an entrée.*

Al dente

Al dente is a term used to describe pasta that has been cooked "firm to the bite." It describes the texture which has a "tooth" when bitten into that is not overdone or mushy.

RED PEPPER AND TOMATO COUSCOUS SALAD

FOR THE DRESSING

> 3 tablespoons olive oil
> 1/4 cup lemon juice
> 1/2 teaspoon salt
> 1/8 teaspoon pepper
> 1/2 teaspoon Dijon mustard

FOR THE SALAD

> 2 large red bell peppers
> 3 cups water
> 1 1/2 cups couscous
> 1 small unpeeled cucumber, chopped
> 1/2 medium Vidalia onion, chopped
> 3/4 cup chopped fresh basil
> 1/4 cup chopped fresh parsley
> 1 large tomato, chopped

[SERVES 8
PREPARATION TIME:
20 MINUTES,
PLUS 1 HOUR
CHILLING TIME]

Helpful Hint

Always store onions in a cool dark place with air circulation to prevent sprouting.

TO PREPARE THE DRESSING

• Combine the olive oil, lemon juice, salt, pepper and Dijon mustard in a jar with a tight-fitting lid, shaking until blended.

TO PREPARE THE SALAD

• Roast the red peppers over a gas flame or grill or broil until charred on all sides. Place the red peppers in a sealable plastic bag; seal tightly. Place in the freezer for 15 minutes; remove from freezer. Let stand until completely cool. Peel and seed the red peppers; chop into 1/2-inch pieces.
• Bring the water to a boil in a saucepan; remove from heat. Stir in the couscous. Let stand, covered, for 5 to 10 minutes or until the water is absorbed.
• Combine the couscous, red peppers, cucumber, onion, basil, parsley and tomato in a bowl; mix well. Add the dressing, tossing to coat.
• Chill, covered, for 1 to 12 hours.

ROASTED NEW POTATO SALAD

INGREDIENTS

[
SERVES 6
PREPARATION TIME:
1 1/2 HOURS
]

11 tablespoons olive oil
6 cloves of garlic, chopped
1 teaspoon salt
1/2 teaspoon pepper
1/2 teaspoon dried thyme
1/2 teaspoon dried rosemary
2 1/2 pounds small new potatoes, cut into wedges
2 tablespoons white wine vinegar
2 teaspoons Dijon mustard
Salt and pepper to taste
1/2 cup finely chopped green onions

DIRECTIONS

• Combine 6 tablespoons of the olive oil, the garlic, 1 teaspoon salt,
1/2 teaspoon pepper, thyme and rosemary in a bowl; mix well. Add the
new potatoes, tossing to coat. Arrange in a greased baking pan.
• Bake at 375 degrees for 55 minutes or until the new potatoes are
brown and tender. Let stand until cool. Transfer the new potatoes
to a bowl.
• Scrape the pan drippings into a measuring cup. Add enough of the
remaining olive oil to measure 6 tablespoons.
• Whisk the wine vinegar and Dijon mustard in a bowl until smooth.
Add the olive oil mixture, whisking until blended. Pour over the new
potatoes, tossing to coat. Season with salt and pepper to taste; sprinkle
with the green onions.
• Serve at room temperature.

Helpful Hint

To peel a clove of garlic, lay
the clove on a cutting board
and with the palm of your
hand hit the flat edge of a
knife to crush the garlic. The
skin will peel right off.

SESAME SALAD

SERVES 6
PREPARATION TIME:
20 MINUTES,
PLUS 3 HOURS
MARINATING TIME

FOR THE DRESSING

1 clove of garlic, minced
1/3 cup vegetable oil
2 tablespoons rice wine vinegar
1 1/2 tablespoons lemon juice
1 tablespoon sugar
1/2 teaspoon salt

FOR THE SALAD

8 ounces snow peas, trimmed
12 ounces fresh mushrooms, sliced
1 large red bell pepper, cut into thin strips
3 tablespoons sesame seeds, toasted

TO PREPARE THE DRESSING

• Whisk the garlic, oil, wine vinegar, lemon juice, sugar and salt
  in a bowl.

TO PREPARE THE SALAD

• Blanch the snow peas in boiling water to cover in a saucepan for
  1 minute; rinse with cold water. Cut the snow peas into halves
  diagonally.
• Combine the snow peas, mushrooms, red pepper and sesame seeds in
  a bowl; mix well. Add the dressing, tossing to coat.
• Marinate, covered, for 3 to 4 hours, tossing occasionally. Drain and
  spoon into a serving bowl.

*Honey and Lime
Dressing*

For Honey and Lime Dressing,
process 2 tablespoons soy
sauce, 2 tablespoons lime
juice, 1 teaspoon honey,
1 tablespoon minced fresh
gingerroot and 2 teaspoons
sesame seeds in a blender for
10 seconds. Add a mixture
of 2 teaspoons sesame oil and
2/3 cup olive oil gradually,
processing constantly for
5 seconds.

SNOW PEA SALAD

1 tablespoon vegetable oil
1 teaspoon mild chili powder
1 clove of garlic, finely minced
1/4 cup white wine vinegar
1/4 cup soy sauce
3 tablespoons sesame oil
1 1/2 tablespoons brown sugar

6 ounces snow peas, trimmed
1 medium carrot, peeled, julienned
2 medium cucumbers, peeled, julienned

TO PREPARE THE DRESSING

• Heat the oil in a skillet. Stir in the chili powder.
• Cook until heated, stirring constantly. Add the garlic, wine vinegar, soy sauce, sesame oil and brown sugar; mix well. Remove from heat.
• Let stand until cool.

TO PREPARE THE SALAD

• Blanch the snow peas in boiling water to cover in a saucepan for 2 minutes. Drain and rinse the snow peas with cold water.
• Combine the snow peas, carrot and cucumbers in a salad bowl. Add the dressing, tossing to coat.
• Chill, covered, for 1 hour.

SERVES 4
PREPARATION TIME:
15 MINUTES,
PLUS 1 HOUR
CHILLING TIME

Helpful Hint

Prevent garlic cloves from drying out by storing them in a bottle of cooking oil. After the garlic is used, use the garlic-flavored oil as a salad dressing.

GREEN SALAD WITH LEMON DRESSING

FOR THE DRESSING

> 2 teaspoons grated lemon rind
> 1/4 cup lemon juice
> 2/3 cup olive oil
> 1 teaspoon sugar
> 1 1/2 teaspoons salt
> 1 teaspoon mustard
> 1 teaspoon chopped fresh chives
> 1/2 teaspoon pepper

[
SERVES 8
PREPARATION TIME:
20 MINUTES
]

FOR THE SALAD

> 2 (10-ounce) packages fresh spinach, trimmed, torn into
> bite-size pieces
> 1 head Boston lettuce, torn into bite-size pieces
> 8 ounces fresh mushrooms, sliced

TO PREPARE THE DRESSING

- Whisk the lemon rind, lemon juice, olive oil, sugar, salt, mustard, chives and pepper in a bowl.

TO PREPARE THE SALAD

- Combine the spinach, lettuce and mushrooms in a salad bowl; mix well. Add the dressing, tossing gently to coat.
- *Variation: Add chopped cooked chicken, shrimp or grilled fish for a main dish.*

Helpful Hint

Tear—never chop—lettuce. Chopping causes the edges to turn brown.

SPINACH AND PASTA SALAD

SERVES 12
PREPARATION TIME:
1 HOUR

FOR THE DRESSING

2 eggs
2 cups vegetable oil
1 cup grated Parmesan cheese
1/2 cup red wine vinegar
2 teaspoons pepper
1 teaspoon salt
2 cloves of garlic, minced

FOR THE SALAD

1 (16-ounce) package pasta ruffles, cooked, drained, cooled
1 (10-ounce) package fresh spinach, torn into bite-size pieces
8 ounces mozzarella cheese, shredded
1 (14-ounce) can artichoke hearts, drained, chopped
1 (14-ounce) can hearts of palm, drained, chopped
1 (4-ounce) can chopped green chiles, drained

TO PREPARE THE DRESSING

• Process the eggs in a food processor for 5 seconds. Add the oil gradually, processing constantly until thickened. Add the Parmesan cheese, wine vinegar, pepper, salt and garlic. Process until thickened.

TO PREPARE THE SALAD

• Combine the pasta, spinach, mozzarella cheese, artichoke hearts, hearts of palm and green chiles in a salad bowl. Add the dressing, tossing to coat.
• *Note: This salad may be served immediately, but the flavor is enhanced if prepared 24 hours before serving.*

Peanut Vinaigrette
South City Kitchen

Serve Peanut Vinaigrette, a specialty of the South City Kitchen, over romaine lettuce topped with grilled chicken strips and julienned red and yellow bell peppers. To prepare, combine 2/3 cup balsamic vinegar, 1/4 cup peanut butter, 3 tablespoons brown sugar, 1 tablespoon honey, 1 tablespoon finely chopped fresh chives, 1 tablespoon finely chopped fresh parsley and 1 teaspoon finely chopped gingerroot. Add 2 cups peanut oil in a fine stream, beating constantly until blended.

SPINACH AND STRAWBERRY SALAD

FOR THE DRESSING

[
SERVES 8
PREPARATION TIME:
30 MINUTES
]

3/4 cup sugar
1/4 teaspoon paprika
1/2 teaspoon dry mustard
1/2 teaspoon Worcestershire sauce
3/4 cup vegetable oil
1 teaspoon minced onion
1/2 cup vinegar
3 tablespoons poppy seeds
3 tablespoons sesame seeds, toasted

FOR THE SALAD

1 pound fresh spinach, trimmed
1 pint fresh strawberries, sliced
4 medium bananas, sliced
1 cup chopped walnuts, toasted

TO PREPARE THE DRESSING

• Process the sugar, paprika, dry mustard, Worcestershire sauce, oil, onion, vinegar, poppy seeds and sesame seeds in a blender until thickened.

TO PREPARE THE SALAD

• Layer the spinach, strawberries, bananas and walnuts on a large platter. Serve the dressing separately.
• *Note: If the salad is prepared in advance, dip the banana slices in lemon juice to prevent browning.*

WARM SPINACH AND BASIL SALAD

INGREDIENTS

6 cups spinach leaves
2 cups fresh basil
1/2 cup olive oil
2 cloves of garlic, minced
1/2 cup pine nuts
4 ounces prosciutto, chopped
Salt and pepper to taste
3/4 cup grated Parmesan cheese

SERVES 6
PREPARATION TIME:
15 MINUTES

DIRECTIONS

• Combine the spinach and basil in a large salad bowl.
• Heat the olive oil in a skillet over medium heat. Add the garlic and pine nuts; mix well.
• Sauté until the pine nuts are brown. Add the prosciutto; mix well.
• Cook just until heated through, stirring constantly. Pour over the spinach mixture, tossing to coat. Season with the salt and pepper; sprinkle with the Parmesan cheese.

Helpful Hint

When buying spinach, remember that one pound fresh spinach yields about one and one-half cups cooked spinach.

DOUBLE TOMATO SALAD

INGREDIENTS

SERVES 4
PREPARATION TIME:
10 MINUTES

4 large tomatoes, sliced
4 ounces mozzarella cheese, sliced
2 tablespoons oil from sun-dried tomatoes
1 tablespoon olive oil
1 tablespoon red wine vinegar
Salt and pepper to taste
$^1/_4$ cup chopped drained oil-pack sun-dried tomatoes
2 tablespoons capers, rinsed, drained
2 tablespoons chopped fresh basil

DIRECTIONS

• Arrange the sliced tomatoes and sliced mozzarella cheese on a serving platter, alternating slices.
• Whisk the oil from the sun-dried tomatoes, olive oil and wine vinegar in a bowl. Drizzle over the tomatoes and cheese.
• Season with salt and pepper. Sprinkle with the sun-dried tomatoes, capers and basil.

*Tarragon
Chicken Salad*

For a quick and easy entrée, try Tarragon Chicken Salad. Combine 4 chopped poached chicken breasts, $^1/_2$ cup finely chopped celery, 1 tablespoon chopped fresh parsley, $^1/_2$ teaspoon dried tarragon, $^1/_2$ to $^3/_4$ cup mayonnaise, salt, white pepper, $^1/_4$ cup chopped pecans and $^1/_2$ cup green grape halves.

CHICKEN SALAD WITH WILD RICE

FOR THE DRESSING

$^1/_4$ cup white wine vinegar
$^1/_2$ cup olive oil
1 tablespoon chopped fresh tarragon
  or 1 teaspoon dried tarragon
1 teaspoon salt
$^1/_2$ teaspoon pepper

FOR THE SALAD

1 $^1/_2$ cups water
Salt to taste
$^1/_2$ cup wild rice, rinsed
2 cups chopped cooked chicken breasts
1 cup watercress leaves
$^1/_2$ cup thinly sliced green onions
$^1/_2$ cup chopped celery
$^1/_2$ cup chopped blanched almonds, toasted

TO PREPARE THE DRESSING

• Pour the wine vinegar into a bowl. Whisk in the olive oil 1 drop at a time until blended. Stir in the tarragon, salt and pepper.

TO PREPARE THE SALAD

• Bring the water and salt to a boil in a saucepan. Stir in the wild rice. Bring to a boil; stir with a fork. Reduce heat.
• Simmer for 30 to 40 minutes or until tender. Rinse with cold water; drain well.
• Combine the wild rice, chicken, watercress, green onions, celery and almonds in a large bowl; mix well. Add a small amount of the dressing, tossing gently. Continue adding small amounts of the dressing until well coated.
• Chill slightly before serving.

> SERVES 4
> PREPARATION TIME:
> 1 HOUR,
> PLUS CHILLING TIME

Helpful Hint

Lengthen the life of olive oil by adding a cube of sugar to the bottle.

GRILLED JADE CHICKEN SALAD

FOR THE DRESSING

1 1/2 tablespoons grated gingerroot
3/4 cup soy sauce
6 tablespoons sugar
6 tablespoons white vinegar
1/2 cup plus 1 tablespoon vegetable oil
1/4 cup peanut butter

SERVES 8
PREPARATION TIME:
45 MINUTES,
PLUS 6 HOURS
MARINATING TIME

FOR THE SALAD AND ASSEMBLY

6 boneless skinless chicken breast halves
1 (3-ounce) package ramen noodles
1 head romaine, torn into bite-size pieces
1/2 head Napa cabbage, cut into bite-size pieces
6 green onions, sliced
1 (8-ounce) can sliced water chestnuts, drained
4 plum tomatoes, sliced
1 cucumber, sliced

TO PREPARE THE DRESSING

• Combine the gingerroot, soy sauce, sugar, white vinegar and oil in a bowl; mix well. Reserve 1/2 cup of the dressing. Stir the peanut butter into the remaining dressing.

TO PREPARE THE SALAD

• Rinse the chicken and pat dry. Arrange in a shallow dish. Pour the reserved dressing over the chicken, tossing to coat.
• Marinate, covered, in the refrigerator for 6 hours, turning occasionally. Drain the chicken and pat dry.
• Grill over hot coals for 6 minutes per side or until cooked through. Let stand until cool. Cut into thin slices.
• Arrange the ramen noodles on a baking sheet. Bake at 350 degrees for 12 minutes or until golden brown.

TO ASSEMBLE

• Combine the romaine, cabbage, green onions, water chestnuts, plum tomatoes and cucumber in a large salad bowl. Add the dressing, tossing to coat. Top with sliced chicken and ramen noodles.

Helpful Hint

To remove the core of a head of lettuce, hit the core end once sharply against the kitchen countertop. The core can then be easily removed by twisting out. This method prevents the brown spots that result when the core is removed with a knife.

GRILLED SHRIMP SALAD WITH LEMON LIME VINAIGRETTE

FOR THE VINAIGRETTE

SERVES 2
PREPARATION TIME:
50 MINUTES

1 tablespoon lemon juice
2 teaspoons lime juice
1/4 teaspoon grated lemon rind
1/4 cup light olive oil
Salt and pepper to taste

FOR THE SALAD

8 ounces shrimp, peeled, deveined
2 tablespoons (about) olive oil
Garlic salt to taste
1/2 head romaine, torn into bite-size pieces
2 large enoki or button mushrooms, sliced
2 medium slices red onion, chopped
1/3 cup grated carrot
1/3 cup torn radicchio or red cabbage

TO PREPARE THE VINAIGRETTE

- Combine the lemon juice, lime juice and lemon rind in a bowl; mix well. Whisk in the olive oil gradually. Stir in salt and pepper.

TO PREPARE THE SALAD

- Brush the shrimp with the olive oil; sprinkle with garlic salt.
- Grill the shrimp over medium-hot coals or broil until the shrimp turn pink. Let stand until room temperature.
- Combine the shrimp, romaine, mushrooms, onion, carrot and radicchio in a salad bowl; mix well. Add the vinaigrette, tossing to coat.

Helpful Hint

Store lemons in a tightly sealed jar of water in the refrigerator. They will yield more juice than when first purchased.

CHICKEN AND SNOW PEA SALAD WITH GINGER

GERRY KLASKALA, CANOE

INGREDIENTS

SERVES 3
PREPARATION TIME:
30 MINUTES

8 ounces boneless skinless chicken breasts
2 tablespoons salad oil
1 red onion, sliced
1 zucchini, sliced
1 yellow squash, sliced
2 shallots, minced
1 cup snow peas, blanched
1 tablespoon finely minced gingerroot
1 tablespoon chopped fresh coriander
2 tablespoons sherry vinegar
Salt and pepper to taste

DIRECTIONS

- Rinse the chicken and pat dry; cut into thin slices. Sauté the chicken in the oil in a sauté pan until cooked through.
- Remove to a platter; keep warm.
- Sauté the red onion in the pan drippings in the sauté pan until tender. Add the zucchini and yellow squash. Cook just until tender-crisp, stirring frequently. Stir in the shallots. Remove from heat.
- Toss the chicken, onion mixture, snow peas, gingerroot, coriander and sherry vinegar in a serving bowl. Season with the salt and pepper.
- *Variation: Serve chilled over mixed salad greens.*

In Search of Grits

BY ANNE RIVERS SIDDONS
ILLUSTRATION BY ELIZABETH TRAYNOR

I've been doing cross-country book tours every summer for the past six or seven years now, and a large part of that time has been spent trying to fit the Southern culinary ideal to the Northern and Western reality of it. This began, basically, as an attempt to get some grits for breakfast north of Richmond and west of Little Rock, but it has expanded into a sort of a cultural-ideological standoff that I don't

have a prayer of winning but refuse to abandon, either. Did Great-great-great-granddaddy Brown give up before Appomattox?

(No, my husband points out, but his side didn't win either.)

At first it didn't seem so bad. I was titillated by the newness of touring and the abundance (to me) of untried, sophisticated regional cuisine, especially at breakfast. Scrapple in Philadelphia, codfish cakes in Boston, assorted wursts in St. Louis, sushi and miso in Los Angeles and San Francisco. Terrific. Came the morning, however, in Minneapolis, that I wanted grits. Nothing else. Right then.

"Do you have any grits?" I asked the room service telephone person.

"What's that?" I heard for the first of a hundred times.

"It's like...well, it's ground corn, I think..."

"Oh, of course. Hominy grits."

"Well, I guess so..."

What arrived was steaming yellow hominy, just out of the Jolly Green Giant's grasp, with red and green ▶

VEGETABLES

peppers and some kind of thick orange sauce on it.

I tried again in Seattle.

"Grits? What's that?"

"Never mind," I said, and ordered the abalone.

Next tour out I carried along some packets of instant grits, a pale substitute for the real thing, but better, I figured, than nothing. The first morning I asked for a pot of hot water with my breakfast and poured my grits and hot water into an empty cup.

"What is that, some kind of health thing?" the waitress said, eyeing me warily.

"No. It's some kind of Southern thing."

"Oh," she said, reassured. "Southern. You know, I ate some rattlesnake meat in Alabama once."

"Real Southern," I nodded. "How was it?"

"Tasted just like chicken," she said. "So that's grits, huh?"

She pointed to the watery mess in my cup. "What's that taste like?"

"Chicken," I said. "Just like chicken."

By far the worst offender in this new Battle of Bull Run is my New York editor, a relentlessly parochial Manhattanite who thinks we all eat possum and roadkill armadillo down here. He will only eat grits if they are billed as Grits Roulade with Braised Leeks and Etoufee and come from a haute little diner in TriBeCa. He teases me mercilessly about what Southerners ingest.

SAUTEED ARTICHOKES

INGREDIENTS

8 small artichokes, trimmed
1 quart water
1 tablespoon lemon juice
2 tablespoons olive oil
2 tablespoons butter or margarine
3 cloves of garlic, minced
1/4 cup chopped fresh parsley
1/2 teaspoon dried basil
2 teaspoons dried oregano
1/2 teaspoon dried rosemary
Salt and pepper to taste
1/2 cup white wine

SERVES 4
PREPARATION TIME:
40 MINUTES

DIRECTIONS

- Cut the artichokes into quarters. Place in a mixture of the water and lemon juice in a bowl. Let stand for several minutes; drain well.
- Heat the olive oil and butter in a medium skillet. Add the artichokes and garlic. Brown lightly on all sides.
- Stir in the parsley, basil, oregano, rosemary, salt, pepper and wine. Steam, covered, over low heat for 20 minutes or until the artichokes are tender-crisp. Cook, uncovered, for several minutes longer if necessary to reduce excess liquid.
- *Note: You may substitute canned artichoke hearts if small fresh artichokes are not available.*

Asparagus and Mushroom Saute

INGREDIENTS

Serves 6
Preparation Time:
25 minutes

1 pound tender asparagus spears
1/2 cup chopped green onions
3 tablespoons olive oil
1 pound mushrooms, cut into halves
2 tablespoons chopped fresh thyme
* or 2 teaspoons dried thyme*
1 teaspoon salt
1/2 teaspoon pepper
6 tablespoons dry white wine
1/2 cup grated Parmesan cheese
2 teaspoons grated lemon zest

DIRECTIONS

- Trim the asparagus and cut into 1-inch pieces.
- Cook the green onions in the olive oil in a skillet over medium heat for 1 minute, stirring constantly. Add the asparagus, mushrooms, thyme, salt and pepper. Cook for 3 minutes, stirring constantly.
- Stir in the wine. Cook, covered, for 2 minutes; drain.
- Spoon into a serving dish. Sprinkle with the cheese and lemon zest to serve.

When at last he visited, I got my revenge.

"What's that?" he said suspiciously, poking at his steaming plate at Deacon Burton's.

"Soul food," I said. "The real thing. You'd pay a fortune for it in New York. Eat up. You can tell everybody at Michael's about it when you get home."

He took a bite. And then another.

"Mmmmm. It's good. What is it?"

"Well, that's collards, and that's Hoppin' John, and what you just ate is a thing called chitlings."

"Terrific," he said, digging in. "Tastes just like chicken."

"Close," I grinned. "But no cigar."

GREEN BEANS WITH PEPPERS AND LEEKS

INGREDIENTS

1 1/2 pounds fresh green beans, trimmed
1 small red bell pepper, cut into strips
1 small yellow bell pepper, cut into strips
1 large leek, white portion only, sliced
2 tablespoons olive oil
1/4 cup white wine
1 teaspoon leaf marjoram
1 teaspoon salt
1/2 teaspoon pepper

> SERVES 6
> PREPARATION TIME:
> 1 1/4 HOURS

DIRECTIONS

- Cut an 18x48-inch piece of heavy-duty foil. Fold in half to measure 18x24 inches. Place the beans, bell peppers and leek lengthwise down the foil.
- Drizzle the vegetables with the olive oil and wine; sprinkle with the marjoram, salt and pepper. Wrap the foil to enclose the vegetables; seal well.
- Bake at 350 degrees for 30 minutes; unwrap. Bake for 30 minutes longer. May roast on a grill with the lid closed.

Herbed Caper Butter

Drizzle this delicious butter over artichokes, asparagus, broccoli, cauliflower, corn, green beans, peas and summer squash. Combine 1/4 cup butter with 2 teaspoons small capers, 1/2 teaspoon dried oregano and 1/8 teaspoon pepper in a saucepan. Heat just until the butter melts, stirring to mix well.

GREEN BEANS PROVENCAL

INGREDIENTS

1/2 cup water
1 pound fresh green beans, trimmed
1 onion, chopped
4 cloves of garlic, minced
2 tablespoons olive oil
4 large tomatoes, peeled, seeded, chopped
1/2 cup dry white wine
1 (2-ounce) can sliced black olives, drained
1 tablespoon lemon juice
1/4 teaspoon pepper

DIRECTIONS

• Bring the water to a boil in a large saucepan. Add the beans; reduce the heat to medium. Simmer, covered, for 10 minutes or until tender. Drain and keep warm.

• Sauté the onion and garlic in the olive oil in a large skillet over high heat for 5 minutes or until tender. Stir in the tomatoes and wine. Bring to a boil; reduce the heat. Simmer for 20 minutes, stirring occasionally. Stir in the olives.

• Spoon the sauce over the green beans in a serving bowl. Sprinkle with the lemon juice and pepper.

Helpful Hint

Cooking vegetables with the least amount of water possible will preserve the vitamins and maintain the flavor.

GARLIC BRUSSELS SPROUTS

INGREDIENTS

[
SERVES 8
PREPARATION TIME:
30 MINUTES
]

3 pounds brussels sprouts
8 cloves of garlic, chopped
2 1/2 tablespoons unsalted butter
2 1/2 tablespoons olive oil
1 cup chicken broth
Salt and pepper to taste
2 tablespoons melted butter or margarine
2 tablespoons chopped fresh parsley

Helpful Hint

Remove the green sprout from the center of a clove of garlic to eliminate a bitter taste.

DIRECTIONS

• Cut off the stems of the brussels sprouts and cut a small x in the base of each sprout, discarding outer leaves. Rinse in cold water and pat dry.
• Cook the garlic in the unsalted butter and olive oil in a saucepan over low heat for 2 to 3 minutes or until the garlic begins to brown. Add the brussels sprouts; toss to coat well.
• Stir in the chicken broth, salt and pepper. Cook, covered, over medium heat for 10 to 15 minutes or until the brussels sprouts are done to taste; drain.
• Add the melted butter and parsley; toss to coat well.

FRUITED CARROTS

INGREDIENTS

8 medium carrots, peeled, diagonally sliced
2 tablespoons butter or margarine
2 tablespoons brown sugar
3 tablespoons vermouth or dry white wine
2 teaspoons cornstarch
3 tablespoons water
3/4 cup green grape halves
3/4 cup red grape halves

SERVES 4
PREPARATION TIME:
30 MINUTES

DIRECTIONS

- Cook the carrots in boiling water to cover in a saucepan for 8 minutes; drain well.
- Melt the butter in a saucepan. Stir in the brown sugar and wine.
- Blend in a mixture of the cornstarch and 3 tablespoons water. Cook until thickened, stirring constantly and adding additional water if needed for desired consistency.
- Stir in the carrots. Cook until heated through. Add the grapes just before serving.

Helpful Hint

To keep the flavor of carrots, peas, beets and corn, add a small amount of sugar to the water after cooking.

CARROT SOUFFLE

INGREDIENTS

1 pound carrots, peeled, sliced
Salt to taste
$1/2$ cup melted butter or margarine
$1/2$ cup sugar
1 teaspoon baking powder
3 tablespoons flour
3 eggs
1 teaspoon vanilla extract

SERVES 8
PREPARATION TIME:
1 $1/4$ HOURS

DIRECTIONS

- Cook the carrots in salted water to cover in a saucepan until tender; drain. Combine with the butter in a blender or food processor container; process until smooth.
- Combine the sugar, baking powder, flour, eggs and vanilla in a bowl; mix well. Add the carrot mixture; mix well.
- Spoon into a greased baking dish. Bake at 350 degrees for 45 minutes.

Pecan Butter

For Pecan Butter, combine $1/2$ cup melted butter, $1/2$ cup toasted chopped pecans, 3 tablespoons lemon juice, 2 tablespoons chopped chives, $1/4$ teaspoon dried marjoram, $1/2$ teaspoon salt and $1/4$ teaspoon pepper in a saucepan and mix well. Heat just until the flavors blend. Serve with artichokes, asparagus, carrots, green beans, peas, potatoes, squash and sweet potatoes.

CAULIFLOWER DIJON

INGREDIENTS

Serves 8
Preparation Time:
30 minutes

2 medium heads cauliflower
2 tablespoons butter or margarine
3 tablespoons flour
1 cup chicken broth
1 cup half-and-half
1/4 cup Dijon mustard
2 teaspoons lemon juice
Freshly ground pepper to taste

DIRECTIONS

- Cut the cauliflower into florets. Steam in a saucepan for 12 minutes or until tender-crisp.
- Melt the butter in a saucepan. Stir in the flour. Cook for 1 minute, stirring constantly. Add the chicken broth and half-and-half. Bring to a boil, stirring constantly; reduce heat. Simmer for 5 minutes, stirring occasionally. Remove from heat.
- Whisk in the mustard, lemon juice and pepper. Spoon over the warm cauliflower in a serving bowl.
- *Note: The sauce can be prepared in advance and reheated over low heat.*

Sherry Supreme Sauce

Sherry Supreme Sauce is delicious over broccoli or cauliflower. Stir 2 tablespoons flour into 2 tablespoons melted butter in a saucepan. Add 1/2 cup half-and-half and 1/2 cup chicken broth gradually. Cook until thickened, stirring constantly. Stir in 1/4 cup shredded Swiss cheese, 2 tablespoons sherry and salt to taste.

STUFFED COLLARD ROLLS WITH TOMATO SAUCE

SERVES 6
PREPARATION TIME:
2 HOURS

FOR THE SAUCE

1 cup chopped onion
2 tablespoons butter or margarine
3 tablespoons dry red wine
1 (28-ounce) can plum tomatoes, drained, chopped
$^1/_8$ teaspoon sugar
$^1/_4$ teaspoon crushed rosemary
$^1/_2$ teaspoon dried oregano
Red pepper flakes, salt and black pepper to taste

FOR THE COLLARD ROLLS

24 collard leaves
1 (10-ounce) package frozen corn, thawed
15 ounces ricotta cheese
8 ounces mozzarella cheese, cut into $^1/_4$-inch cubes
1 egg, beaten
2 small red bell peppers, chopped
$^1/_2$ cup sliced scallions
Salt and pepper to taste
$^1/_4$ cup minced fresh parsley

TO PREPARE THE SAUCE

- Sauté the onion in the butter in a saucepan over medium-low heat until tender. Add the wine. Simmer for 2 minutes.
- Add the tomatoes, sugar, rosemary, oregano, red pepper flakes, salt and black pepper; mix well. Simmer until the mixture is thickened and most of the liquid has evaporated, stirring occasionally.
- Spread the sauce in a large shallow baking dish.

Lemon Sauce

Serve Lemon Sauce over asparagus or broccoli. Stir 2 tablespoons flour into 3 tablespoons melted butter in a saucepan. Add $^1/_4$ cup lemon juice and 1 cup boiling water. Cook until thickened, stirring constantly. Add $^1/_2$ cup cream, a dash of hot sauce and $^1/_4$ teaspoon salt and simmer for 5 minutes. Whisk in 1 tablespoon butter just before serving.

TO PREPARE THE COLLARD ROLLS

- Cook the collard leaves in water in a saucepan for 10 minutes or until tender-crisp. Drain and refresh in cold water. Remove each stem and ⅓ of the tough center rib; pat dry.
- Drain the corn and pat dry.
- Combine the corn, ricotta cheese, mozzarella cheese, egg, bell peppers, scallions, salt and pepper in a bowl; mix well.
- Spoon 2 tablespoons of the cheese mixture at the top end of each collard leaf; roll the leaves to enclose the filling, tucking the ends under. Arrange in a single layer in the sauce in the prepared dish.
- Bake, covered, at 375 degrees for 45 to 50 minutes or until the rolls are cooked through and the sauce is bubbly.
- Remove the rolls to a serving plate; keep warm. Spoon the sauce into a saucepan. Cook until thickened to the desired consistency.
- Stir in the parsley. Spoon over the rolls.

SPICY CORN STIR-FRY

INGREDIENTS

1 red bell pepper, chopped
1 tablespoon minced jalapeño
2 tablespoons butter or margarine
1½ teaspoons ground cumin
2 cups cooked fresh corn or 1 (16-ounce)
  package frozen corn

SERVES 4
PREPARATION TIME:
20 MINUTES

DIRECTIONS

- Stir-fry the bell pepper and jalapeño in the butter in a heavy skillet over medium heat for 5 minutes. Add the cumin. Stir-fry for 30 seconds.
- Add the corn. Stir-fry for 2 minutes or until heated through.

Helpful Hint

You will get more juice if you roll lemons, grapefruit or oranges on the counter to soften them before cutting.

SAUTE OF EGGPLANT WITH SHIITAKE MUSHROOMS AND PEPPERS

ROBIN CHURCHILL, TO DINE FOR

> SERVES 6
> PREPARATION TIME:
> 30 MINUTES,
> PLUS 1 HOUR
> STANDING TIME

INGREDIENTS

8 small dried shiitake mushrooms
1 cup warm water
2 tablespoons dry vermouth or dry white wine
1 tablespoon soy sauce
1 tablespoon red wine vinegar
2 teaspoons chile paste
1 medium eggplant
2 teaspoons salt
6 tablespoons peanut oil
4 shallots, sliced
4 cloves of garlic, minced
1 red bell pepper, cut into 1 1/2-inch pieces
1 yellow bell pepper, cut into 1 1/2-inch pieces
10 fresh shiitake mushrooms, cut into quarters

DIRECTIONS

- Rinse the dried mushrooms. Soak in the warm water in a bowl for 30 minutes or until softened. Squeeze the mushrooms dry, discarding the tough stems; cut the caps into quarters.
- Combine the wine, soy sauce, vinegar and chile paste in a bowl; mix well. Set aside.
- Peel the eggplant and cut into 1 1/2-inch cubes. Sprinkle with the salt in a large bowl. Let stand for 30 minutes; drain and pat dry.
- Fry the eggplant in the oil in a skillet over high heat until golden brown. Remove the eggplant with a slotted spoon. Add the bell peppers, shallots, garlic and fresh mushrooms to the oil in the skillet. Stir-fry until tender; drain in a colander.
- Combine with the eggplant, soaked mushrooms and wine sauce in the skillet, tossing to coat well. Cook until heated through. Serve hot or at room temperature.
- *Note: Do not refrigerate this dish, as it dulls the flavor.*

Helpful Hint

Sand and dirt can be easily removed from fresh vegetables by soaking the vegetables in salted warm water for five minutes.

Vidalia Onion Tart

GUENTER SEEGER, EXECUTIVE CHEF—THE DINING ROOM,
THE RITZ-CARLTON® BUCKHEAD

SERVES 6
PREPARATION TIME:
1 HOUR, PLUS
2 HOURS
CHILLING TIME

INGREDIENTS

10 1/2 tablespoons butter or margarine,
   chilled, chopped
2 cups plus 1 tablespoon flour
Salt to taste
1/4 cup ice water
3 Vidalia onions, chopped
2 tablespoons butter or margarine
1 cup whipping cream
1 egg
1 egg yolk
Nutmeg and pepper to taste
Cumin seeds to taste

DIRECTIONS

- Cut the chilled butter into the flour and salt in a bowl until crumbly. Add the ice water; mix lightly to form a dough. Chill for 2 hours or longer.
- Roll the dough 1/8 inch thick on a floured surface. Fit into a pie plate. Prick all over with a fork and set aside.
- Sauté the onions in 2 tablespoons butter in a skillet until tender. Add the cream. Cook until thickened and reduced to the desired consistency. Stir in the egg and egg yolk. Season with nutmeg, salt and pepper.
- Spoon into the prepared pie plate; sprinkle with cumin seeds.
- Bake at 400 degrees on lower oven rack for 25 minutes or until set.

The Vidalia Onion

The Vidalia® Onion story takes root in Toombs County, Georgia over 60 years ago, when a farmer by the name of Mose Coleman discovered in the late spring of 1931 that the onions he had planted were not hot, as he expected. They were *sweet!*

In the 1940s, the State of Georgia built a Farmers' Market in Vidalia, and because the small town was at the juncture of some of South Georgia's most widely traveled highways, the market had a thriving tourist business. Word began to spread about "those Vidalia onions." Consumers, then, gave the onions their famous name.

In 1986, Georgia's state legislature passed legislation giving the Vidalia Onion legal status and defining the 20-county production area. The Vidalia Onion was named Georgia's Official State Vegetable by the state legislature in 1990.

®Vidalia is a registered U.S. Certification mark
of the Georgia Department of Agriculture.

SUGAR SNAP PEAS WITH LEMON AND BASIL

INGREDIENTS

SERVES 4
PREPARATION TIME:
30 MINUTES

1 1/2 pounds sugar snap peas, trimmed
2 teaspoons olive oil
1 teaspoon grated lemon zest
1/2 cup chopped fresh basil
1/2 teaspoon salt
1/2 teaspoon white pepper

DIRECTIONS

- Sauté the peas in heated olive oil in a skillet over medium heat for 3 minutes or until tender-crisp.
- Sprinkle with the lemon zest, basil, salt and white pepper.
- Sauté for 1 minute longer.

Vidalia Onions

A fresh Vidalia Onion has a light golden-brown bulb and a white interior. Its shape is rounded on the bottom and somewhat flat on the top or stem end. Ordinary storage onions are darker, have a thicker skin and are generally more round or oblong.

BLEU CHEESE VIDALIA ONIONS

INGREDIENTS

SERVES 4
PREPARATION TIME:
35 MINUTES

2 large Vidalia onions
6 ounces bleu cheese, crumbled
2 tablespoons unsalted butter, softened
2 teaspoons Worcestershire sauce
1/2 teaspoon dillweed
Freshly ground pepper to taste

DIRECTIONS

- Slice the onions into a 9x13-inch baking dish. Combine the bleu cheese, butter, Worcestershire sauce, dillweed and pepper in a bowl; mix well. Spread over the onions.
- Bake at 425 degrees for 20 minutes. Broil just until the top is brown and bubbly.

STUFFED YELLOW PEPPERS

INGREDIENTS

SERVES 4
PREPARATION TIME:
1 1/4 HOURS

3/4 cup uncooked long grain rice
3 tablespoons dried currants
1/4 cup orange juice
1 large onion, chopped
2 cloves of garlic, minced
2 tablespoons olive oil
1 tablespoon chopped sun-dried tomatoes
1 teaspoon ground coriander
1 tablespoon chopped fresh basil or 1 teaspoon dried basil
1 tablespoon chopped fresh parsley
Salt and pepper to taste
4 large yellow bell peppers

DIRECTIONS

- Cook the rice using the package directions; set aside.
- Soak the currants in the orange juice for several minutes; drain.
- Cook the onion and garlic in heated olive oil in a large skillet for 10 minutes, stirring occasionally. Add the rice, currants, tomatoes, coriander, basil, parsley, salt and pepper; mix well.
- Cut the tops from the peppers, reserving the tops; discard the seeds and membranes. Fill with the rice mixture; replace the tops. Place in a deep baking dish rubbed with additional olive oil; peppers should fit snugly.
- Bake, covered, at 350 degrees for 35 minutes or until the peppers are tender. Bake, uncovered, for 15 minutes longer or until light brown. Serve warm or at room temperature.

Confetti Dressing

Process 8 ounces cream cheese, 1/2 cup sour cream, 1/2 cup loosely packed fresh parsley, 1/2 cup loosely packed fresh rosemary, dillweed or thyme, 1/4 teaspoon salt, 1/2 cup chopped scallions and 1 tablespoon white pepper in a food processor until smooth. Add 1 tablespoon white wine vinegar, 1/4 cup olive oil and 2 tablespoons milk, processing constantly until blended. Sprinkle with 1/2 cup chopped red or yellow bell pepper. Great topping for baked potatoes or use as a dip with fresh vegetables.

SCALLOPED POTATOES WITH GARDEN TOMATOES

INGREDIENTS

SERVES 8
PREPARATION TIME:
2 HOURS

2 pounds tomatoes
3 cups thinly sliced onions
2 cloves of garlic, minced
2 tablespoons olive oil
2 tablespoons butter or margarine
2 tablespoons chopped parsley
1/2 teaspoon basil
1/2 teaspoon oregano
1 1/2 teaspoons salt
Freshly ground pepper to taste
2 1/2 pounds potatoes, peeled, thinly sliced
1 cup shredded Swiss cheese
2 tablespoons grated Parmesan cheese
2 tablespoons butter or margarine

DIRECTIONS

- Peel the tomatoes and cut into halves, discarding the seeds. Invert to drain for 1 minute. Chop the tomatoes.
- Sauté the onions and garlic in the olive oil and 2 tablespoons butter in a skillet until tender but not brown. Add the tomatoes, parsley, basil, oregano, salt and pepper; mix gently.
- Spoon 1/3 of the tomato mixture into a greased 3-quart baking dish.
- Layer the potatoes, Swiss cheese, Parmesan cheese and remaining tomato mixture 1/2 at a time in the prepared dish. Dot with 2 tablespoons butter.
- Bake at 375 degrees for 1 1/2 hours or until the potatoes are tender.

Goat Cheese Sauce

Try Goat Cheese Sauce over asparagus, broccoli or potatoes. Combine 3 ounces cream cheese, 3 ounces goat cheese and 1/4 cup mayonnaise in a saucepan. Heat over medium heat until smooth, stirring to blend well. Stir in 1/4 cup milk and 1 tablespoon chopped chives.

MARBLED POTATOES

INGREDIENTS

SERVES 6
PREPARATION TIME:
2 HOURS

1 pound red potatoes
1 pound sweet potatoes
2 large scallions, chopped
1/4 cup butter or margarine
1/2 cup sour cream or plain yogurt
1/2 cup whipping cream, whipped
Nutmeg to taste
1 teaspoon salt
1/2 teaspoon pepper
1/4 cup fresh bread crumbs
2 tablespoons melted butter or margarine
2 tablespoons minced fresh parsley

Helpful Hint

Use a couple of tablespoons of
cream cheese in place of butter
for mashed potatoes.

DIRECTIONS

- Cook the red potatoes and the sweet potatoes separately in water to
  cover in saucepans until tender; drain. Cool slightly and peel.
  Mash in separate bowls.
- Sauté the scallions in 1/4 cup butter in a skillet until tender.
  Stir half the scallions into each bowl of potatoes.
- Whisk the sour cream with the whipped cream in a bowl. Fold half
  gently into each bowl of potatoes. Add half the nutmeg, salt and pepper
  to each bowl.
- Layer the potatoes 1/2 at a time in a greased 1-quart soufflé dish.
  Swirl with a knife to marbleize. Sprinkle with a mixture of the bread
  crumbs, melted butter and parsley.
- Bake at 350 degrees for 30 to 35 minutes or until the topping is
  golden brown.
- *Note: This casserole freezes well before baking.*

SPINACH AND ARTICHOKE TART

INGREDIENTS

1 small onion, chopped
1 clove of garlic, minced
2 tablespoons melted butter or margarine
1 (14-ounce) can artichokes, drained
1 (10-ounce) package frozen spinach, thawed, drained
1/2 cup sliced mushrooms
1/4 cup grated Parmesan cheese
Salt and pepper to taste
1 sheet frozen puff pastry, thawed
1 egg
1 tablespoon water

Helpful Hint

Before trying out a new recipe, read through it once to make sure that you have all the ingredients on hand.

DIRECTIONS

- Sauté the onion and garlic in the butter in a saucepan until tender. Add the artichokes, spinach, mushrooms, cheese, salt and pepper; mix well.
- Roll the puff pastry to an 11x14-inch rectangle on a lightly floured surface. Spread the vegetable filling on half the pastry, leaving a 1/2-inch edge. Fold the remaining half of the pastry over the filling, pressing the edges to seal.
- Make several diagonal slashes in the top. Brush with a mixture of the egg and water. Place on a baking sheet.
- Bake at 400 degrees for 30 minutes or until golden brown. Cool slightly. Slice with a bread knife to serve. Serve warm or cool.

SPINACH WITH OLIVES AND PINE NUTS

INGREDIENTS

SERVES 8
PREPARATION TIME:
45 MINUTES

4 large bunches spinach, trimmed
4 large cloves of garlic, chopped
1/3 cup black olives, cut into quarters
1/3 cup raisins
1/4 cup olive oil
1/4 cup pine nuts, toasted
1 1/2 tablespoons balsamic vinegar
Salt and pepper to taste

DIRECTIONS

- Toss 1/3 of the undrained spinach at a time in a heavy saucepan over high heat for 3 minutes or until wilted but still green. Drain and cool in a colander lined with a kitchen towel, pressing to remove the excess moisture.
- Sauté the garlic, olives and raisins in heated olive oil in a large skillet over medium heat for 3 minutes or until the garlic begins to brown.
- Add the spinach and pine nuts. Cook until heated through, tossing to mix well. Add the vinegar, salt and pepper; mix lightly.

Helpful Hint

To save the unused portions of olives or pimentos, cover them with a little vinegar, seal them tightly and refrigerate.

ACORN SQUASH WITH APPLE STUFFING

INGREDIENTS

2 medium acorn squash
2 McIntosh or Red Delicious apples, chopped
1/2 cup chopped walnuts or pecans
1/2 cup raisins
5 tablespoons brown sugar
3 tablespoons melted butter or margarine

[
SERVES 4
PREPARATION TIME:
1 HOUR AND
20 MINUTES
]

DIRECTIONS

- Slice the squash into halves, discarding the seeds. Place in a baking dish. Bake for 30 minutes.
- Combine the apples, walnuts, raisins and brown sugar in a bowl; mix well. Spoon into the squash. Drizzle with the melted butter.
- Bake at 350 degrees for 25 to 30 minutes or until done to taste.

Helpful Hint

When making squash casseroles, save time and add a nice crunch by grating the squash instead of slicing and adding to the dish uncooked.

BAKED YELLOW SQUASH AND ZUCCHINI

INGREDIENTS

4 medium yellow squash, sliced
3 medium zucchini, sliced
1 medium yellow onion, chopped
2 cloves of garlic, crushed, chopped
1 tablespoon butter or margarine
8 ounces white Cheddar cheese, shredded
1 egg, beaten
Salt and pepper to taste
1/4 cup grated Parmesan cheese

[
SERVES 8
PREPARATION TIME:
1 1/4 HOURS
]

DIRECTIONS

- Cook the yellow squash and zucchini in water in a saucepan just until tender; drain well.
- Sauté the onion and garlic in the butter in a skillet just until light brown. Add the squash, Cheddar cheese, egg, salt and pepper; mix well. Spoon into a 9x13-inch baking dish; top with the Parmesan cheese.
- Bake at 350 degrees for 30 minutes.

Sweet Potato Souffle

Marge Klepinger, Mary Mac's Tea Room

INGREDIENTS

[
Serves 8
Preparation Time:
1 3/4 hours
]

2 pounds small sweet potatoes
1/4 cup butter or margarine
1/4 cup sugar
1/3 cup light cream
2 eggs, beaten
Cinnamon and/or allspice to taste
2 cups miniature marshmallows

DIRECTIONS

- Cook the sweet potatoes in water to cover in a saucepan for 1 hour or until tender; drain. Peel the potatoes and mash in a large bowl.
- Add the butter, sugar, cream, eggs and cinnamon; mix well. Spoon into a greased 2-quart baking dish.
- Bake at 350 degrees for 30 to 40 minutes or until the center is set. Increase the oven temperature to 475 degrees. Top with the marshmallows. Bake for 3 to 5 minutes or until golden brown.
- *Variation: Omit the marshmallows, reduce the sugar slightly and fold in 1/2 cup raisins and 1/2 cup toasted pecans.*

Orange Butter

Try Orange Butter on asparagus, carrots, winter squash and sweet potatoes. Squeeze an orange and strain the juice, reserving the pulp and juice separately. Combine the juice with 1 tablespoon Grand Marnier and 1 tablespoon white wine vinegar and cook over medium heat until reduced to about 2 tablespoons; remove it from the heat. Whisk in 1/2 cup cold butter 1 tablespoon at a time until thick and creamy. Stir in the orange pulp.

Sweet Potato Hash

TRAVIS HOLEWINSKI, SOUTH CITY KITCHEN

INGREDIENTS

4 sweet potatoes, peeled
2 cups dried cranberries
2 cups corn, blanched
1 cup chopped red bell pepper
2 cups chopped pecans
2 cups finely chopped parsley
1 cup honey

[
SERVES 14
PREPARATION TIME:
40 MINUTES
]

DIRECTIONS

• Cut the sweet potatoes into cubes the size of the dried cranberries. Cook in water to cover in a saucepan until tender but still firm; drain.
• Mix the cranberries, corn, bell pepper, pecans and parsley in a large bowl. Add the sweet potatoes and honey; mix lightly to coat well.

Orange Glaze

For Orange Glaze, combine 3 tablespoons orange juice, 1¹/₂ tablespoons sugar, ¹/₄ cup butter, 6 cloves and ¹/₄ teaspoon salt in a saucepan. Heat until the butter melts and flavors blend. Remove the cloves before serving over carrots, winter squash or sweet potatoes.

Curried Green Tomatoes

INGREDIENTS

2 green onions, sliced
2 tablespoons melted butter or margarine
³/₄ teaspoon curry powder
¹/₄ teaspoon lemon pepper
¹/₄ teaspoon garlic powder
¹/₄ teaspoon seasoned pepper
3 green tomatoes, sliced ¹/₄ inch thick
¹/₂ cup vegetable broth

[
SERVES 4
PREPARATION TIME:
30 MINUTES
]

DIRECTIONS

• Sauté the green onions in the butter in a large skillet over medium heat until tender. Stir in the seasonings. Stir in the green tomatoes and half the vegetable broth.
• Simmer for 10 minutes or until the green tomatoes are tender, adding additional vegetable broth as needed for desired consistency.

TOMATOES ROCKEFELLER

INGREDIENTS

1 (10-ounce) package frozen chopped spinach
1/3 cup herb stuffing, crushed
3 green onions, minced
1 egg, beaten
3 tablespoons melted butter or margarine
2 tablespoons grated Parmesan cheese
1/4 teaspoon salt
1/4 teaspoon black pepper
6 thick tomato slices
Garlic salt to taste
Cayenne to taste

SERVES 6
PREPARATION TIME:
1 HOUR

DIRECTIONS

- Cook the spinach using the package directions; drain. Combine with the herb stuffing, green onions, egg, butter, cheese, salt and black pepper in a bowl; mix well.
- Arrange the tomato slices in a greased baking dish; sprinkle with the garlic salt. Top with the spinach mixture.
- Bake at 350 degrees for 15 minutes or until the tomatoes are tender. Sprinkle with the cayenne.
- *Note: The spinach mixture can be made in advance and refrigerated.*

Herbed Butter

Herbed Butter is good with any vegetable. Combine 1/2 cup softened butter with 2 tablespoons each chopped parsley and watercress; 1 1/2 teaspoons each minced tarragon, minced mint, grated Parmesan cheese and Pernod; 1/2 teaspoon grated lemon zest; 1/4 teaspoon each salt and hot sauce; and a pinch of white pepper. Shape the butter into a 1x6-inch roll on waxed paper to chill. Serve at room temperature.

STUFFED TOMATOES

INGREDIENTS

SERVES 6
PREPARATION TIME:
50 MINUTES

6 firm ripe tomatoes
1 cup corn kernels
1 jalapeño, minced
1/4 cup chopped green onions
1/4 cup minced green bell pepper
3 tablespoons chopped fresh basil
4 ounces Monterey Jack cheese, shredded
1/2 teaspoon salt
Pepper to taste
1 tablespoon cornmeal
1 tablespoon butter or margarine

Helpful Hint
___

Warmth rather than sunlight ripens tomatoes, so place them near the stove or dishwasher to receive heat.

DIRECTIONS

- Slice off the top quarter of each tomato. Scoop the pulp from each tomato, reserving half the pulp. Invert the tomato shells to drain.
- Combine the reserved pulp with the corn, jalapeño, green onions, green pepper, basil, cheese, salt and pepper in a bowl; toss to mix well.
- Spoon into the tomato shells. Sprinkle with the cornmeal and dot with butter. Arrange on a lightly greased baking sheet.
- Bake at 400 degrees for 25 minutes or until the topping is golden brown and the tomatoes are tender.

TOMATO AND CHEESE HERB TART

FOR THE PASTRY

1 1/4 cups flour
1/4 teaspoon salt
1/2 cup butter or margarine, chilled, chopped

> SERVES 8
> PREPARATION TIME:
> 1 1/2 HOURS, PLUS
> 1 1/2 HOURS
> CHILLING, FREEZING
> AND DRAINING TIME

FOR THE FILLING

5 medium tomatoes
9 ounces Gruyère cheese, thinly sliced
1 tablespoon minced fresh basil or 1 teaspoon dried basil
1 teaspoon minced fresh thyme or 1/4 teaspoon dried thyme
1 teaspoon minced fresh oregano or 1/4 teaspoon dried oregano
Pepper to taste
3 tablespoons grated Parmesan cheese

TO PREPARE THE PASTRY

- Combine the flour and salt in a food processor. Add the butter. Pulse until the mixture resembles coarse meal. Add ice water 1 tablespoon at a time until moistened.
- Shape into a ball and wrap in plastic wrap. Chill for 30 minutes. Roll the pastry into a 13-inch circle on a lightly floured surface.
- Place in an 11-inch tart pan with a removable side; trim the edges. Freeze for 15 minutes.
- Line the pastry with foil and fill with dried beans. Bake at 375 degrees for 15 minutes or until set. Remove the beans and foil.
- Bake for 15 minutes longer or until golden brown. Cool on a wire rack.

TO PREPARE THE FILLING

- Slice the tomatoes 1/2 inch thick; cut the slices into halves.
- Drain on paper towels for 45 minutes.
- Layer the Gruyère cheese and tomatoes in the tart shell; sprinkle the basil, thyme, oregano, pepper and Parmesan cheese over the tomatoes.
- Bake at 375 degrees for 35 minutes or until the cheese melts and the tomatoes are tender. Cool slightly. Remove the side of the pan and cut the tart into wedges.

Sun-Dried Tomato Butter

For Sun-Dried Tomato Butter, combine 1/2 cup softened butter or margarine, 1 minced clove of garlic, 1 1/2 teaspoons lemon juice, 2 tablespoons minced drained oil-pack sun-dried tomatoes, 1 small chopped, cored, seeded fresh tomato and 1/4 cup chopped parsley. Shape the butter into a 1x8-inch log on waxed paper to chill. Serve at room temperature on artichokes, asparagus, broccoli, cauliflower, corn, green beans, peas, spinach or summer squash.

ZUCCHINI PIE

SERVES 6
PREPARATION TIME:
45 MINUTES

INGREDIENTS

1 unbaked (9-inch) deep-dish pie shell
2 teaspoons Dijon mustard
4 cups thinly sliced zucchini
1 cup chopped onion
1/3 cup butter or margarine
1/2 cup chopped parsley
1/4 teaspoon garlic powder
1/4 teaspoon dried basil
1/4 teaspoon dried oregano
1/2 teaspoon salt
1/2 teaspoon pepper
2 eggs, beaten
2 cups shredded mozzarella cheese

DIRECTIONS

- Bake the pie shell at 375 degrees for 5 to 7 minutes or just until set; do not brown. Brush with the mustard.
- Sauté the zucchini and onion in the butter in a skillet for 10 minutes, stirring occasionally. Stir in the parsley, garlic powder, basil, oregano, salt and pepper.
- Beat the eggs with the cheese in a bowl. Add to the zucchini mixture; mix well. Spoon into the pie shell.
- Bake at 375 degrees for 20 minutes. Let stand for 10 minutes before serving.

Sesame Seed and Lemon Butter

Sesame Seed and Lemon Butter is a delicious addition to most vegetables. Combine 5 tablespoons melted butter with 2 tablespoons toasted sesame seeds, 1 tablespoon lemon juice and salt and pepper to taste in a saucepan. Heat until the flavors are blended.

GRILLED VEGETABLE KABOBS

INGREDIENTS

> Serves 4
> PREPARATION TIME:
> 40 MINUTES, PLUS
> 2 HOURS CHILLING
> AND MARINATING

1 cup oil-free Italian salad dressing
1 tablespoon lemon juice
1 tablespoon chopped fresh parsley
1 tablespoon chopped fresh basil
2 medium yellow squash, sliced 1 inch thick
2 medium zucchini, sliced 1 inch thick
8 small boiling onions
8 cherry tomatoes
8 mushrooms

DIRECTIONS

- Combine the salad dressing, lemon juice, parsley and basil in a bowl; mix well. Chill in the refrigerator.
- Thread the yellow squash, zucchini, onions, tomatoes and mushrooms onto 8 skewers. Combine with the marinade in a shallow dish.
- Marinate for 1 hour or longer.
- Spray the grill with nonstick cooking spray. Grill the kabobs for 15 minutes or until tender, turning frequently and basting with the marinade.

Helpful Hint

Keep parsley fresh longer by storing it in an airtight container. Add salt to parsley to make the chopping easier.

VEGETABLE PAELLA

INGREDIENTS

SERVES 6
PREPARATION TIME:
1 HOUR AND
10 MINUTES

2 (14-ounce) cans artichoke hearts
Lemon juice to taste
2 onions, chopped
2 tablespoons olive oil
2 (15-ounce) cans tomatoes, drained, chopped
3 leeks, white portion only, chopped
3 green bell peppers, cut into strips
6 asparagus spears, cut into pieces
1/2 cup thawed frozen peas
4 (10-ounce) cans chicken or vegetable broth
1 clove of garlic, minced
2 sprigs of parsley, minced, or 1 teaspoon dried parsley
Salt and pepper to taste
3 (5-ounce) packages yellow rice

DIRECTIONS

- Drain the artichoke hearts. Cut the artichoke hearts into halves and sprinkle with the lemon juice. Set aside.
- Sauté the onions in heated olive oil in a large skillet.
- Stir in the tomatoes, leeks, artichoke hearts, green peppers, asparagus, peas and 1 can of the chicken broth.
- Bring to a boil. Simmer for 10 minutes. Stir in the remaining 3 cans broth, garlic, parsley, salt and pepper. Add the rice.
- Simmer, covered, over medium heat for 20 to 25 minutes or until the rice is tender and the liquid has been absorbed. Let stand, covered, for 5 minutes before serving.
- *Variation: Substitute 1 2/3 cups long grain rice and 1/4 teaspoon turmeric for the packaged yellow rice.*

Fresh Asparagus

First snap off the tough ends of the spears and wash the spears in tepid water, removing any scales, which harbor grit. You may peel the stems if you like, using a vegetable peeler. An easy method of cooking asparagus is to cook in a wide skillet with a small amount of water for 6 to 8 minutes or until tender-crisp. Asparagus also may be cooked on a rack in a steamer over boiling water. If using an asparagus pan to steam the spears, tie them loosely and place in the wire basket. Place the basket in the pan with enough water to cover the ends of the spears. Cook for 10 to 15 minutes or until the stems are tender.

To microwave the asparagus, layer the spears 2 or 3 deep in a microwave-safe dish and microwave 8 ounces at a time on High for 2 1/2 minutes.

CHEESY BEAN AND WHEAT BERRY TIMBALE

SERVES 4
PREPARATION TIME:
1 1/4 HOURS, PLUS
8 HOURS
STANDING TIME

INGREDIENTS

1/2 cup dried black or kidney beans
1/2 cup wheat berries (see note)
2 eggs, beaten
1 cup milk
2 cups shredded sharp Cheddar cheese
1 teaspoon dried tarragon
1 teaspoon salt
1/8 teaspoon cayenne
2 medium onions, chopped
2 carrots, sliced
2 tablespoons olive oil

DIRECTIONS

- Sort and rinse the beans. Soak in water to cover in a saucepan for 8 hours or longer; drain.
- Cook the beans in fresh water to cover in a saucepan for 30 minutes; drain. Cook the wheat berries in water to cover for 30 minutes or until slightly softened; drain.
- Combine the beans and wheat berries with the eggs, milk, cheese, tarragon, salt and cayenne in a bowl; mix well.
- Sauté the onions and carrots in the olive oil in a skillet. Add to the bean mixture; mix well.
- Spoon into a greased baking dish. Bake at 325 degrees for 30 minutes or until set.
- *Note: Wheat berries are whole grain wheat; they can be found at health food stores.*

Helpful Hint

For an easy cleanup, brush a small amount of oil on the grater before shredding cheese.

Nut and Vegetable Roast in Puff Pastry

INGREDIENTS

3 stalks celery, finely chopped
1 tablespoon vegetable oil
10 ounces carrots, grated
4 ounces mushrooms, thickly sliced
5 ounces bread crumbs
4 ounces hazelnuts, crushed
2 teaspoons mixed Italian herbs
1 tablespoon soy sauce
2 tomatoes, peeled, chopped
1 tablespoon lemon juice
1 tablespoon Worcestershire sauce
Freshly ground pepper to taste
2 eggs, beaten separately
12 ounces puff pastry

Helpful Hint

Hazelnuts are sometimes called filberts.

DIRECTIONS

- Sauté the celery in heated oil in a skillet. Add the carrots and mushrooms; sauté for 2 to 3 minutes. Add a mixture of the bread crumbs and hazelnuts gradually, mixing well. Stir in the mixed herbs, soy sauce, tomatoes, lemon juice, Worcestershire sauce, pepper and 1 of the eggs.
- Roll the pastry into an 11x15-inch rectangle on a lightly floured surface. Spoon the vegetable mixture down the center of the pastry.
- Brush the edges of the pastry with a portion of the remaining beaten egg. Fold the edges of the pastry over the filling and draw up the ends to enclose the filling completely; press to seal. Decorate with leaves made from pastry trimmings.
- Place the pastry on a lightly oiled baking sheet. Make 4 diagonal slits on the top; brush with the remaining egg.
- Bake at 425 degrees for 25 to 30 minutes or until golden brown.
- Cool slightly. Slice with a bread knife.

Notes from a Reconstructed Yankee

BY BILL DIEHL
ILLUSTRATION BY NIP ROGERS

I have been graced with great luck and good fortune through the years, but one of the luckiest days in my life was September 23, 1949, a day that began as a disaster.

I had been working for a small daily newspaper in Pennsylvania since graduating from the University of Missouri and was lured to Atlanta with the promise of a job on the Atlanta Constitution. My editor told me it was a great opportunity so I borrowed 75 ▶

dollars from the local bank and took the train South, arriving at the old Union Station which was next door to the Constitution building.

Unfortunately, when I arrived I discovered there had been a misunderstanding. Nobody at the paper had ever heard of me and there was no job waiting. I stood in front of the building, hundreds of miles from home, with eighteen dollars in my pocket and fear in my heart.

Even worse, I was a Yankee.

In desperation, I invested a dime in the morning paper and there on the front page was Ralph McGill's column and picture. So I stood in the lobby watching every face until he suddenly appeared on his way to lunch. I approached him and he stared at me from under those shaggy eyebrows as I told him my problem.

"Were you in the war?" he asked, a natural question since World War II had ended only four years earlier.

"Yes sir," I answered, " I was a ball turret gunner in the Fifteenth Air Force in Italy."

His expression suddenly became grave. ▶

PASTA DINNER
WITH FRIENDS

Mixed Green Salad with Honey Lime Dressing, page 62

————

Southwestern Spaghetti, page 118

————

Crusty Bread

————

Low-Fat Crème Caramel, page 227

————

Sangria, page 121

PASTA & GRAINS

"How many missions did you fly?"

"Twenty-nine."

I didn't know it at the time, but Mr. McGill had flown several combat missions over Europe as a war correspondent. He knew that the ball turret was the most vulnerable position in a bomber and those who occupied it roughly had the life expectancy of a flea.

"You have a job, son," he said. "Come back at four o'clock."

Thus my career as a writer and journalist began on the obit desk for 25 bucks a week. Celestine Sibley occupied the desk next to mine. And in the years that followed, McGill became my mentor. He frequently asked me to drive him to speeches and during those drives along two-lane blacktops to Rome or Athens, he would talk, describing a wedding he had recently witnessed in Bombay or a chat with Carl Sandburg or explaining to me the traumatic and historic changes occurring in the South—changes which, as a Northerner, were alien to me at the time. I treasure those memories.

Years later, when I was travelling and shooting photographs with Dr. Martin Luther King, I got a note from him. "I see you got the message," was all it said.

The fact that I have lived the past 45 years as a Southerner still has not altered my roots. My wife, Virginia, and my daughter, Temple, still refer to me at times when

BEEF BIACOILE WITH FARFALLE AND TOMATO FONDUE

TOM MINCHELLA, EXECUTIVE CHEF, CHOPS RESTAURANT

SERVES 6
PREPARATION TIME:
1 HOUR, PLUS
1 HOUR
CHILLING TIME

FOR THE BEEF BIACOILE

1 pound sirloin steak, sliced into 12 very
  thin slices
1 tablespoon olive oil
1 tablespoon chopped garlic
2 tablespoons chopped fresh basil
1/4 cup grated Parmesan cheese
Salt and pepper to taste

FOR THE TOMATO FONDUE

1 tablespoon chopped garlic
1/4 cup olive oil
3 large tomatoes, peeled, seeded, chopped (page 30)
1 tablespoon tomato paste
1/4 cup chopped fresh basil

FOR THE PESTO SAUCE AND PASTA

1 cup packed basil leaves
4 cloves of garlic
1/4 cup grated Parmesan cheese
1/2 cup olive oil
1/4 cup pine nuts
16 ounces farfalle (bow tie pasta), cooked

TO PREPARE THE BEEF BIACOILE

- Sprinkle the beef slices evenly with the olive oil, garlic, basil, cheese, salt and pepper. Roll each slice and secure with a wooden pick. Chill the rolls, covered, for 1 hour.
- Sauté the rolls in a large nonstick skillet over medium heat until done to taste; keep warm.

TO PREPARE THE TOMATO FONDUE

- Sauté the garlic in heated olive oil in a medium sauté pan over medium heat for 2 to 3 minutes. Add the tomatoes and tomato paste. Cook for 10 to 12 minutes, stirring occasionally. Stir in the basil; keep warm.

- Process the basil, garlic, cheese, olive oil and pine nuts in a blender or food processor until smooth.
- Combine with the hot pasta in a bowl; toss to coat well.
- Spoon the pasta onto serving plates. Top with the tomato fondue and beef biacoile. Serve immediately.

ANGEL HAIR PASTA WITH MUSSELS AND TOMATOES

DANIEL O'LEARY, BUCKHEAD DINER

[
SERVES 2
PREPARATION TIME:
15 MINUTES
]

INGREDIENTS

16 to 20 fresh mussels
1 tablespoon chopped shallot
1 tablespoon chopped garlic
1 tablespoon olive oil
3/4 cup white wine
16 to 20 fresh mussels
1/2 cup chopped Roma plum tomatoes
2 tablespoons chopped fresh basil
Salt and pepper to taste
8 ounces angel hair pasta, cooked

DIRECTIONS

- Scrub the mussels well and rinse in 3 changes of water.
- Sauté the shallot and garlic in heated olive oil in a large sauté pan over medium-high heat for 15 to 20 seconds or until tender.
- Add the wine and mussels. Steam, covered, for 3 to 4 minutes or until the mussel shells open. Remove the mussels with a slotted spoon, discarding any with closed shells.
- Boil the remaining cooking liquid for 8 to 10 minutes or until reduced to 1/2 cup. Stir in the tomatoes, basil, salt, pepper and pasta.
- Spoon the pasta mixture into a serving bowl; top with the mussels.

I get a little too brash for my own good as a "Yankee." But I remember something Mr. McGill once wrote in a column. I dug it out and I think it is worth repeating here:

"Certainly I love the South," he wrote. "I fancy I can detect the beginning of its fields and the colors of its soils high up from an airplane when flying from a distant region. They seem to call out to me, saying, 'You're back home.' One always has a sentiment for one's own people and one's own land. I long ago came to the conclusion that all of us ought to think first of ourselves as Americans, and secondly as residents of our region. We must work to make a better North, South, West or New England, because in so doing we make a better America."

One final note. That long-ago day in 1949 was twice-blessed for me. At almost the precise moment I disembarked from that train, my wife, Virginia Gunn, was born at Piedmont Hospital. ∎

COMPANY LASAGNA

INGREDIENTS

SERVES 10
PREPARATION TIME:
1 1/2 HOURS

1 large onion, chopped
2 cloves of garlic, minced
3 tablespoons olive oil
1 (28-ounce) can Italian-style stewed tomatoes
1 (6-ounce) can tomato paste
1 teaspoon sugar
1 tablespoon fresh oregano or 1 teaspoon dried oregano
1 tablespoon fresh basil or 1 teaspoon dried basil
1 teaspoon salt
1 pound mild sausage
8 ounces hot sausage
2 cups drained small curd cottage cheese or low-fat cottage cheese
1/2 cup grated Parmesan cheese
1 egg, beaten
1/2 cup chopped fresh parsley
6 lasagna noodles, cooked
12 ounces mozzarella cheese, thinly sliced
1 tablespoon chopped fresh parsley

DIRECTIONS

- Sauté the onion and garlic in heated olive oil in a large skillet until tender. Stir in the tomatoes, tomato paste, sugar, oregano, basil and salt. Simmer until thickened to the desired consistency.
- Brown the sausage in a medium skillet, stirring until crumbly; drain. Add to the tomato mixture; mix well.
- Combine the cottage cheese, Parmesan cheese, egg and 1/2 cup parsley in a bowl; mix well.
- Spread a thin layer of the sausage mixture in an oiled 9x13-inch baking dish. Layer half the noodles, half the cottage cheese mixture, half the mozzarella cheese and half the sausage mixture in the prepared dish. Add layers of the remaining noodles, cottage cheese mixture, sausage mixture and mozzarella cheese. Sprinkle with 1 tablespoon parsley.
- Bake, covered with foil, at 350 degrees for 35 minutes or until bubbly.
- *Variation: Try ground beef in this recipe for a milder taste, extra-hot sausage for a spicy dish, or any combination you like.*

Helpful Hint

To hold noodles for later use, add one tablespoon olive oil to the cooking water. Drain the noodles well and arrange on a plate under a warm damp paper towel.

PASTA WITH ITALIAN SAUSAGE AND VEGETABLES

LINDA EASTERLIN, CATERER

SERVES 5
PREPARATION TIME:
1 1/2 HOURS

INGREDIENTS

8 ounces hot Italian sausage
8 ounces mild Italian sausage
1 medium onion, sliced
1 small red bell pepper, sliced
1 large zucchini, sliced
1 small eggplant, peeled, chopped
2 tablespoons olive oil
1 (16-ounce) can chopped tomatoes
1/4 cup chopped fresh basil
1/4 cup chopped fresh parsley
12 ounces bow tie or corkscrew pasta, cooked
1/4 cup grated Parmesan cheese

DIRECTIONS

- Remove the casings from the sausage and crumble. Brown the sausage in a medium skillet over medium heat. Drain and set aside the sausage; wipe out the skillet.
- Sauté the onion, red pepper, zucchini and eggplant in heated olive oil in the skillet for 5 to 7 minutes or until tender-crisp. Add the tomatoes and basil.
- Simmer for 30 minutes. Stir in the parsley and sausage. Add the pasta; toss to coat well.
- Spoon into a serving bowl; sprinkle with the cheese.

Helpful Hint

Dried herbs are more concentrated than fresh herbs. To substitute, use three times the amount of fresh herbs as dried.

CHICKEN AND PESTO PASTA

FOR THE PESTO

1/2 cup packed fresh basil leaves
1/2 cup packed fresh parsley leaves
4 cloves of garlic
1/2 cup grated Romano cheese
1/2 cup pine nuts, toasted
2 tablespoons fresh lemon juice
1/2 cup olive oil

[
SERVES 6
PREPARATION TIME:
1 1/2 HOURS
]

FOR THE CHICKEN SAUCE AND PASTA

2 boneless skinless
   chicken breast halves
1 teaspoon paprika
1/4 teaspoon cayenne
3 tablespoons olive oil
4 green onions, chopped
2 cloves of garlic, minced

8 ounces fresh mushrooms, sliced
2 medium zucchini, sliced
6 ounces cream cheese, softened
3/4 cup half-and-half
16 ounces herb-flavored fettuccini, cooked
1/4 cup grated Romano cheese

Toasted Pine Nuts

To toast pine nuts, spread the nuts on a baking sheet or a microwave-safe dish. Toast at 350 degrees for 6 to 8 minutes or microwave on High for 1 1/2 minutes or until light brown. Watch the nuts carefully to prevent overbrowning.

TO PREPARE THE PESTO

• Process the basil, parsley, garlic, Romano cheese and pine nuts in a food processor fitted with a steel blade until finely minced.
• Add the lemon juice and olive oil gradually, processing constantly until smooth.

TO PREPARE THE CHICKEN SAUCE AND PASTA

• Cut the chicken into bite-size pieces; rinse and pat dry. Season with paprika and cayenne. Sauté in half the olive oil in a large skillet until cooked through; remove with a slotted spoon.
• Heat the remaining olive oil in the same skillet. Add the green onions and garlic. Sauté until tender. Add the mushrooms. Sauté for 5 minutes or until tender.
• Stir in the zucchini, cream cheese and half-and-half. Bring to a boil, stirring to mix the cream cheese well. Add the chicken; mix well. Simmer for 4 minutes or until slightly thickened.
• Toss the hot pasta with the pesto in a large serving bowl. Top with the chicken sauce; sprinkle with the Romano cheese.

CRAWFISH LASAGNA

INGREDIENTS

8 uncooked lasagna noodles
1/2 teaspoon shrimp boil
1 cup chopped onion
3/4 cup chopped celery
3/4 cup chopped green bell pepper
1/3 cup melted butter or margarine
3 cloves of garlic, minced
1 teaspoon dried basil
1 teaspoon dried oregano
1/4 teaspoon salt
1/4 teaspoon pepper
Hot pepper sauce to taste
1/3 cup flour
3 cups milk
1 cup sour cream
3 cups shredded Monterey
   Jack cheese

2 pounds peeled crawfish tails
2/3 cup chopped green onions
1 tablespoon vegetable oil
1/3 cup chopped fresh parsley
1 teaspoon dried basil
1 teaspoon dried oregano
1/2 teaspoon salt
1/2 teaspoon pepper
1 cup shredded Monterey
   Jack cheese

> SERVES 10
> PREPARATION TIME:
> 1 3/4 HOURS

DIRECTIONS

- Cook the noodles using the package directions and adding the shrimp boil; drain.
- Sauté the onion, celery and green pepper in the butter in a large skillet. Add the garlic, 1 teaspoon basil, 1 teaspoon oregano, 1/4 teaspoon salt, 1/4 teaspoon pepper and pepper sauce to taste. Sprinkle with the flour, stirring to mix well.
- Stir in the milk gradually. Cook over medium heat until thickened, stirring constantly. Whisk in the sour cream and 3 cups Monterey Jack cheese.
- Sauté the crawfish tails and green onions in the vegetable oil in a large skillet. Add to the cheese sauce. Stir in the parsley, 1 teaspoon basil, 1 teaspoon oregano, 1/2 teaspoon salt, 1/2 teaspoon pepper and pepper sauce to taste. Simmer for 5 to 6 minutes.
- Layer the noodles and crawfish mixture 1/2 at a time in a lightly greased 9x13-inch baking dish.
- Bake at 350 degrees for 40 minutes. Sprinkle with 1 cup Monterey Jack cheese. Bake for 5 minutes longer. Let stand for 10 minutes before serving.

Shrimp Cocktail Pasta

Marinate 15 large shrimp in a mixture of 1/4 cup hot cocktail sauce and 1 tablespoon lemon juice. Sauté 1 thinly sliced red bell pepper and 1/4 teaspoon minced garlic in 1 tablespoon olive oil in a skillet until tender-crisp. Add the shrimp with the marinade and 1/4 cup balsamic vinegar. Cook for 3 minutes or until heated through. Serve over 4 ounces cooked linguini on 2 serving plates; sprinkle with Parmesan cheese.

Fettuccini with Scallops

INGREDIENTS

SERVES 6
PREPARATION TIME:
30 MINUTES

1 pound bay scallops
1 tablespoon olive oil
1/2 cup chopped green onions
1 cup sliced mushrooms
3 cloves of garlic, minced
2 medium tomatoes, peeled, seeded, chopped
1/8 teaspoon pepper
1/4 cup dry white wine
1 tablespoon cornstarch
1/2 cup plain nonfat yogurt
1 (14-ounce) can artichoke hearts
3 tablespoons chopped fresh basil
9 ounces fresh fettuccini, cooked
1/4 cup grated Parmesan cheese

DIRECTIONS

- Sauté the scallops in heated olive oil in a large skillet for 2 minutes; remove with a slotted spoon.
- Add the green onions, mushrooms, garlic, tomatoes and pepper to the skillet. Sauté for 1 to 2 minutes or until tender-crisp.
- Add the wine. Cook over medium heat for 2 to 3 minutes. Stir in a mixture of the cornstarch and yogurt. Add the artichoke hearts, basil and scallops. Cook for 3 to 4 minutes or until thickened, stirring constantly.
- Spoon the pasta onto serving plates. Spoon the scallop mixture over the top; sprinkle with the cheese.

How to Cook Perfect Pasta

Bring 4 quarts of water to a boil for every pound of pasta to be cooked. Add 1 heaping tablespoon of salt (optional) and bring water to a rapid boil. Add pasta to water all at once and return to a boil. Cook, uncovered, until it is *al dente*.

Al dente simply means "firm to the bite" and that equals perfect pasta. Test a piece after a few minutes. When you can bite through without snapping it, it is done. Generally, fresh pasta will cook in about 1-2 minutes while dried pasta usually will cook in 5-8 minutes depending upon its size and shape. When the pasta is done, drain it in a colander and serve immediately.

PAN-SEARED CRAB CAKES
WITH LEMON LINGUINI

ROGER M. KAPLAN, CITY GRILL

SERVES 4

PREPARATION TIME:

1 HOUR

INGREDIENTS

1 1/2 cups whipping cream
16 ounces linguini
Salt to taste
8 (2 1/2-ounce) Jumbo Lump Crab Cakes
Canola oil for sautéing
1 teaspoon minced garlic
1 tablespoon lemon zest
1 cup fresh spinach leaves
Pepper to taste
1 tablespoon basil oil
1 tablespoon red chile oil
3 tablespoons chopped fresh parsley
4 teaspoons (1/4-inch pieces) tomato

DIRECTIONS

- Heat the whipping cream in a saucepan until reduced by 1/3.
- Cook the linguini in boiling salted water to cover in a saucepan until al dente.
- Sear the crab cakes in canola oil in a skillet until golden brown on both sides; reduce heat. Cook until heated through.
- Sauté the garlic in canola oil in a saucepan. Stir in the whipping cream, lemon zest and spinach. Add the linguini, tossing to coat. Season with salt and pepper.
- Place the linguini in the centers of 4 warm dinner plates, spooning excess sauce over the top of the linguini. Drizzle with some of the basil oil and the red chile oil; sprinkle with the parsley. Arrange the crab cakes on opposing sides of the linguini; sprinkle with the tomato. Drizzle with the remaining basil oil and red chile oil.

Jumbo Lump Crab Cakes
City Grill

Roger Kaplan of the City Grill prepares Jumbo Lump Crab Cakes by combining 1 1/2 pounds lump crab meat, 1 tablespoon finely chopped red bell pepper, 1 tablespoon finely chopped green bell pepper, 1 tablespoon finely chopped yellow bell pepper, 1 teaspoon chopped seeded jalapeño, 1 tablespoon finely chopped red onion, 2 tablespoons mayonnaise, 2 tablespoons finely chopped fresh cilantro, 1/2 cup (or more) bread crumbs, salt, pepper and Old Bay seasoning. Shape into 8 crab cakes. Sauté in canola oil until brown on both sides and heated through.

SEAFOOD PASTA CAKES

LINDA BEIGH, LINDY'S RESTAURANT

INGREDIENTS

SERVES 6
PREPARATION TIME:
20 MINUTES

3 ounces scallops

3 ounces peeled shrimp

16 ounces fresh angel hair pasta,
  cooked al dente

4 eggs, beaten

3 ounces lump crab meat, shredded

1 clove of garlic, minced

1 teaspoon grated onion

Salt and pepper to taste

1 teaspoon chicken base or crab base

1/4 cup olive oil

Helpful Hint

Don't try to cook pasta in a
saucepan that is too small; you
will have to lower the
temperature to avoid boil-overs
and this will result in a
sticky pasta.

DIRECTIONS

- Sauté the scallops and shrimp in a nonstick skillet over medium-high heat just until cooked through. Chop the shrimp and scallops.
- Combine the warm pasta with the eggs in a large bowl; mix gently. Stir in the crab meat, sautéed seafood, garlic, onion, salt, pepper and chicken base.
- Heat the olive oil in a large skillet over high heat. Drop the pasta mixture into mounds 3 inches in diameter in the skillet. Cook for 3 to 4 minutes or until golden brown on the bottom. Turn the cakes and cook until golden brown.
- Serve immediately with lemon butter, hollandaise sauce or lemon wedges.
- Note: Chicken and crab base are pastes similar in flavor to instant bouillon and can be found in most supermarkets. If the base is unavailable, substitute one crushed bouillon cube.

ARTICHOKE AND TOMATO PASTA SUPREME

INGREDIENTS

[
SERVES 4
PREPARATION TIME:
20 MINUTES
]

1 (6-ounce) jar marinated artichoke hearts
$1/4$ cup chopped green onions
3 cloves of garlic, pressed
2 tablespoons chopped fresh basil
Pepper to taste
$1/3$ cup olive oil
3 large tomatoes, peeled, chopped
8 oil-cured black olives, sliced
8 ounces herb-flavored angel hair pasta, cooked
$1/2$ cup toasted pine nuts (page 112)

DIRECTIONS

• Drain and chop the artichoke hearts, reserving the marinade.
• Sauté the green onions and garlic with the basil and pepper in heated olive oil in a large skillet over medium heat just until heated through. Add the artichoke hearts. Cook for 1 minute.
• Add the reserved marinade. Cook, covered, for 2 minutes. Stir in the tomatoes and olives. Cook, covered, for 2 minutes.
• Add the pasta; mix gently. Spoon into a serving dish; sprinkle with the pine nuts.

Cucumber and Sour Cream Rotini

For a quick pasta dish for 8, cream $1/2$ cup butter or margarine with $1/2$ cup grated Parmesan cheese. Stir in 2 cups regular or nonfat sour cream, $1/3$ cup chopped unpeeled cucumber, $1/4$ cup chopped chives and 1 teaspoon salt. Toss with 16 ounces cooked spinach rotini and serve with additional Parmesan cheese. The cucumber mixture will keep for several days in the refrigerator and is also good over baked potatoes.

SOUTHWESTERN SPAGHETTI

INGREDIENTS

SERVES 3
PREPARATION TIME:
30 MINUTES,
PLUS 1 HOUR
STANDING TIME

1 (16-ounce) can whole peeled tomatoes
2 tablespoons olive oil
3 cloves of garlic, minced
1 tablespoon minced jalapeño
3 tablespoons chopped fresh cilantro
1 tablespoon lime juice
1 tablespoon chili powder
$1/2$ teaspoon cumin
$1/4$ teaspoon salt
$1/4$ teaspoon white pepper
8 ounces thin spaghetti, cooked
3 ounces goat cheese
3 tablespoons pine nuts, toasted (page 112)

DIRECTIONS

• Drain and chop the tomatoes, reserving half the juice. Combine the tomatoes, reserved juice, olive oil, garlic, jalapeño, cilantro, lime juice, chili powder, cumin, salt and white pepper in a medium non-reactive bowl; mix well. Let stand at room temperature for 1 hour or longer.
• Spoon the warm pasta onto serving plates. Top with the sauce. Sprinkle with the cheese and pine nuts. Serve immediately.
• *Note: Tomatoes and other acidic foods can react with aluminum cookware, leaving an unpleasant taste and color. Use stainless, coated enamel or nonmetallic bowls for foods with a high acid content.*

Lemon Cream Pasta

For an easy dish for 4 to 6 people, combine 1 cup whipping cream, $1/2$ cup half-and-half, 2 tablespoons grated lemon rind and $1/4$ teaspoon red pepper flakes in a saucepan and cook for 20 minutes or until reduced to 1 cup. Toss with 12 ounces cooked bow tie pasta, $1/2$ cup grated Parmesan cheese and $1/3$ cup minced parsley. As a variation, you may add 1 cup cooked shredded chicken or fish just before serving.

TORTELLINI WITH SPINACH AND MUSHROOM SAUCE

SERVES 8
PREPARATION TIME:
30 MINUTES

INGREDIENTS

3 large shallots, sliced
2 cloves of garlic, minced
$^1/_4$ cup butter or margarine
1 $^1/_2$ pounds fresh mushrooms, sliced
$^1/_4$ cup dry sherry
$^1/_2$ cup chicken broth
1 cup whipping cream
2 tablespoons lemon juice
1 envelope Alfredo sauce mix
10 ounces fresh spinach, chopped
3 tablespoons chopped fresh basil
2 pounds cheese tortellini, cooked
$^1/_2$ cup grated Parmesan cheese

DIRECTIONS

• Sauté the shallots and garlic in the butter in a medium saucepan until tender. Add the mushrooms. Sauté for 2 minutes.
• Stir in the wine, chicken broth, cream, lemon juice and Alfredo sauce mix. Bring to a boil. Add the spinach, basil and tortellini.
• Cook for 3 to 4 minutes or just until the spinach is wilted, stirring occasionally. Sprinkle with the cheese to serve.

Red Pepper and Saffron Sauce

Make a delicious sauce to serve over pasta, chicken or seafood. Sauté 1 chopped onion and 1 minced clove of garlic in 2 tablespoons butter until tender. Add 2 chopped red bell peppers, 3 saffron threads, $^1/_2$ cup chicken stock and salt and cayenne to taste. Simmer for 10 minutes. Add $^1/_2$ cup whipping cream and bring just to a boil. Process in a food processor until smooth.

TORTELLINI WITH PROSCIUTTO AND PEAS

INGREDIENTS

[SERVES 4
PREPARATION TIME:
40 MINUTES]

1 (10-ounce) package frozen peas
1 cup sliced mushrooms
2 tablespoons melted butter or margarine
4 ounces thinly sliced prosciutto, chopped
1 cup half-and-half
Pepper to taste
1/4 cup grated Parmesan cheese
12 ounces frozen tortellini, cooked

DIRECTIONS

- Thaw the peas under running warm water; drain. Sauté the mushrooms in the melted butter in a medium skillet over medium heat for 3 to 5 minutes or until tender.
- Add the prosciutto and peas. Sauté for 3 to 5 minutes or until heated through. Stir in the half-and-half. Simmer for 6 to 8 minutes or until thickened to the desired consistency, stirring frequently. Add the pepper and cheese.
- Add the pasta; mix gently. Serve garnished with additional Parmesan cheese.

Helpful Hint

Prolonged heat will destroy the flavor of spices and herbs, so store them away from heat in a cool dry place.

PAELLA VALENCIANA

INGREDIENTS

8 very large shrimp, peeled, deveined
1 tablespoon lemon juice
2 red bell peppers
6 small pieces chicken
Salt and pepper to taste
5 tablespoons olive oil
1 medium onion, finely chopped
3 cloves of garlic, crushed
4 ounces chorizo, chopped
2 large tomatoes, peeled, seeded, chopped
8 ounces grouper, cut into pieces
2 cups uncooked short grain rice
3 1/2 cups chicken stock
3/4 cup dry vermouth
15 to 25 strands Spanish saffron
1 cup fresh green peas
12 fresh mussels
1/4 cup chopped curly parsley

> SERVES 6
> PREPARATION TIME:
> 2 1/2 HOURS

DIRECTIONS

- Combine the shrimp with the lemon juice in a bowl; set aside.
- Roast the bell peppers on all sides under a broiler or over a gas burner. Remove and discard skins, seeds and stems; cut into vertical strips.
- Rinse the chicken and pat dry. Season with salt and pepper. Sauté in heated olive oil in a paella pan for 10 minutes or until light brown on all sides. Remove to a platter.
- Add the onion, garlic and chorizo to the pan. Cook for 3 minutes or until the onion is tender. Add the tomatoes and red peppers. Sauté for 2 minutes.
- Add the shrimp and grouper. Cook for 2 minutes or just until the shrimp are pink; remove to a platter. Add the rice to the pan. Sauté for 3 to 4 minutes or until the grains are well coated and opaque.
- Stir in the chicken stock, wine and saffron. Bring to a boil. Stir in the peas. Cook over medium heat for 8 minutes or until the liquid has been absorbed but the mixture is not dry, stirring occasionally.
- Arrange the shrimp, chicken and grouper over the rice, pushing in to cover halfway. Arrange the mussels hinge side down over the top.
- Bake at 350 degrees for 15 minutes. Let stand, loosely covered with foil, for 5 to 7 minutes before serving. Sprinkle with the parsley.

Sangria

For a refreshing drink, combine 1/2 cup orange juice, 1/2 cup lime juice, 1/2 cup light rum, 1/2 cup sugar and 1 fifth burgundy, stirring until sugar dissolves. Add 1/2 cup maraschino cherries, 1 thinly sliced orange and 1 cinnamon stick. Let stand at room temperature for 1 hour; discard cinnamon stick.
Pour over ice in glasses.

SHRIMP AND ASPARAGUS RISOTTO

INGREDIENTS

SERVES 6
PREPARATION TIME:
1 1/2 HOURS

1/2 cup minced onion
1 tablespoon olive oil
3 tablespoons butter or margarine
2 cups uncooked arborio rice
1 pound asparagus, cut into 2-inch pieces
Salt and pepper to taste
6 cups chicken broth
1 1/2 pounds large shrimp, peeled, deveined
Paprika, chopped fresh basil and oregano to taste
4 cloves of garlic, chopped
1/2 teaspoon white wine vinegar
1/4 cup butter or margarine
Juice of 1/2 lemon
1/2 cup grated Parmesan cheese
2 tablespoons chopped fresh parsley

Helpful Hint

Use only the short grain Italian rice known as arborio for risotto dishes. Long grain rice will never achieve a properly creamy texture.

DIRECTIONS

- Sauté the onion in the olive oil and 3 tablespoons butter in a saucepan. Add the rice, asparagus, salt and pepper. Sauté for 3 minutes.
- Add the chicken broth 1/2 cup at a time, stirring constantly. Cook for 25 minutes or until the liquid has been absorbed and the rice is tender.
- Sauté the shrimp in a nonstick skillet for 6 to 8 minutes or until pink. Sprinkle with paprika, basil, oregano, salt and pepper. Add the garlic, vinegar and 1/4 cup butter. Cook for 2 to 3 minutes or until heated through. Stir in the lemon juice.
- Add to the rice mixture. Stir in the cheese. Spoon onto a serving platter; sprinkle with the parsley.

WILD RICE WITH OYSTERS

INGREDIENTS

6 ounces uncooked wild rice
3 cups chicken stock
1 1/2 teaspoons butter or margarine
16 ounces shelled fresh oysters, drained
8 ounces fresh mushrooms, sliced
1/4 cup chopped celery
1/4 cup chopped onion
1/4 cup flour
2 tablespoons melted butter or margarine
1/2 cup chicken stock
1/2 cup milk
1/2 teaspoon dried thyme
1/4 teaspoon salt
1/8 teaspoon pepper
1/8 teaspoon hot sauce
1/4 cup chopped fresh parsley

SERVES 6
PREPARATION TIME:
2 HOURS

DIRECTIONS

- Rinse the wild rice well. Add to 3 cups boiling stock in a large saucepan. Bring to a boil; reduce heat. Simmer, tightly covered, for 50 to 60 minutes or until tender. Drain if necessary. Toss with 1 1/2 teaspoons butter; set aside.
- Sauté the oysters, mushrooms, celery and onion in a large skillet over medium heat just until the edges of the oysters begin to curl, stirring occasionally; drain.
- Stir the flour into 2 tablespoons melted butter in a large saucepan. Cook for 1 minute, stirring until smooth. Whisk in 1/2 cup chicken stock and milk gradually. Cook until thickened, whisking constantly.
- Stir in the thyme, salt, pepper, hot sauce, rice and oyster mixture. Spoon into a greased 2 1/2-quart baking dish.
- Bake at 350 degrees for 30 minutes or until bubbly. Sprinkle with the parsley.

BUCKHEAD RICE

INGREDIENTS

SERVES 8
PREPARATION TIME:
1 1/4 HOURS

3 cups warm cooked rice
1/4 cup butter or margarine
4 eggs, beaten
1 cup milk
16 ounces sharp Cheddar cheese, shredded
1 (10-ounce) package frozen chopped spinach, cooked, drained
1 tablespoon chopped onion
1 tablespoon Worcestershire sauce
1/2 teaspoon dried marjoram
1/2 teaspoon dried thyme
1/2 teaspoon dried rosemary
1/2 teaspoon salt

DIRECTIONS

• Combine the rice and butter in a large bowl. Combine the eggs, milk and cheese in a medium bowl. Stir in the spinach.
• Stir the egg mixture into the rice mixture; mix well. Add the onion, Worcestershire sauce, marjoram, thyme, rosemary and salt; mix well.
• Spoon into a greased 2 1/2-quart baking dish. Set in a large pan with 2 inches warm water.
• Bake at 350 degrees for 45 minutes or until set.

Sun-dried Tomato Vinaigrette
Atlanta Catering Company

Process 1 cup balsamic vinegar, 1/2 cup chopped shallots, 25 oil-pack sun-dried tomatoes, 1 1/2 tablespoons dried basil, 1 tablespoon chopped garlic, 1/2 cup red wine vinegar, 3/4 cup water and 2 cups olive oil in a food processor until smooth. Pour into a saucepan. Cook over high heat until reduced by 1 cup, stirring constantly. Cool in refrigerator. May store in refrigerator for up to 2 months.

HEARTY MUSHROOM RISOTTO

INGREDIENTS

SERVES 8
PREPARATION TIME:
1 HOUR

3 large shallots, chopped

1/2 tablespoon olive oil

8 ounces portobello or shiitake mushrooms
with stems, sliced

1 cup white wine

12 ounces button mushrooms with stems, sliced

1 1/4 cups uncooked arborio rice

1 tablespoon olive oil

3 to 4 cups chicken stock

2 tablespoons grated Parmesan cheese

2 teaspoons butter or margarine

1/4 cup white wine

1/4 teaspoon salt

1/2 teaspoon pepper

DIRECTIONS

- Sauté the shallots in 1/2 tablespoon olive oil in a nonstick skillet over medium heat for 1 to 2 minutes or until tender. Stir in the portobello mushrooms and 1/2 cup of the wine. Cook for 4 minutes. Add the remaining 1/2 cup wine and the button mushrooms. Pour into a large saucepan.
- Sauté the rice in 1 tablespoon olive oil in the same skillet for 2 minutes, stirring constantly. Stir into the mushroom mixture.
- Heat the chicken stock in a saucepan to just below the simmering point. Stir 1/2 cup of the stock into the rice. Cook until most of the liquid has been absorbed, stirring constantly.
- Add the remaining chicken stock 1/2 cup at a time. Cook until the stock is absorbed after each addition. Cook until the rice is tender and the mixture is creamy. Stir in the cheese, butter, 1/4 cup wine, salt and pepper.
- Garnish with additional Parmesan cheese.

PECAN AND LEMON WILD RICE

INGREDIENTS

[
SERVES 8
PREPARATION TIME:
1 HOUR AND
20 MINUTES
]

1 cup uncooked wild rice
3 cups chicken stock
1 1/2 tablespoons grated lemon rind
1 tablespoon lemon juice
1 tablespoon butter or margarine
1/2 cup chopped pecans, toasted
3 tablespoons minced green onions
1/4 cup minced fresh parsley

DIRECTIONS

- Rinse the rice in hot water 3 times and drain.
- Bring the chicken stock, 2 1/2 teaspoons of the lemon rind, lemon juice and butter to a boil in a medium saucepan.
- Add the rice; reduce the heat. Simmer, covered, for 1 hour or until the liquid is absorbed and the rice is tender. Stir in the pecans, remaining lemon rind, green onions and parsley.

Toasted Pecans

To toast pecans, spread them on a baking sheet or in a microwave-safe dish. Toast at 350 degrees for 5 to 7 minutes or microwave on High for 1 minute or until light brown. Watch carefully to prevent overbrowning.

Corn and Grits Timbales

Gary Ronin, Gary and Forsythia, Inc.

INGREDIENTS

[
SERVES 12
PREPARATION TIME:
35 MINUTES
]

3 cups water
3/4 cup quick-cooking grits
1/2 teaspoon salt
1 cup shredded sharp Cheddar cheese
1/2 cup whipping cream
1/2 cup minced chives or green onions
4 eggs, lightly beaten
2 cups whole kernel corn
Salt and pepper to taste

DIRECTIONS

- Bring the water to a boil in a medium saucepan. Stir in the grits and salt. Simmer, covered, for 5 minutes or until the water is absorbed; remove from the heat.
- Add the cheese, cream, chives, eggs, corn, salt and pepper; mix well. Spoon into 12 muffin cups sprayed with nonstick cooking spray. Place in a larger pan with 1 1/2 inches warm water.
- Bake at 350 degrees for 20 to 30 minutes or until set. Cool slightly before unmolding.
- *Note: These may be made in advance, unmolded and chilled until needed. Reheat to serve.*

The Nitty Gritty of Grits

It is correct to say that "grits are." It is also correct to say that "grits is a favorite food of Southerners." In other words, grits has its own grammar and can be used with either a plural or singular verb. One source we consulted with at Martha White Foods (a Nashville company in the grits business for a long time) says the term is believed to have originated from the Old English "grytt," which means bran and has been used since at least the end of the 18th century.

CREAMY POLENTA WITH MINT AND CHERVIL

CHEF JACK SHOOP, VININGS CLUB

SERVES 6
PREPARATION TIME:
30 MINUTES

INGREDIENTS

8 ounces imported polenta cornmeal
3 cups milk
2 tablespoons butter or margarine
1/3 cup grated Parmesan cheese
2 tablespoons whipping cream
2 tablespoons chopped fresh mint
1 tablespoon chopped fresh chervil
Salt and white pepper to taste

DIRECTIONS

- Combine the polenta cornmeal with 1$\frac{1}{2}$ cups of the milk in a bowl. Bring the remaining 1$\frac{1}{2}$ cups milk to a boil in a medium saucepan. Add the polenta mixture gradually, stirring constantly.
- Simmer for 5 to 7 minutes or until smooth, stirring constantly; remove from heat. Add the butter, cheese, cream, mint, chervil, salt and white pepper. Serve immediately.
- *Note: This is good served with lamb or with smoked or roasted poultry.*

Polenta

Polenta, the Italian first cousin to grits, is very much like the cornmeal mush of the South. Simply put, polenta is slow-cooked cornmeal—from 45 minutes to as much as 2$\frac{1}{2}$ hours. The attraction of polenta is its rather neutral taste: like pasta or mashed potatoes, it depends for its goodness on the sauce or dish which accompanies it.

How to Grill Out in the South

BY EUGENIA PRICE
ILLUSTRATION BY DIANE BOROWSKI

Among my earliest childhood memories are the happy moments leading up to delicious steak dinners cooked on an outdoor grill by my adored father, who aside from his expertise in his dental office, was normally all thumbs. But that wonderful man knew how to grill steaks! I'm supposed to be a lot like him and so have lived a long life believing I inherited his genius with charcoal.

While living in Chicago, I set up my first grill in the drafty basement coal entrance of my great old restored

▶

townhouse. Often garbed in goggles against the smoke billowing up, a knit cap to save my ears from the cold and asbestos gloves to protect my hands, I turned out not only luscious steaks, but memorable lamb chops—both of which are praised to this day by editors and friends lucky enough to have shared them.

By the time I lived temporarily in a beach cottage on St. Simons Island while our house was being built, I was quite confident of my practiced outdoor cooking skills. Anyone who knows me knows I fell hopelessly in love with the South I had shunned for so many years, fearing its ultra-conservative politics and segregated facilities. The very fact that my native state of West Virginia had separated from Virginia in order to avoid seceding from the Union back in the 1860s made me leery of the soft, sweet-smelling air of the American South. But finding St. Simons Island and a whole raft of stories for novels I longed to write was like young romance and I took for granted that because of the balmy weather most of the year, I'd really get to be a whiz at my grill.

▶

EARLY SUMMER EVENING

Red Pepper and Tomato Couscous Salad, page 60

———

New Potatoes with Dill, page 139

———

Salmon with Vegetable Topping, page 139

———

Raspberry Mousse, page 238

———

Chardonnay

SEAFOOD

My dear friend, Richard Baltzell, then with the house that published my early novels, knew my culinary reputation from firsthand experience and to celebrate his first Island visit he and Joyce bought a huge aged porterhouse to cook on a cheap wire grill purchased at the drugstore. The super steak was pronounced ready for our feast at the very moment when we realized we'd forgotten to bring out a platter for our sizzling treat. Richard hurried in the house to get one and, so help me, as I stood guard beside the aromatic wonder still on the live charcoal, the entire steak vanished! An old Georgia liver-spotted hound-dog appeared out of nowhere and stole it right before my unbelieving eyes!

My second defeat at the grill found Richard beside me again as months later I tried to celebrate the move into our new house in the woods at Frederica by christening our elegant grill. In anticipation of preparing my specialties, we had commissioned Lamar Webb, our architect, to design a special outdoor grill, complete with its own chimney and separate flue. Another catastrophe? Yes. While cooking the first steaks on the never-before-used grill, Richard and I, both wearing shorts, were attacked by "nature" entirely foreign to Yankee chefs. With tree branches we were forced to "sweep" our bare legs and arms free of hundreds of sticky little green peepers (tree frogs) and

GRILLED SEA BASS WITH PINK-EYED RAGOUT

CHEF CLIFFORD, BACCHANALIA

[
SERVES 4
PREPARATION TIME:
1 HOUR
]

INGREDIENTS

2 tablespoons extra-virgin olive oil
¹/₄ cup finely chopped pancetta or bacon (see note)
¹/₄ cup finely chopped carrot
¹/₄ cup finely chopped celery
¹/₄ cup finely chopped gala apple
¹/₄ cup finely chopped yellow onion
1 teaspoon minced fresh thyme
1 cup veal stock
2 cups pink-eyed or black-eyed peas, shelled, blanched
1 cup diagonally sliced pole beans, blanched
Salt and pepper to taste
4 (6-ounce) sea bass fillets
4 teaspoons olive oil

DIRECTIONS

- Heat 2 tablespoons olive oil in a large sauté pan. Add the pancetta. Cook until crisp, stirring constantly. Stir in the carrot, celery, apple and onion.
- Cook over medium heat for 5 minutes, stirring frequently. Add the thyme and veal stock; mix well.
- Cook for 5 minutes or until the liquid is reduced slightly, stirring constantly. Stir in the peas and pole beans. Cook until heated through. Season with salt and pepper.
- Brush the fillets with 4 teaspoons olive oil; sprinkle with salt and pepper.
- Grill over hot coals for 3 minutes per side or until the fillets flake easily. May continue the cooking process in a 400-degree oven if fillets are over 2 inches thick and not cooked through.
- Ladle the ragout into soup bowls. Arrange the fillets over the top. Garnish with sprigs of thyme.
- *Variation: Chicken stock may be substituted for veal stock.*
- *Note: Pancetta is Italian bacon.*

PECAN-CRUSTED GROUPER

INGREDIENTS

¹/₂ cup pecan pieces
¹/₂ cup bread crumbs
1 (1-pound) grouper fillet, cut diagonally
  into 4 (4-ounce) pieces
Salt and pepper to taste
¹/₄ to ¹/₃ cup flour
2 eggs, beaten
³/₄ cup butter or margarine
Juice of 1 lemon
1 bunch Italian parsley, chopped

[
SERVES 4
PREPARATION TIME:
1 HOUR
]

DIRECTIONS

• Process the pecans and bread crumbs in a food processor just until a coarse mixture forms.
• Season the fillet pieces with salt and pepper. Dredge in the flour; dip in the egg. Coat with the pecan mixture.
• Melt ¹/₄ cup of the butter in a nonstick ovenproof skillet over medium-high heat. Sauté the fish on 1 side until brown. Turn the fish.
• Bake at 400 degrees for 10 minutes or until the fillet pieces flake easily. Remove the fish to a warm platter; wipe the skillet.
• Add the remaining butter to the skillet. Cook over high heat until the butter is foamy and dark brown, stirring constantly. Add the lemon juice and parsley, stirring until combined. Pour over the grouper. Serve immediately.

both of us were so shocked and distracted by the frogs that three thick would-be glorious filet mignon steaks did the unforgivable—they overcooked! The very next day, before we'd had time to clean the grill from its first use, a wren began busily building a nest in—you guessed it —the flue that vented the charcoal grill.

More than twenty-five years have passed since that wren moved in with us to lay claim forever to the outdoor grill and my lesson has been well-learned: I love the New South and I live in the most beautiful spot on earth as long as I stay safely inside away from the jungle-like attacks of Georgia hounds and tree frogs. (In case you're wondering, yes, I had used my head enough to have an indoor grill built in the corner of my thick-walled fortified country kitchen.) ■

Spanish-Style Orange Roughy

INGREDIENTS

$^1/_4$ cup chopped green onions
1 tablespoon margarine
2 medium tomatoes, chopped
3 tablespoons fresh lime juice
1 ounce canned green chiles, chopped
1 tablespoon minced fresh parsley
$^1/_8$ teaspoon salt
$^1/_8$ teaspoon garlic powder
$^1/_8$ teaspoon pepper
4 (4-ounce) orange roughy fillets
4 lime wedges

SERVES 4
PREPARATION TIME:
50 MINUTES

DIRECTIONS

- Sauté the green onions in the margarine in a skillet until tender. Stir in the tomatoes, lime juice, green chiles, parsley, salt, garlic powder and pepper. Bring to a boil; reduce heat.
- Simmer for 10 minutes, stirring occasionally. Add the fillets, spooning the sauce over the fish.
- Simmer, covered, for 10 minutes or until the fish flakes easily. Top with the lime wedges.

Mango Vinaigrette

Try Mango Vinaigrette over mixed greens. Combine $^1/_2$ cup red wine vinegar, $1^1/_2$ cups olive oil, $^1/_4$ cup bottled lime juice, 2 peeled and sliced mangoes, 1 minced clove of garlic, $^1/_8$ teaspoon dried or rubbed sage and salt and pepper to taste in a bowl; mix well. Pour over greens and garnish with sliced avocado, sliced nectarines and walnut pieces.

REDFISH WITH SUN-DRIED TOMATO SAUCE

INGREDIENTS

SERVES 4
PREPARATION TIME:
30 MINUTES

¹/₄ cup unsalted butter or margarine
4 redfish fillets
Salt and pepper to taste
1 tablespoon lemon juice
¹/₄ cup finely chopped green onions
2 tablespoons unsalted butter or margarine
¹/₂ cup clam juice
¹/₂ cup white wine
3 tablespoons chopped drained oil-pack sun-dried tomatoes
1 cup whipping cream

DIRECTIONS

- Melt ¹/₄ cup butter in a 9x13-inch baking dish in a 425-degree oven.
- Season the fillets with salt and pepper; drizzle with the lemon juice. Place in the prepared baking dish.
- Bake the fillets for 5 to 7 minutes on each side or until the fish flakes easily. Arrange the fillets on warm plates.
- Sauté the green onions in 2 tablespoons butter in a saucepan until tender. Add the clam juice and white wine; mix well. Bring to a boil; reduce heat slightly.
- Cook until the sauce is reduced to ¹/₂ cup, stirring frequently. Add the sun-dried tomatoes and cream. Bring to a boil, stirring constantly; reduce heat.
- Cook until the sauce is reduced to ³/₄ cup, stirring frequently. Pour over the fillets.

GRILLED SALMON BLT

DANIEL O'LEARY, BUCKHEAD DINER

INGREDIENTS

1/3 cup mayonnaise
1/2 teaspoon minced fresh tarragon
2 shallots, minced
3/4 teaspoon lemon juice
Salt and pepper to taste
2 (4-ounce) salmon fillets
1 teaspoon olive oil
4 slices potato-dill bread, toasted
1 cup shredded lettuce
2 tomatoes, sliced
4 slices crisp-fried bacon

Helpful Hint

When buying seafood for two, use these helpful guidelines: 1 1/3 pounds whole fish or 1/2 to 2/3 pounds fish fillets; 1/2 to 1 pound shucked or shelled crab, lobster, scallops, oysters or shrimp.

DIRECTIONS

- Combine the mayonnaise, tarragon, shallots and lemon juice in a bowl; mix well. Season with salt and pepper.
- Brush the fillets with the olive oil; sprinkle with salt and pepper.
- Grill the salmon over medium-high coals just until slightly underdone.
- Spread the 4 slices of bread generously with the mayonnaise mixture. Layer 2 slices with the lettuce, tomatoes, salmon and bacon.
- Serve open-face with the 2 remaining slices of bread cut into halves and arranged around the sides of the sandwiches.

MESQUITE GRILLED SALMON FILLETS

FOR THE MARINADE

1 cup soy sauce
¹/2 cup sake
¹/4 cup Japanese sesame oil
¹/4 cup peanut oil
4 large cloves of garlic, finely minced
2 tablespoons finely chopped gingerroot
3 green onions with tops, cut into ¹/2-inch slices
1 tablespoon sugar

SERVES 4
PREPARATION TIME:
40 MINUTES, PLUS
30 MINUTES
MARINATING TIME

FOR THE SALMON

4 (8-ounce) king, coho or sockeye salmon fillets

TO PREPARE THE MARINADE

• Combine the soy sauce, sake, sesame oil, peanut oil, garlic, gingerroot, green onions and sugar in a bowl; mix well.
• Let stand at room temperature for 10 minutes to enhance the flavor.

TO PREPARE THE SALMON

• Arrange the fillets in a shallow dish. Pour the marinade over the salmon, tossing to coat.
• Let stand at room temperature for 30 minutes, turning occasionally; drain. Place the fillets in a grilling basket brushed with olive oil.
• Place 3 briquettes of mesquite in the grill. Arrange the grilling basket on the grill rack.
• Grill, covered, over hot coals for 10 minutes. Turn the grill basket. Grill, covered, for 10 minutes or until the salmon flakes easily.

Helpful Hint

Prevent fish from curling during frying by first placing skin side down in the skillet.

SALMON WITH BASIL CHAMPAGNE CREAM SAUCE

[SERVES 4
PREPARATION TIME:
1 HOUR]

FOR THE SAUCE

2 tablespoons butter or margarine
1/4 cup chopped shallots
2 cups dry Champagne
2 cups whipping cream
Salt and pepper to taste

FOR THE BASIL-PINE NUT MIXTURE

2 tablespoons olive oil
1 cup pine nuts
1 cup packed fresh basil leaves
Salt and pepper to taste

FOR THE SALMON AND ASSEMBLY

4 (8-ounce) salmon steaks, 3/4 inch thick
2 tablespoons olive oil
Salt and pepper to taste
1/2 cup chopped chives or green onions

TO PREPARE THE SAUCE

- Melt the butter in a heavy skillet over medium heat. Stir in the shallots.
- Sauté for 3 minutes. Increase heat to high. Stir in the Champagne. Boil for 10 minutes or until the liquid is reduced to 1/2 cup. Add the cream; mix well.
- Cook for 8 minutes or until thickened and of sauce consistency, stirring constantly. Remove from heat. Season with salt and pepper. May cover and store in the refrigerator at this point for 1 day.

TO PREPARE THE BASIL-PINE NUT MIXTURE

- Process the olive oil, pine nuts and basil in a food processor until finely chopped. Season with salt and pepper.

Helpful Hint

Fresh fish has practically no "fish odor." The odor becomes more pronounced with the passage of time, but should not be strong when fish is bought.

TO PREPARE THE SALMON

- Brush the steaks with the olive oil; sprinkle with salt and pepper. Arrange on a rack in a broiler pan.
- Broil for 3 minutes on each side or until the salmon flakes easily.

TO ASSEMBLE

- Sprinkle the salmon with the basil-pine nut mixture, pressing gently to adhere.
- Bring the sauce to a simmer. Stir in the chives or green onions. Spoon the sauce onto plates; top with the salmon.

SALMON WITH VEGETABLE TOPPING

INGREDIENTS

2 (8-ounce) salmon fillets
3 tablespoons fresh lemon juice
1/2 cup finely grated carrot
1/2 cup finely chopped tomato
3 tablespoons chopped green onions
3 tablespoons mayonnaise
2 tablespoons cream cheese, softened
2 tablespoons minced fresh parsley
1/4 teaspoon pepper

[
SERVES 2
PREPARATION TIME:
1 HOUR
]

DIRECTIONS

- Arrange the fillets in a baking dish; drizzle with the lemon juice.
- Combine the carrot, tomato and green onions in a bowl; mix well. Stir in a mixture of the mayonnaise, cream cheese, parsley and pepper. Mound on top of each fillet, covering completely.
- Bake at 400 degrees for 20 minutes or until the salmon flakes easily.
- *Variation: Substitute halibut or other thick-cut fish fillets for the salmon.*
- *Note: May be prepared 1 day in advance, covered and chilled overnight and baked the next day.*

New Potatoes with Dill

For an easy potato recipe to accompany salmon, try New Potatoes with Dill. Melt 1 stick of butter in a dutch oven or casserole, add 2 dozen new potatoes— unpeeled, cleaned and dried. Salt, pepper and coat with butter. Cook, covered, over low heat for 30 to 45 minutes. Toss with 1/4 cup chopped fresh dill just before serving.

GRILLED SWORDFISH

INGREDIENTS

1 1/2 to 2 pounds swordfish steaks
6 sprigs of rosemary, minced
1/3 cup olive oil
Salt and pepper to taste

SERVES 4
PREPARATION TIME:
25 MINUTES,
PLUS 1 HOUR
MARINATING TIME

DIRECTIONS

• Rinse the fish with cold water and pat dry. Arrange in a shallow dish.
• Pour a mixture of rosemary, olive oil, salt and pepper over the fish.
• Marinate, covered, in the refrigerator for 1 hour, turning occasionally.
• Grill the steaks over hot coals for 4 to 5 minutes per side or until the fish flakes easily.

Helpful Hint

Do not thaw fish at room temperature or in warm water. This causes the fish to lose moisture and flavor. Thaw frozen fish in the refrigerator, allowing eighteen to twenty-four hours per pound thawing time. For the best quality, cook immediately after thawing. Never refreeze thawed fish.

GRILLED GROUPER

INGREDIENTS

1/4 cup sour cream
1 tablespoon Dijon mustard
2 teaspoons lemon juice
1 clove of garlic, minced
1/4 teaspoon dried dillweed
1 pound grouper fillets
2 tablespoons melted butter or margarine
Salt and pepper to taste

SERVES 4
PREPARATION TIME:
30 MINUTES

DIRECTIONS

• Combine the sour cream, Dijon mustard, lemon juice, garlic and dillweed in a bowl; mix well.
• Brush the fillets with the melted butter; sprinkle with the salt and pepper.
• Grill the grouper over hot coals until the fillets flake easily, basting frequently with the sour cream mixture.
• *Variation: Substitute swordfish steaks or mahimahi for the grouper.*

SAVORY ST. PETER'S BROIL

INGREDIENTS

4 (8-ounce) St. Peter's red tilapia fillets
1/2 cup butter or margarine
1/2 cup olive oil
3 tablespoons wine vinegar
1 teaspoon dry mustard
1 teaspoon salt
1/2 teaspoon lemon juice
1/2 teaspoon dried tarragon
1/2 teaspoon dried basil
1/4 teaspoon pepper
1 clove of garlic, minced
1/4 teaspoon hot pepper sauce

SERVES 4
PREPARATION TIME:
20 TO 30 MINUTES

DIRECTIONS

• Arrange the fillets in a single layer in a shallow baking dish.
• Combine the butter, olive oil, wine vinegar, dry mustard, salt, lemon juice, tarragon, basil, pepper, garlic and hot pepper sauce in a saucepan; mix well.
• Simmer over medium heat for 2 minutes or until the butter melts and the mixture is combined, stirring frequently. Pour over the fish, tossing to coat.
• Broil 4 to 5 inches from the heat source for 5 minutes or until the fish flakes easily. Serve immediately.

Citrus and Herb
Tartar Sauce

Process 4 thinly sliced green onions, 1/4 cup chopped sweet gherkins, 1/4 cup chopped French or Italian green olives, 3 tablespoons chopped fresh parsley, 3 tablespoons chopped fresh tarragon and 3 tablespoons chopped fresh dillweed in a food processor until mixed. Add 2/3 cup homemade mayonnaise, 1/2 cup sour cream, 2 tablespoons fresh lemon juice and 2 teaspoons grated lemon rind. Process just until blended. Season with salt and pepper. Chill, covered, for 4 hours to 3 days.

TUNA STEAKS WITH SOY CILANTRO SAUCE

SERVE THIS AT YOUR NEXT PARTY. SIMPLY BROIL OR GRILL
THE TUNA, CUT INTO THIN SLICES, DRIZZLE WITH THE MARINADE
AND GARNISH WITH GREEN ONIONS.

> SERVES 6
> PREPARATION TIME:
> 20 MINUTES, PLUS
> MARINATING TIME

FOR THE MARINADE

1/2 cup peanut oil
1/4 cup soy sauce
1/2 cup rice vinegar
1/4 cup dry sherry
2 green onions with tops, minced
2 cloves of garlic, minced
1 tablespoon chopped fresh cilantro or 2 teaspoons dried coriander

FOR THE TUNA

6 (6- to 8-ounce) tuna steaks, 1 inch thick

TO PREPARE THE MARINADE

- Process the peanut oil, soy sauce, rice vinegar, sherry, green onions, garlic and cilantro in a food processor until blended.

TO PREPARE THE TUNA

- Arrange the tuna steaks in a shallow dish. Pour the marinade over the fish, turning to coat. Marinate, covered, in the refrigerator for several hours, tossing occasionally; drain. Place the tuna on a rack in a broiler pan.
- Broil 4 inches from the heat source for 4 to 5 minutes per side or until flaky but not dry.
- *Note: May grill 1 1/2-inch tuna steaks over hot coals for 4 to 5 minutes per side or until the fish flakes easily.*

Mango Sauce

Mango Sauce is delicious served with grilled fish. Process 1 chopped and peeled mango and 1/4 cup fresh lemon juice in a blender until smooth. Combine the mango mixture with 1 small chopped red onion, 1 1/2 cups coarsely chopped fresh pineapple, 1 chopped tomato, 1 teaspoon chicken bouillon granules, 1 teaspoon chili powder and 1/4 teaspoon hot sauce in a skillet. Bring to a boil; reduce heat. Simmer for 4 to 5 minutes or until the onion is tender.

SEARED TUNA WITH WILTED GREENS AND TOMATO SAGE OIL

Bistango Restaurant

INGREDIENTS

1 cup sun-dried tomatoes
4 cloves of garlic, chopped
1/2 cup extra-virgin olive oil
2 tablespoons chopped fresh sage
1 (8-ounce) tuna fillet
8 ounces mixed escarole, red kale and spinach
1 clove of garlic, chopped
1 tablespoon olive oil

> SERVES 2
> PREPARATION TIME:
> 45 MINUTES,
> PLUS 2 DAYS
> MARINATING TIME

DIRECTIONS

- Combine the sun-dried tomatoes, 4 cloves of garlic, 1/2 cup olive oil and sage in a bowl; mix well. Let stand, covered, for 2 days.
- Sear the tuna on both sides in a skillet until the tuna flakes easily but is not dry.
- Sauté the greens and 1 clove of garlic in 1 tablespoon olive oil in a skillet until the greens are wilted.
- Arrange the greens on a serving platter; top with the tuna. Drizzle with the tomato-sage oil. Garnish with fried ramen noodles.

ROASTED BLEU CHEESE OYSTERS

INGREDIENTS

12 fresh oysters on the half shell
12 (2-inch) slices bacon
1/4 cup crumbled bleu cheese

> SERVES 6
> PREPARATION TIME:
> 20 MINUTES

DIRECTIONS

- Arrange the oysters on a baking sheet. Layer each oyster with 1 slice of the bacon and 1 teaspoon of the cheese.
- Broil for 10 minutes or until oyster edges curl and the cheese is bubbly. Serve immediately.

Helpful Hint

———

Although the most familiar oyster is the bluepoint, now a generic term for any large oyster from Long Island Sound, there are many other varieties of oysters, including Wellfleets, Belons, Kumamotos, Quilcenes, Hog Island Sweetwaters, Olympias, Westcott Bay Petites, Minterbrooks, Kent Islands, Pine Islands, Caraquets, Golden Mantles and Willapa Bays. Some oyster suppliers now offer as many as nineteen varieties to suit the tastes of oyster fanciers.

Oak-Roasted Georgia Mountain Trout

Gerry Klaskala, Canoe

This recipe is best prepared in a wood-fired oven. The fortunate few who own wood-fired ovens know of the intense high heat which quickly sears and cooks, leaving the finished product very juicy. Start the wood oven's fire 4 to 5 hours in advance of cooking. If you do not own a wood oven, a conventional oven will be satisfactory. Preheat the conventional oven to 500 degrees 20 minutes in advance of cooking the trout.

[
Serves 4
Preparation Time:
1 hour
]

INGREDIENTS

2 whole trout with heads and tails, boned
Olive oil to taste
Freshly ground salt and pepper
Whole leaves of 2 branches fresh tarragon
1 shallot, minced
1 tablespoon olive oil
6 Vidalia spring onions, white part only
1 1/2 cups small fresh chanterelles
1 fennel bulb, cut into halves, cut into 3/8-inch slices
3 small artichokes, cut into 1/4-inch slices
1/2 bunch Italian parsley, coarsely chopped
Leaves of 1/2 branch fresh tarragon, coarsely chopped

DIRECTIONS

- Brush both the inside and outside of the trout with olive oil to taste. Season the inside cavity with salt and pepper. Place the whole tarragon leaves in the trout cavity.
- Sauté the shallot in 1 tablespoon olive oil in a sauté pan for 3 to 4 minutes or until tender; do not brown. Add the spring onions; mix well.
- Sauté for 4 minutes; increase heat. Stir in the chanterelles, fennel and artichokes. Season with salt and pepper.
- Cook for 3 to 4 minutes, stirring frequently. Stir in the parsley and chopped tarragon leaves. Cook for 1 to 2 minutes, stirring frequently.
- Spoon a heaping tablespoon of the vegetable mixture into the cavities of the trout. Spoon the remainder into the bottom of a baking pan; arrange the trout over the prepared layer.
- Place the baking pan in the center of the wood oven. Bake for 10 to 12 minutes or until the fish flakes easily. Bake in a conventional oven for 22 to 25 minutes. Garnish with additional tarragon sprigs. Serve immediately.

SOUTHWEST CRAB CAKES WITH LIME AND CHILES

INGREDIENTS

SERVES 6
PREPARATION TIME:
45 MINUTES,
PLUS 30 MINUTES
CHILLING TIME

1 egg, beaten
1 tablespoon mayonnaise
2 teaspoons Dijon mustard
¹/8 teaspoon cayenne
¹/2 teaspoon Worcestershire sauce
¹/2 teaspoon freshly ground white pepper
¹/8 teaspoon salt
1 pound fresh lump or backfin crab meat
¹/4 cup chopped fresh parsley
¹/4 cup chopped green onions
8 to 10 saltines, crushed
1 to 2 (2-inch) fresh serrano chiles, seeded, minced
2 tablespoons unsalted butter or margarine
2 tablespoons vegetable oil
12 lime wedges

DIRECTIONS

- Combine the egg, mayonnaise, Dijon mustard, cayenne, Worcestershire sauce, white pepper and salt in a bowl; mix well.
- Stir in the crab meat, parsley, green onions, crackers and chiles. Shape into 12 patties. Place on a foiled-lined tray.
- Chill, covered, for 30 minutes or longer.
- Sauté the crab cakes on both sides in the butter and oil in a skillet over medium-high heat until brown and crisp; drain.
- Serve with lime wedges.

Avocado Coriander Salsa

———

This salsa is delicious served with grilled fish or chicken. Combine 1 chopped ripe avocado, 3 tablespoons olive oil, 2¹/2 tablespoons fresh lemon juice, ¹/3 cup chopped green onions, 1 clove of crushed garlic, ¹/4 teaspoon salt, 3 dashes of hot pepper sauce and 2 tablespoons chopped fresh coriander, Chinese parsley, cilantro or culantro.

AMERICAN SNAPPER AND MUSSEL STEW

ROGER M. KAPLAN, CITY GRILL

INGREDIENTS

SERVES 4
PREPARATION TIME:
1 1/2 HOURS

12 mussels, cultured, scrubbed
1 teaspoon minced shallot
1/2 cup white wine
1/4 cup (1/4-inch pieces) bacon
1 teaspoon minced garlic
1/4 cup (1/4-inch pieces) onion
1/4 cup (1/4-inch pieces) leek
1/4 cup (1/4-inch pieces) celery
1 cup (1/4-inch pieces) potato
1 cup chopped tomato with juice
1 quart fish stock
1 tablespoon chopped fresh thyme
Salt and pepper to taste
4 (2-ounce) snapper fillets with skin
Olive oil for sautéing
1 tablespoon chopped fresh parsley

DIRECTIONS

• Steam the mussels with the shallot and white wine in a steamer. Remove the mussels to a bowl. Strain the broth, reserving the liquid.
• Fry the bacon in a stockpot until crisp. Add the garlic, onion, leek and celery; mix well. Cook over low heat until tender but not brown, stirring frequently. Add the reserved mussel broth, potato, tomato with juice and fish stock.
• Simmer until the potato is tender but firm, stirring occasionally. Add the thyme, salt and pepper; mix well. Keep warm.
• Place the snapper fillets skin side down in the olive oil in a skillet. Sauté until the fish flakes easily, turning once. Ladle the stew into 4 soup bowls. Add 3 mussels to each serving. Arrange the snapper fillets in the centers of the bowls; sprinkle with the parsley. Garnish with saffron mayonnaise and potato-dill croutons.

SCAMPI WITH ARTICHOKES

INGREDIENTS

1 pound medium shrimp, peeled, deveined
¹/₄ cup butter or margarine
1 tablespoon minced green onions
3 tablespoons olive oil
5 cloves of garlic, minced
2 tablespoons fresh lemon juice
Salt to taste
¹/₄ cup dry white wine
2 (16-ounce) cans artichoke hearts, drained
3 tablespoons minced fresh parsley
¹/₂ teaspoon grated lemon rind
Freshly ground pepper to taste

[
SERVES 4
PREPARATION TIME:
1 HOUR
]

DIRECTIONS

• Rinse the shrimp and pat dry.
• Heat the butter in a saucepan until melted. Stir in the green onions, olive oil, garlic, lemon juice and salt.
• Cook until heated through, stirring constantly. Add the shrimp; mix well.
• Cook for 4 to 5 minutes or until the shrimp turn pink, stirring occasionally. Add the wine and artichoke hearts; mix well.
• Cook until heated through, stirring frequently. Stir in the parsley, lemon rind and pepper. Serve immediately.
• *Note: Serve alone or over hot cooked fresh pasta sprinkled with grated fresh Parmesan cheese.*

Homemade Mayonnaise

Serve Homemade Mayonnaise with your favorite seafood salad. Process 1 egg, 2 egg yolks, 1 tablespoon Dijon mustard, 3 (or more) tablespoons fresh lemon juice and salt and pepper to taste in a food processor until smooth. Add 2 cups vegetable oil in a fine stream, processing constantly at a high speed until blended; adjust the seasonings.

GRILLED SAVANNAH WHITE SHRIMP WITH CORN PANCAKES AND RED PEPPER COULIS

MAURO CANAGLIA, EXECUTIVE CHEF, THE RITZ-CARLTON® BUCKHEAD

[
SERVES 4
PREPARATION TIME:
1 1/4 HOURS
]

FOR THE SAUCE

2 red bell peppers, chopped
1 teaspoon chopped garlic
1 tablespoon chopped shallot
1/2 cup olive oil
2 cups chicken stock
Salt and pepper to taste

FOR THE PANCAKES

2 cups flour
1/4 cup cornmeal
1 teaspoon baking powder
1 teaspoon salt
1 egg, lightly beaten
1/2 cup milk

1 teaspoon baking soda
1 cup buttermilk
1 cup fresh yellow corn kernels
1 cup finely chopped Vidalia onion
2 tablespoons melted butter
 or margarine

FOR THE ONION RINGS

1 medium Vidalia onion,
 thinly sliced into rings
1/3 cup flour
2 cups vegetable oil

FOR THE SHRIMP AND ASSEMBLY

20 large Savannah white shrimp, peeled, deveined, grilled

TO PREPARE THE SAUCE

- Sauté the red peppers, garlic and shallot in 2 tablespoons of the olive oil in a skillet for 5 minutes. Add the chicken stock, stirring to deglaze the skillet. Cook until the vegetables are tender, stirring frequently.
- Process the red pepper mixture in a blender until smooth. Add the remaining olive oil, salt and pepper. Process until blended.

TO PREPARE THE PANCAKES

- Sift the flour, cornmeal, baking powder and salt into a bowl; mix well. Stir in the egg and milk.

- Dissolve the baking soda in the buttermilk; stir into the flour mixture. Add the corn and onion; mix well. Stir in the melted butter.
- Pour 1/4 cup of the batter onto a hot greased griddle. Bake until golden brown and the top starts to bubble; turn. Bake until golden brown.
- Repeat the process with the remaining batter.

TO PREPARE THE ONION RINGS

- Coat the onion rings with the flour.
- Fry in 400-degree oil in a deep fryer until brown on both sides; drain.

TO ASSEMBLE

- Place 3 pancakes in the center of each plate. Arrange the shrimp around the pancakes. Top with the onion rings; drizzle with the sauce.
- Garnish with additional fresh vegetables.

LIME AND GARLIC SHRIMP

INGREDIENTS

4 cloves of garlic, crushed
1 cup finely chopped green onions
1/4 cup butter or margarine
2 pounds medium shrimp, peeled, deveined
1/2 cup fresh lime juice
Coarsely ground pepper to taste
Hot pepper sauce to taste
1/4 cup chopped fresh parsley
2 cups cooked wild rice

SERVES 4
PREPARATION TIME:
1 HOUR

DIRECTIONS

- Sauté the garlic and green onions in the butter in a skillet until the green onions turn bright green. Stir in the shrimp and lime juice.
- Cook until the shrimp turn pink, stirring constantly. Stir in the pepper, hot pepper sauce and parsley.
- Serve over the wild rice.

LEMON AND GINGER SHRIMP

INGREDIENTS

SERVES 4
PREPARATION TIME:
1 HOUR AND 10
MINUTES

1/4 cup butter or margarine
4 shallots, minced
1/2 teaspoon ground ginger
1/2 teaspoon cinnamon
1/4 teaspoon nutmeg
2 cloves of garlic, minced
1 tablespoon minced lemon rind
1/2 cup brewed dark roast coffee
1/4 cup lemon juice
2 pounds shrimp, peeled, deveined
1 1/2 tablespoons brown sugar
Salt and pepper to taste

Helpful Hint

Store peeled and sliced fresh ginger in sherry in a covered glass jar in the refrigerator. After the ginger is depleted, flavor oriental dishes with the sherry.

DIRECTIONS

- Heat the butter in a saucepan until melted. Stir in the shallots, ginger, cinnamon and nutmeg.
- Cook over medium-low heat for 5 minutes or until the shallots are tender, stirring constantly. Add the garlic, lemon rind, coffee, lemon juice and shrimp; mix well. Increase the heat.
- Sauté just until the shrimp are barely cooked; remove the shrimp to a platter. Cook until the liquid is reduced to 1 to 2 tablespoons.
- Return the shrimp to the saucepan. Add the brown sugar, tossing to coat the shrimp.
- Cook until the brown sugar melts and glazes the shrimp. Sprinkle with salt and pepper. Serve immediately.

GRILLED SHRIMP WITH BLACK BEAN SALAD

INGREDIENTS

3 cups canned black beans, rinsed, drained
1/2 teaspoon salt
2 cloves of garlic, minced
2 mangoes, peeled, chopped
1 red onion, chopped
1 red bell pepper, chopped
1/2 cup chopped fresh cilantro
1 tablespoon ground cumin
1 tablespoon chili powder
2 tablespoons olive oil
1/2 cup fresh lime juice
1 pound medium shrimp, peeled, deveined
Salt and pepper to taste

[
SERVES 4
PREPARATION TIME:
45 MINUTES
]

DIRECTIONS

- Combine the black beans, salt and garlic in a bowl; mix well. Stir in the mangoes, red onion and red pepper.
- Whisk the cilantro, cumin, chili powder, olive oil and lime juice in a bowl. Stir into the black bean mixture.
- Season the shrimp with salt and pepper. Thread the shrimp on bamboo skewers.
- Grill over hot coals for 3 minutes on each side or until the shrimp turn pink.
- Spoon the black bean mixture onto a serving platter; top with the shrimp.
- *Note: For variety, serve the shrimp over hot cooked white rice and garnish with sour cream.*

SHRIMP IN BASIL BUTTER

INGREDIENTS

SERVES 6
PREPARATION TIME:
20 MINUTES,
PLUS 1 HOUR
MARINATING TIME

6 tablespoons melted butter or margarine
1/2 cup chopped fresh basil
1/2 cup chopped fresh parsley
4 cloves of garlic
1/2 teaspoon salt
2 teaspoons lemon pepper
1 1/2 to 2 pounds medium shrimp, peeled, deveined
3/4 cup whipping cream
1/2 cup grated Parmesan cheese
Salt and pepper to taste
9 ounces fresh pasta, cooked, drained
2 tablespoons chopped fresh parsley

DIRECTIONS

- Process the butter, basil, parsley, garlic, salt and lemon pepper in a food processor until blended. Pour over the shrimp in a shallow dish, tossing to coat.
- Marinate, covered, in the refrigerator for 1 hour, tossing occasionally. Drain, reserving the marinade.
- Sauté the shrimp in a skillet sprayed with nonstick cooking spray until the shrimp turn pink. Remove the shrimp to a bowl.
- Add the cream, Parmesan cheese and reserved marinade to the skillet; mix well.
- Cook over medium heat until heated through, stirring constantly. Stir in the shrimp. Add salt and pepper; mix well.
- Serve over the pasta; sprinkle with the parsley.

Fresh Tomato and Spinach Sauce

For an easy sauce, sauté 1/2 cup chopped pecans or walnuts and 1 chopped clove of garlic in 3 tablespoons olive oil until the nuts are lightly toasted. Stir in 2 tablespoons tomato paste, 5 chopped seeded peeled tomatoes and 1 cooked bunch chopped fresh spinach. Cook for 3 to 5 minutes or until heated through. Serve over pasta, grilled chicken or seafood. You may also substitute one 10-ounce package frozen spinach and one 15-ounce can tomato sauce for the fresh spinach and tomatoes, omitting the tomato paste.

Mama Zone's Fried Chicken vs. My Cholesterol

BY JOHNNETTA COLE
ILLUSTRATION BY KAREN STRELECKI

I'm not sure how old I was when the practice began, or when it stopped, but as best I can remember, it went on for as long as my hair was in childhood braids. Every Sunday after church at Mt. Olive A.M.E. Church, which of course had followed Sunday School, my sister and I went to the home of our great-grandfather, A. L. Lewis, a mighty yet gentle man we always called "FaFa." That is where Mama Zone prepared that special fried chicken that would send my

▶

taste buds into ecstasy, but today, it would do-in my cholesterol level.

I never knew my great-grandmother, Mary Lewis, because she passed away before I was born, but Mama Zone, A. L. Lewis' second wife, was very much a part of my life as a child. After all, she could cook the best fried chicken on the face of the earth. At least my sister and I thought so.

Now A. L. Lewis was considered by most, if not all folks, to be the most outstanding Black man in our home town of Jacksonville, Florida. After all, in 1901, with a small group of other Black men, he had founded a firm that would become the very first insurance company in the state of Florida. Many years later, I would almost burst with pride in recalling that A. L. Lewis long before it was popular to use the term Afro-American, had named that company the Afro-American Life Insurance Company.

A. L. Lewis, FaFa to me, was the superintendent of the Sunday School at Mt. Olive A.M.E. Church; and besides, he was a deacon of the church and the head of the finance

A DINNER PARTY
TO IMPRESS

Grilled Lettuce with Stilton Cheese, page 53

Cornish Hens with Crab Meat Stuffing, page 168

Warm Roasted New Potato Salad, page 61

Asparagus Bundles

Chocolate White Chocolate Cheesecake, page 222

Pinot Noir

POULTRY

committee too. FaFa took his religion quite seriously, and when my sister and I went to his big house at 1748 Jefferson Street after church, we could only play two games—church or school—because after all, it was the holy day, and the Lord didn't want any card playing, loud talking or horsing around.

While I took turns with my sister, being first the teacher then the pupil, first the preacher and then the congregation, that's when Mama Zone would be in the kitchen, doing up that fried chicken that I wish my cholesterol level would let me eat every Sunday. Oh well, for ole times' sake, I might as well tell you how Mama Zone did it.

After the chicken was carefully washed and cut into pieces for frying, she would fill a big cast iron skillet with olive oil. That's right, "pure de" olive oil. While that olive oil got as hot as it could be, she would dip each piece of chicken, first into a bowl into which she had beated some eggs, then into a brown paper bag with a mixture of flour, salt, pepper and paprika. And now she slid those pieces of fully coated chicken, one by one, into the hot boiling oil. Somehow, Mama Zone knew just how to control the heat of the stove so that the chicken always came out juicy on the inside—without a speck of red of course—and golden brown on the outside.

Humph, humph, humph: sure wish my cholesterol level would permit just one piece of that kind of chicken every now and then.

BASIL ORANGE CHICKEN

INGREDIENTS

[SERVES 8
PREPARATION TIME:
45 MINUTES,
PLUS 6 HOURS
MARINATING TIME]

8 boneless skinless chicken breast halves
$1/3$ cup orange juice
3 tablespoons canola oil
3 tablespoons honey
$2 1/4$ teaspoons chopped fresh basil or $3/4$ teaspoon dried basil
3 tablespoons vegetable oil

DIRECTIONS

- Rinse the chicken and pat dry. Place in a sealable plastic food storage bag.
- Pour a mixture of the orange juice, canola oil, honey and basil over the chicken, tossing to coat; seal tightly.
- Marinate in the refrigerator for 6 to 8 hours, tossing occasionally. Drain, reserving the marinade.
- Brown the chicken on both sides in the vegetable oil in a skillet; drain. Arrange the chicken in a glass baking dish. Pour the reserved marinade over the chicken.
- Bake at 350 degrees for 25 minutes or until tender. Serve hot or cold.

BREASTS OF CHICKEN IN CHAMPAGNE SAUCE

INGREDIENTS

[SERVES 6
PREPARATION TIME:
30 MINUTES]

6 boneless skinless chicken breast halves
1 tablespoon paprika
Salt and white pepper to taste
Juice of 1 lemon
2 teaspoons chopped shallot
1/4 cup butter or margarine
2 cups extra-dry Champagne
4 cups whipping cream
Chopped green onions or capers

DIRECTIONS

- Rinse the chicken and pat dry. Sprinkle both sides with the paprika, salt and white pepper. Place in a saucepan. Add the lemon juice, shallot, butter and Champagne; mix well.
- Poach, covered, for 10 minutes or until the chicken is cooked through. Remove the chicken with a slotted spoon to a platter.
- Cook the pan juices until reduced by 2/3, stirring constantly.
- Stir in the cream. Cook until the liquid is reduced by 1/2, stirring constantly. Add the chicken; mix well.
- Cook just until the chicken is heated through, stirring occasionally.
- Arrange the chicken on a serving platter; drizzle with the Champagne sauce.
- Sprinkle with the green onions or capers.

Helpful Hint

———

Keep raw meat, fish and poultry and their juices away from other foods. Always wash your hands after handling them to prevent contamination of other foods.

CHICKEN MACADAMIA

INGREDIENTS

SERVES 4
PREPARATION TIME:
45 MINUTES

4 boneless skinless chicken breast halves
1 egg, beaten
2/3 cup bread crumbs
1/2 cup chopped macadamia nuts
1/4 teaspoon salt
2 tablespoons butter or margarine
2 tablespoons olive oil
1/2 cup chicken broth
1/2 cup orange juice
2 tablespoons butter or margarine

DIRECTIONS

- Rinse the chicken and pat dry. Dip the chicken in the egg; coat with a mixture of the bread crumbs, macadamia nuts and salt.
- Sauté the chicken in 2 tablespoons butter and olive oil in a skillet until brown on all sides; reduce heat.
- Cook, covered, over low heat for 5 to 7 minutes or until the chicken is cooked through, turning occasionally. Remove the chicken to a serving platter; keep warm.
- Stir the chicken broth and orange juice into the pan juices. Cook over high heat until reduced by 1/3, stirring constantly. Stir in 2 tablespoons butter 1 tablespoon at a time until blended. Serve the sauce with the chicken.

Helpful Hint

Remove the skin from chicken before cooking rather than after; otherwise the fat will be absorbed by the chicken.

CHICKEN IN PHYLLO

INGREDIENTS

4 boneless skinless chicken breast halves
1 onion, finely chopped
3 tablespoons butter or margarine
8 ounces mushrooms, chopped
3 tablespoons butter or margarine
1 clove of garlic, minced
1 tablespoon plus $3/4$ teaspoon flour
$1/3$ cup white wine
2 tablespoons vegetable oil
2 tablespoons butter or margarine
8 sheets phyllo pastry
$1/4$ cup melted butter or margarine
$1/4$ cup bread crumbs

[
SERVES 4
PREPARATION TIME:
1 $1/4$ HOURS
]

DIRECTIONS

- Rinse the chicken and pat dry.
- Sauté the onion in 3 tablespoons butter in a skillet until brown. Remove the onion with a slotted spoon to a bowl. Sauté the mushrooms in 3 tablespoons butter in the skillet until tender; drain. Add the garlic. Sauté for 2 minutes.
- Stir in the onion and flour until mixed. Add the wine; mix well.
- Cook until thickened, stirring constantly. Remove from heat.
- Sauté the chicken in the oil and 2 tablespoons butter in a skillet for 1 minute on each side; drain.
- Brush 1 sheet of the phyllo pastry with the melted butter; sprinkle lightly with the bread crumbs. Top with another sheet of phyllo. Arrange a chicken breast in the center of the phyllo pastry; spoon $1/4$ of the mushroom mixture over the chicken. Roll up the pastry to enclose the filling; tuck ends. Arrange seam side down on buttered baking sheet. Brush top and sides with melted butter. Repeat with remaining ingredients.
- Bake at 350 degrees for 35 minutes.
- *Note: Keep the phyllo pastry moist while working by covering with a damp cloth or paper towel.*

Helpful Hint

If you are unable to cook fresh chicken or ground meat right away, salt them immediately to prevent spoilage. This allows you to store in the refrigerator for a day or two longer.

SUMMER STYLE CHICKEN CUTLETS

GERRY KLASKALA, CANOE

FOR THE CHICKEN

[
SERVES 2
PREPARATION TIME:
40 MINUTES
]

2 whole boneless skinless chicken breasts
Salt and pepper to taste
1 cup flour
2 eggs, beaten
1/4 cup milk
1 cup dry bread crumbs
1/4 cup grated Parmesan cheese
1/3 cup olive oil
1 teaspoon unsalted butter
1 sprig fresh rosemary
2 sprigs fresh thyme

FOR THE SALAD AND ASSEMBLY

1 large tomato, chopped
1 bunch arugula
1 bunch endive, torn into bite-size pieces
1 tablespoon chopped fresh basil
1 clove of garlic, minced
1/2 teaspoon grated Parmesan cheese
1 tablespoon extra-virgin olive oil
1 teaspoon red wine vinegar
1 lemon, cut into halves

TO PREPARE THE CHICKEN

- Rinse the chicken and pat dry. Pound between sheets of waxed paper until doubled in size. Sprinkle with the salt and pepper.
- Coat the chicken with the flour. Dip in a mixture of the eggs and milk; shake off the excess. Dredge the chicken in a mixture of the bread crumbs and cheese.
- Heat the olive oil in a large skillet until hot. Add the butter.
- Heat until the butter begins to brown. Add the rosemary and thyme; reduce heat. Add the chicken.
- Cook until brown on both sides, turning once. Remove to a platter; keep warm.

Nonfat Raspberry Vinaigrette Dressing

—

Drizzle Nonfat Raspberry Vinaigrette Dressing over poached or grilled chicken. Combine 1/2 cup raspberry vinegar, 1/4 teaspoon salt, 1/4 teaspoon pepper, 4 teaspoons sugar, 2 minced cloves of garlic, 2 teaspoons Worcestershire sauce and 1 tablespoon Dijon mustard in a bowl; mix well. Chill until serving time.

- Toss the tomato, arugula, endive, basil, garlic and cheese in a bowl. Drizzle with a mixture of the olive oil and wine vinegar, tossing to coat.
- Arrange the chicken on dinner plates. Top with the salad. Arrange lemon along side of chicken.

CREAMY CHICKEN AND CHEESE ENCHILADAS

INGREDIENTS

SERVES 5
PREPARATION TIME:
1 HOUR

4 boneless skinless chicken breast halves
3 tablespoons olive oil
3 cups shredded Monterey Jack cheese
1/2 cup chopped onion
10 flour tortillas
1/4 cup butter or margarine
1/4 cup flour
2 cups chicken broth
1 cup sour cream
1 (4-ounce) can chopped green chiles, drained

DIRECTIONS

- Rinse the chicken and pat dry; cut into thin slices.
- Sauté the chicken in the olive oil in a skillet until brown; drain. Combine the chicken, cheese and onion in a bowl; mix well.
- Spoon the chicken mixture onto the center of each tortilla; roll the tortilla to enclose the filling. Place the enchiladas seam side down in a 9x13-inch baking dish.
- Heat the butter in a saucepan until melted. Stir in the flour until blended. Add the chicken broth; mix well.
- Cook until thickened, stirring constantly. Stir in the sour cream and chiles. Spoon the sauce over the enchiladas.
- Bake at 350 degrees for 20 minutes or until bubbly.

Helpful Hint

Marinate chicken in a sealable plastic food storage bag. Chicken will stay covered in the marinade and tightly sealed.

FRIED CHICKEN

HORSERADISH GRILL, SCOTT PEACOCK

INGREDIENTS

SERVES 8
PREPARATION TIME:
1 HOUR, PLUS
30 HOURS
MARINATING TIME

1 (3-pound) chicken
1 cup kosher salt
1 gallon water
2 cups buttermilk
6 cups lard
1 cup butter
2 cups flour
1 tablespoon cornstarch
1/2 teaspoon salt
Pepper to taste
1/2 cup flour
2 to 3 cups chicken stock, chilled
1/4 cup milk
Salt to taste

DIRECTIONS

- Rinse the chicken. Dissolve the kosher salt in the water in a large container; mix well. Add the chicken. Let stand in the refrigerator for 24 hours; drain.
- Cut the chicken into 8 pieces. Marinate, covered, in the buttermilk in a shallow dish in the refrigerator for 6 to 8 hours, turning occasionally.
- Heat the lard and butter in a skillet over low heat for 20 minutes, skimming off butter solids as needed.
- Drain the chicken. Coat with a mixture of 2 cups flour, cornstarch, 1/2 teaspoon salt and pepper; shake off excess. Arrange the chicken skin side down in the hot lard mixture. Fry for 15 to 20 minutes or until brown on both sides, turning once; drain.
- Drain the skillet drippings, reserving 1/2 cup. Combine the reserved drippings and 1/2 cup flour in the skillet. Cook over medium-low heat until brown and of roux consistency, stirring constantly. Stir in the chicken stock, whisking constantly until blended. Simmer for 20 minutes, stirring frequently. Stir in the milk. Season with salt and pepper to taste. Cook until of the desired consistency, stirring constantly. Serve with the fried chicken.

Biscuits
Horseradish Grill

The Horseradish Grill Biscuits may be prepared by combining 3 3/4 cups sifted White Lily® flour, 2 1/2 tablespoons baking powder and 1 1/2 teaspoons kosher salt. Cut in 1/2 cup lard until crumbly. Stir in 1 1/3 cups buttermilk just until moistened. Roll dough 1 inch thick on lightly floured surface; cut with 3-inch biscuit cutter. Bake at 450 degrees until brown; brush tops with melted butter.

SUCCULENT CHICKEN

INGREDIENTS

[
SERVES 6
PREPARATION TIME:
45 MINUTES
]

4 boneless skinless chicken breast halves
1 bunch green onions, chopped
$^1/_4$ red bell pepper, chopped
$^1/_2$ cup olive oil
$^1/_2$ cup butter or margarine
$^1/_4$ teaspoon dried basil
$^1/_4$ teaspoon dried tarragon
$^1/_4$ teaspoon pepper
$^1/_2$ teaspoon salt
3 ounces sun-dried tomatoes
2 tablespoons fresh minced dillweed
$^1/_4$ cup whipping cream
$^1/_4$ cup sour cream

DIRECTIONS

- Rinse the chicken and pat dry; cut into thin slices.
- Sauté the green onions and red pepper in the olive oil and butter in a skillet. Remove the vegetables with a slotted spoon to a bowl. Add the chicken to the skillet.
- Sauté until the chicken is cooked through; drain. Stir in the basil, tarragon, pepper, salt, sun-dried tomatoes, dillweed and sautéed vegetables. Add the cream and sour cream; mix well.
- Cook over low heat just until heated through, stirring constantly.
- Serve over angel hair pasta or mashed potatoes.

Georgia Peach Salsa

———

Georgia Peach Salsa is delicious served with chicken, ham, pork or seafood. Process 1 teaspoon minced fresh or pickled gingerroot with 1 peeled and chopped Georgia peach in a food processor until smooth. Combine the peach mixture with 4 peeled and chopped Georgia peaches, $^1/_4$ cup minced green onions, $1^1/_2$ tablespoons sugar, 1 teaspoon dry mustard, $1^1/_2$ tablespoons lime juice, $^1/_4$ teaspoon salt and $^1/_4$ teaspoon white pepper. Chill, covered, for 4 hours or longer.

Duck Breasts with Port and Grapefruit Sauce

INGREDIENTS

Serves 4
Preparation Time:
45 minutes,
plus 30 minutes
standing time

4 duck breasts
Salt and pepper to taste
1 cup port
Juice of 1 white grapefruit
1 cup chicken stock
1/3 cup whipping cream

DIRECTIONS

- Rinse the duck and pat dry; score with a sharp knife.
- Season the duck with salt and pepper.
- Let stand for 30 minutes or until the duck has reached room temperature.
- Sauté the duck skin side down in a skillet over medium heat for 5 minutes or until the duck is brown and the pan drippings are reduced by 2/3. Drain, discarding the pan drippings. Arrange the duck in a baking pan. Bake at 350 degrees for 10 to 15 minutes or until cooked through.
- Add the wine and grapefruit juice to the skillet; mix well. Bring to a boil, stirring to deglaze the skillet. Add the chicken stock.
- Cook until reduced by 1/2, stirring constantly. Strain into a saucepan. Bring to a boil. Add the cream; do not stir.
- Boil for 3 to 5 minutes or until the sauce is of the desired consistency; reduce heat.
- Simmer the sauce while slicing the duck, stirring occasionally. Season with salt and pepper.
- Arrange the sliced duck on a serving platter; spoon the port and grapefruit sauce over the duck.

SAUTEED DUCK BREASTS WITH EGGPLANT AND OLIVE-BASIL SAUCE

CIBOULETTE RESTAURANT

SERVES 4
PREPARATION TIME:
45 MINUTES

INGREDIENTS

2 duck breasts
Salt and pepper to taste
1 eggplant, cut into ³/4-inch slices
¹/4 cup flour
1 tablespoon olive oil
2 red bell peppers, julienned
2 onions, sliced
2 tablespoons olive oil
3 ounces port
1 cup duck or veal stock
Chopped fresh basil to taste
¹/2 cup pitted niçoise olives

DIRECTIONS

- Rinse the duck and pat dry. Season with the salt and pepper.
- Coat the sliced eggplant lightly with the flour. Fry in the 1 tablespoon olive oil in a skillet until cooked through; drain. Remove to a platter; keep warm.
- Combine the red peppers, onions and 2 tablespoons olive oil in a saucepan. Cook, covered, over low heat until the vegetables are tender but not brown. Remove from heat; keep warm.
- Sauté the duck skin side down in a skillet until crispy; turn the duck. Sauté for 3 to 4 minutes or until the duck is cooked through. Remove the duck to a platter. Drain the pan drippings from the skillet. Add the port, stirring to deglaze the skillet. Stir in the stock.
- Cook until the liquid is reduced by ¹/2, stirring constantly.
- Strain the sauce into a bowl; stir in the basil and olives.
- Cut the duck into thin slices. Arrange the eggplant in the centers of 4 plates. Spoon the red pepper mixture over the eggplant. Fan the sliced duck over the top. Drizzle the olive and basil sauce around the outer edge of the plates.

Raspberry and Walnut Sauce

Prepare this sauce by melting 1 tablespoon butter in a skillet. Stir in 1 tablespoon sugar. Cook until golden brown. Add ¹/3 cup orange juice, ¹/4 cup chicken broth and 2 tablespoons blackberry brandy gradually. Bring to a boil. Cook for 5 minutes or until the mixture is reduced to ¹/4 cup. Add ¹/4 cup fresh raspberries, ¹/2 cup seedless raspberry preserves, ¹/4 teaspoon ginger and ¹/8 teaspoon allspice. Simmer for 10 minutes. Remove from heat; stir in ³/4 cup fresh raspberries and ¹/4 cup chopped walnuts.

GRILLED COUNTRY HAM-WRAPPED QUAIL WITH SUN-DRIED PEACHES

MARK ERICKSON, CMC, CHEROKEE TOWN AND COUNTRY CLUB

[
SERVES 6
PREPARATION TIME:
1 1/2 HOURS
]

FOR THE GRITS

2 1/2 cups chicken broth
1/2 cup white or yellow grits
1/2 cup shredded Cheddar cheese

FOR THE QUAIL

18 dried peach halves, cut into halves
9 (4-ounce) semi-boneless quail, skinned,
cut into quarters
3 ounces lean country ham, thinly sliced

FOR THE MUSHROOM SAUCE
AND VEGETABLES

2 tablespoons chopped shallot
2 cloves of garlic, minced
1 1/2 teaspoons olive oil
4 ounces wild mushrooms
2 teaspoons balsamic vinegar
3/4 cup brown sauce
1/4 cup coarsely chopped pecans, lightly toasted
Rosemary and sage to taste
Chopped fresh Italian parsley to taste
12 ounces small fresh green beans, blanched
1/2 celery root, julienned
1 bunch collard greens, mustard greens or arugula, trimmed
Freshly ground white pepper
Olive oil to taste

Wild Game Marinade

To make this marinade, combine 2 cups cider vinegar, the juice of 3 lemons, 10 ounces Worcestershire sauce, 5 ounces hot sauce, 2 tablespoons soy sauce, 2 tablespoons sugar, 2 tablespoons salt and 2 tablespoons pepper. Store in an airtight container in the refrigerator.

TO PREPARE THE GRITS

- Bring the chicken broth to a simmer in a saucepan. Add the grits gradually; mix well. Simmer for 20 minutes or until cooked through. Remove from heat. Stir in the cheese. Spoon into 6 demitasse cups which have been lightly coated with olive oil.

TO PREPARE THE QUAIL

- Soften the peaches in water or warm broth to cover in a bowl; drain.
- Rinse the quail and pat dry. Remove any visible fat from the quail. Wrap each quail quarter with a slice of country ham.
- Thread 6 quail pieces (3 breasts and 3 legs) and 6 pieces of peach onto each of 6 skewers.
- Grill the quail over hot coals until the quail is tender.

TO PREPARE THE MUSHROOM SAUCE AND VEGETABLES

- Sauté the shallot and garlic in 1 1/2 teaspoons olive oil in a sauté pan. Add the mushrooms and sauté lightly. Add the balsamic vinegar and the brown sauce. Bring to a boil, reduce heat.
- Simmer until slightly reduced, stirring frequently. Stir in the pecans, rosemary, sage and Italian parsley.
- Sauté the green beans, celery, collard greens and white pepper in a nonstick skillet coated with olive oil until tender-crisp.

TO ASSEMBLE

- Invert the grits into the centers of 6 dinner plates. Arrange the vegetables around the grits. Remove the quail and peaches from the skewers; arrange around the edge of the plates. Drizzle with the mushroom sauce.

One of my favorite dishes ever has a mixed ethnic background: it is from a restaurant in Oxford, England, called Restaurant Elizabeth, owned by a Basque named Antonio Lopez. When I lived in Atlanta, Nathalie Dupree offered to cook me anything I wanted for my fortieth birthday (longer ago than I care to remember), and I immediately called Antonio for the recipe. Here it is:

Poulet au Porto

Bone four chicken thighs, wrap each around a sliver of green pepper and marinate in port wine for twenty-four hours. Season with salt and pepper, brown in butter, then cook in the port with sliced green apples until done. Reduce the sauce and serve with saffron rice and a good red wine. Serves two.

I have always used any excuse to get to Oxford and Restaurant Elizabeth for dinner, and I think you should, too. Tell Antonio I sent you.

CORNISH HENS WITH CRAB MEAT STUFFING

INGREDIENTS

4 (1 1/2-pound) Cornish game hens
1 lemon, cut into halves
Salt and pepper to taste
1 clove of garlic, chopped
2 tablespoons chopped fresh parsley
1/4 cup chopped green onions
1/4 cup chopped celery
1/2 cup butter or margarine
1 cup crab meat
1/2 teaspoon salt
1 cup fine bread crumbs
1/3 cup half-and-half

SERVES 4
PREPARATION TIME:
1 1/4 HOURS

DIRECTIONS

• Rinse the game hens inside and out and pat dry. Rub the game hens with the lemon; sprinkle with salt and pepper to taste.
• Sauté the garlic, parsley, green onions and celery in the butter in a skillet until the vegetables are tender. Stir in the crab meat, 1/2 teaspoon salt and pepper to taste. Stir in the bread crumbs. Add the half-and-half gradually, stirring until mixed.
• Stuff the game hens with the crab meat mixture. Place in a baking pan.
• Bake at 350 degrees for 45 to 60 minutes or until the game hens are cooked through, basting frequently with pan drippings.
• *Variation: Substitute imitation crab meat for fresh crab meat.*

"I come from a long line of outdoor grillers."

BY LEWIS GRIZZARD
ILLUSTRATION BY DON MORRIS

I thought I would bring to this space some of my vast knowledge regarding cooking out on an outdoor grill.

This peculiar American practice actually began on the first Thanksgiving Day when the Pilgrims invited the Indians over for some smoked turkey.

I come from a long line of outdoor grillers. My Uncle Jerome still holds the American record for consecutive days grilling out, 178.

His streak ended when he ran out of beer one night as he cooked over his grill and drank a can of charcoal lighter fluid.

"At least he died doing what he loved the most," said his wife, my Aunt Ashley.

The key to outdoor grilling is the fire itself. As a purist, I never use one of those gas grills. That's cheating. Anybody who can strike a match can start a fire in a gas grill. It's as simple as lighting an oil well in Kuwait.

The biggest mistake beginning grillers make is they light the charcoal too soon after applying the charcoal lighter.

The lighter fluid doesn't have time to soak into the briquettes and quickly burns off. The briquettes, in that case, never get hot enough to attain that glowing heat necessary for an even, slow cook.

Here's the proper way to start a fire in a charcoal grill.

Stack the briquettes into a pyramid in the grill. Pour the lighter fluid evenly on the briquettes. Go away and have several beers.

When you return, the fluid will have soaked into the briquettes and the subsequent fire will be perfect.

▶

A COUNTRY FRENCH DINNER

Warm Spinach and Basil Salad, page 67

———

Country Garden Veal Ratatouille, page 177

———

Herb Foccacia

———

Almond Cakes with Cinnamon Port Wine Pears, page 220

———

Cabernet Sauvignon

MEAT & PORK

Allow the fire to burn for several more beers before putting on the meat. That way, when the fat from the meat hits the fire, it won't flame up and burn your nose hairs.

Of course, you've had so much beer by this time, you won't notice your nasal hairs on fire, but you certainly will feel it the next morning when you try to breathe through the charred wreckage left by the nasal inferno of the night before.

One other note. There're some things not suited for outdoor grilling. Among these are liver, Spam, asparagus, noodles, any variety of cheeses or cats.

Before Uncle Jerome passed from drinking the charcoal lighter, he became disoriented and suffered from blurred vision and put the family cat on the grill.

The poor cat survived but was never the same. After that experience, each time the remaining members of the family tried to grill out the cat became hysterical and began to claw at the living-room photograph of my late Uncle Jerome in his Masonic outfit.

To summarize, outdoor grilling can be lots of fun, but it can be dangerous too. Careful not to drink the lighter fluid, and if you're a cat, stay out of sight lest the drunken jackass wearing the apron mistakes you for a porkchop. ∎

Reprinted with special permission of King Features Syndicate.

BEEF WITH APRICOTS AND LEEKS
THE EASY WAY OUT

INGREDIENTS

2 pounds sirloin, cubed
2 tablespoons vegetable oil
2 cups beef bouillon
1/2 cup packed brown sugar
1/4 cup brandy
2 cups sliced leeks
1 1/2 cups dried apricots

SERVES 6
PREPARATION TIME:
1 1/2 HOURS

DIRECTIONS

• Brown the beef on all sides in the oil in a skillet. Stir in the bouillon, brown sugar, brandy, half the leeks and half the apricots.
• Simmer, covered, for 45 to 60 minutes or until the beef is tender. Add the remaining leeks and apricots; mix well. Serve over rice.

BEEF TENDERLOIN WITH MUSHROOMS

INGREDIENTS

SERVES 10

PREPARATION TIME:

1 HOUR, PLUS

8 HOURS

MARINATING TIME

1 pound fresh mushrooms, sliced
1 cup chopped green onions
¹/4 cup melted butter or margarine
¹/4 cup chopped fresh parsley
1 (6- to 7-pound) beef tenderloin
¹/2 teaspoon seasoned salt
¹/4 teaspoon lemon pepper
4 ounces bleu cheese, crumbled
1 (8-ounce) bottle red wine vinegar and oil salad dressing
¹/4 cup crushed peppercorns
10 whole mushrooms
Several sprigs of fresh watercress

DIRECTIONS

- Sauté the sliced mushrooms and green onions in the butter in a skillet; drain. Stir in the parsley and set aside.
- Trim the excess fat from the tenderloin. Cut a pocket in 1 side, leaving ¹/4 inch or more uncut at each end. Sprinkle with the seasoned salt and lemon pepper. Spoon the mushroom mixture into the pocket.
- Sprinkle the filling with the bleu cheese. Close the pocket and secure at 2-inch intervals with heavy string.
- Place the tenderloin in a shallow dish. Add the salad dressing. Marinate in the refrigerator for 8 hours or longer, basting occasionally.
- Drain the tenderloin; press the peppercorns into the surface.
- Grill, covered, over medium heat for 35 minutes or until done to taste. Remove to a platter, discarding the string. Arrange the whole mushrooms and watercress around the tenderloin.

GRILLED FLANK STEAK

INGREDIENTS

SERVES 4
PREPARATION TIME:
30 MINUTES,
PLUS 12 HOURS
MARINATING TIME

¹/₂ cup vegetable oil
2 tablespoons white wine vinegar
3 tablespoons dry vermouth
2 tablespoons prepared whole-grain mustard
1 teaspoon dry mustard
1¹/₂ tablespoons dried rosemary
¹/₂ teaspoon thyme
¹/₂ teaspoon pepper
1 (1¹/₂- to 2-pound) flank steak

DIRECTIONS

• Combine the oil, vinegar, wine, prepared mustard, dry mustard, rosemary, thyme and pepper in a shallow dish; mix well. Add the steak. Marinate, covered, in the refrigerator for 12 hours. Drain, reserving the marinade.

• Grill the steak over high heat for 5 to 7 minutes on each side or until done to taste, basting with the reserved marinade. Slice thinly on the diagonal. Garnish with fresh herbs.

Dry Rub for Ribs

Combine 2 tablespoons each garlic powder and paprika; 1 tablespoon each onion powder, sugar and celery salt; 1 teaspoon turmeric; ¹/₂ teaspoon each red pepper and black pepper; and 1¹/₂ teaspoons salt. Rub the ribs with the seasoning mixture before grilling.

MARINATED LONDON BROIL WITH PINEAPPLE AND MINT CHUTNEY

CHRIS D. KERR, CEC, HUNTCLIFF SUMMIT

SERVES 12
PREPARATION TIME:
1 HOUR, PLUS
2 HOURS
MARINATING AND
STANDING TIME

FOR THE PINEAPPLE AND MINT CHUTNEY

1 large pineapple
1 1/2 cups loosely packed mint leaves, chopped
1/3 cup minced red onion
1/4 cup (about) sugar
2 tablespoons white vinegar

FOR THE LONDON BROIL

2 cloves of garlic
Salt to taste
1/3 cup Dijon mustard
1/3 cup bourbon
1/4 cup packed brown sugar
1 small onion, thinly sliced
1/4 cup fresh lemon juice
3/4 cup plain yogurt
2 tablespoons olive oil
4 pounds flank steak, cut into 2 pieces

TO PREPARE THE PINEAPPLE AND MINT CHUTNEY

• Peel, core and chop the pineapple. Combine with the mint leaves, onion, sugar and vinegar in a bowl; mix well. Let stand, covered, for 1 hour or longer.

TO PREPARE THE LONDON BROIL

• Mash the garlic with a small amount of salt in a shallow dish. Add the mustard, bourbon, brown sugar, onion, lemon juice, yogurt and olive oil; mix well. Add the flank steak. Marinate for 2 hours or longer.
• Grill the steak for 10 to 12 minutes on each side or to 123 degrees on a meat thermometer. Let stand for 10 minutes before serving. Slice thinly on the diagonal. Serve with the chutney.

Helpful Hint

Lemon juice is a natural tenderizer for beef.

GOURMET MEAT LOAF

INGREDIENTS

[SERVES 8
PREPARATION TIME:
1 3/4 HOURS]

1 pound hot Italian sausage
2 pounds ground chuck
1 medium onion, chopped
4 cloves of garlic, finely chopped
1 1/4 cups dry bread crumbs
1 cup chopped Italian parsley
2 eggs, beaten
1/2 cup tomato sauce
1/2 cup red wine
1 teaspoon dried oregano
1 teaspoon salt
1 teaspoon pepper
2 cups chopped fresh spinach
4 ounces oil-pack sun-dried tomatoes, drained
1/2 cup chopped black olives
1 pound mozzarella cheese, thinly sliced

DIRECTIONS

- Remove the sausage from the casings and crumble. Combine with the ground chuck, onion, garlic, bread crumbs, parsley, eggs, tomato sauce, wine, oregano, salt and pepper in a bowl; mix well.
- Spread into a 12x15-inch rectangle on a large sheet of waxed paper. Spread the spinach on the rectangle, leaving the edges uncovered. Top with the tomatoes and olives; layer 3/4 of the cheese over the filling.
- Roll the meat loaf to enclose the filling, using the waxed paper to begin the roll. Remove the waxed paper; press the edges to seal. Place seam side down in a foil-lined baking pan.
- Bake at 350 degrees for 1 hour or until cooked through. Top with the remaining cheese. Bake just until the cheese melts. Serve hot or cold.

Lemon and Mustard Vinaigrette

Try Lemon and Mustard Vinaigrette on a mixed green salad. Combine 8 chopped scallions, 1 tablespoon prepared mustard, 2 1/2 tablespoons olive oil, 2 tablespoons lemon juice, 1 1/2 teaspoons rinsed capers, 1 tablespoon red wine vinegar and 1/2 cup apple juice in a blender container. Process until smooth.

COUNTRY GARDEN VEAL RATATOUILLE

INGREDIENTS

3 pounds lean veal, cut into 2-inch cubes

Salt and pepper to taste

1/2 cup corn oil

2 cups pearl onions

1 tablespoon minced garlic

1/4 cup flour

1 cup dry white wine

2 cups chicken broth

3 tablespoons tomato paste

1 cup water

1 teaspoon dried thyme

1 large eggplant, cut into 2-inch cubes

2 small zucchini, cut into 1-inch slices

2 green bell peppers, cut into 1 1/2-inch pieces

2 large tomatoes, cut into 1-inch pieces

Helpful Hint

Freeze leftover tomato paste
in one-tablespoon cubes
for later use.

DIRECTIONS

- Sprinkle the veal with salt and pepper. Brown on all sides in the oil in a saucepan. Add the onions and garlic.
- Sprinkle with the flour; mix well. Add the wine, chicken broth, tomato paste, water and thyme. Add the eggplant, zucchini and green peppers to the saucepan.
- Bring to a boil; reduce the heat. Simmer, covered, for 30 minutes, stirring occasionally. Add the tomatoes. Simmer for 15 minutes longer. Adjust the salt and pepper.

VEAL GRILLADES

INGREDIENTS

1 1/2 pounds veal
1/2 cup flour
Salt and pepper to taste
2 tablespoons vegetable oil
1/3 cup chopped onion
1/3 cup chopped celery
1/3 cup chopped green bell pepper
1 (8-ounce) can tomato sauce
1/4 teaspoon dried thyme
1 bay leaf
Creole seasoning to taste

DIRECTIONS

• Cut the veal into 4-inch pieces. Coat with a mixture of the flour, salt and pepper. Brown lightly in the oil in a saucepan; remove with a slotted spoon.
• Add the onion, celery and green pepper to the saucepan. Sauté until the onion is tender. Stir in the tomato sauce.
• Return the veal to the saucepan, stirring to coat well. Add enough water to cover the veal. Add the thyme, bay leaf and Creole seasoning.
• Simmer until the veal is tender and the gravy is brown and of the desired consistency; discard the bay leaf. Serve over hot garlic cheese grits.

Grits and Grillades

Grillades, the New Orleans version of smothered steak, are always served with grits—for the very practical reason of soaking up the gravy. To prepare grillades, brown thinly pounded veal or beef round steak in hot vegetable oil and simmer with onions, fresh tomatoes, garlic and pepper.

MARINATED VEAL CHOPS WITH VIDALIA ONION COMPOTE

MAURO CANAGLIA, EXECUTIVE CHEF,
THE RITZ-CARLTON®, BUCKHEAD

> SERVES 4
> PREPARATION TIME:
> 45 MINUTES,
> PLUS 2 HOURS
> MARINATING TIME

FOR THE VEAL CHOPS

2 cloves of garlic, chopped
1/3 cup balsamic vinegar
1/2 cup olive oil
1/3 cup white wine
1 sprig of fresh rosemary
1 sprig of fresh thyme
Salt and pepper to taste
8 veal chops

FOR THE ONION COMPOTE

4 ounces bacon, cut into small pieces
8 ounces Vidalia onions, chopped
2 tablespoons sugar
2 tablespoons water
1/4 cup sherry vinegar

TO PREPARE THE VEAL CHOPS

- Combine the garlic, vinegar, olive oil, wine, rosemary, thyme, salt and pepper in a shallow dish; mix well. Add the veal chops. Marinate in the refrigerator for 2 hours or longer.
- Grill the veal chops until done to taste.

TO PREPARE THE ONION COMPOTE

- Cook the bacon in a skillet over high heat until nearly crisp; drain. Add the onions. Sauté until the onions are tender.
- Combine the sugar and water in a heavy saucepan. Cook until the mixture begins to caramelize. Add the vinegar. Cook until reduced by 1/2.
- Add the onion and bacon mixture. Bring to a boil. Spoon into a baking dish.
- Bake, covered with parchment paper, at 350 degrees for 20 minutes. Cool slightly. Serve over the veal chops.
- Note: Grill the veal chops for this dish while the compote is cooling.

Vidalia Onions

Since Vidalia Onions are available only a portion of each year, sweet onion lovers buy them in quantity (fifty pounds or more), and store them for extended enjoyment.

The key to preserving Vidalias, and to prevent bruising, is to keep them cool, dry and separated.

The following are several favorite methods of storage:

•

In the refrigerator, wrapped separately in foil.
This method takes up precious refrigerator space, but can preserve Vidalia Onions for as long as a year.

•

Vidalia Onions can also be frozen.
Chop and place on a baking sheet in the freezer. When frozen, remove and place in freezer containers or bags, and seal. This allows you to remove the amount you want when you want it. Or, freeze whole. Jumbos can be peeled, washed, cored and dropped into a plastic bag. Once frozen, they can be removed like ice cubes. Freezing changes the texture of onions, so frozen onions should be used for cooking only. Whole frozen Vidalias can be baked.

Source: Vidalia Onion Committee, Vidalia, Georgia

GRILLED LEG OF LAMB

INGREDIENTS

SERVES 10
PREPARATION TIME:
1 HOUR, PLUS
24 HOURS
MARINATING TIME

3 cups dry red wine
1/2 cup olive oil
2 onions, thinly sliced
1 carrot, thinly sliced
6 sprigs of parsley
2 bay leaves, crumbled
1 tablespoon dried thyme
2 teaspoons salt
1/2 teaspoon pepper
1 (7-pound) leg of lamb, boned, butterflied

Helpful Hint
———
Use a basket grill to keep butterflied lamb flat while grilling.

DIRECTIONS

• Combine the wine, olive oil, onions, carrot, parsley, bay leaves, thyme, salt and pepper in a shallow dish; mix well. Add the lamb, turning to coat well.
• Marinate, covered, in the refrigerator for 24 to 48 hours; drain and pat dry.
• Grill the lamb over medium heat for 10 to 15 minutes on each side for rare or until done to taste.

Lamb Chops with Herb Butter

FOR THE HERB BUTTER

1 tablespoon minced fresh rosemary
1 shallot, minced
1 clove of garlic, minced
1/4 cup water
1 cup unsalted butter, softened
2 tablespoons minced fresh parsley
1/4 teaspoon salt
1/2 teaspoon white pepper

SERVES 4
PREPARATION TIME:
30 MINUTES,
PLUS 1 HOUR
STANDING TIME

FOR THE LAMB CHOPS

4 lamb chops
2 tablespoons olive oil
4 cloves of garlic, crushed
Lemon pepper to taste

Helpful Hint

Seasoned butters freeze well.
They can be used on any
grilled meat.

TO PREPARE THE HERB BUTTER

• Combine the rosemary, shallot and garlic with the water in a small
  saucepan. Boil for 1 minute; strain and cool.
• Combine with the butter, parsley, salt and white pepper in a food
  processor container; process until smooth.
• Shape into a roll on waxed paper. Chill until firm.

TO PREPARE THE LAMB CHOPS

• Rub the lamb chops with the olive oil and crushed garlic; sprinkle with
  lemon pepper. Let stand in the refrigerator for 1 hour.
• Grill the lamb chops for 5 to 7 minutes on each side or until done to
  taste. Serve topped with the herb butter.

LAMB WITH BARLEY RISOTTO

MAURO CANAGLIA, EXECUTIVE CHEF, THE RITZ-CARLTON®, BUCKHEAD

FOR THE LAMB

[
SERVES 6
PREPARATION TIME:
2 HOURS
]

6 cuts lamb shank
Salt and pepper to taste
1/2 cup olive oil
2 tablespoons butter or margarine
1/2 cup chopped celery
1/2 cup chopped peeled carrots
1 cup chopped onion
2 cloves of garlic, chopped
2 cups sliced mushrooms
1 bouquet garni of bay leaf, rosemary and basil
3 cups red wine
1 (28-ounce) can peeled whole tomatoes
2 cups chicken stock

FOR THE BARLEY RISOTTO

1/2 cup finely chopped onion
3 tablespoons olive oil
2 cups uncooked pearl barley
1 cup dry white wine
6 cups chicken stock
1/2 cup grated Parmesan cheese
1/2 cup unsalted butter
Salt and pepper to taste

TO PREPARE THE LAMB

• Season the lamb with salt and pepper. Sear in half the olive oil in a Dutch oven over high heat. Remove the lamb and discard the drippings.
• Heat the remaining olive oil and butter in the Dutch oven. Add the celery, carrots, onion, garlic, mushrooms and bouquet garni. Sauté until the vegetables are tender.
• Return the lamb to the pan. Add the wine, stirring to deglaze. Cook until the liquid is reduced by 2/3. Stir in the tomatoes and chicken stock. Adjust the seasonings. Bring to a boil.
• Bake at 350 degrees for 1 to 1 1/2 hours or until tender, turning the lamb every 30 minutes; discard the bouquet garni.

- Sauté the onion in the olive oil in a saucepan over medium heat until tender. Add the barley. Sauté for 3 minutes.
- Add the wine, stirring to deglaze. Cook until the moisture has evaporated.
- Stir in the chicken stock 2 cups at a time, cooking until the liquid has been absorbed after each addition and stirring constantly; the barley should be creamy but not soupy.
- Remove from the heat. Stir in the cheese and butter; season with salt and pepper. Serve with the lamb.

RACK OF LAMB WITH GEORGIA PECAN CRUST

TERRY COLBY, FOOD STYLIST

INGREDIENTS

[SERVES 4
PREPARATION TIME:
1 HOUR]

Helpful Hint

Always use a meat thermometer when roasting to prevent overcooking.

¹/₄ cup melted butter
³/₄ cup chopped Georgia pecans
¹/₄ cup fresh bread crumbs
2 tablespoons grated Parmesan cheese
2 tablespoons chopped fresh rosemary
2 teaspoons minced garlic
2 racks of young lamb, trimmed
Salt and freshly ground pepper to taste
2 tablespoons peanut oil

DIRECTIONS

- Combine the butter, pecans, bread crumbs, cheese, rosemary and garlic in a bowl; mix well. Pat the pecan mixture onto both sides of the lamb. Season with salt and pepper.
- Brown the lamb on both end sides in the peanut oil in a skillet. Transfer to a baking pan.
- Bake at 350 degrees for 35 minutes or until a meat thermometer inserted in the center of the lamb registers 140 degrees for medium-rare or 160 degrees for medium.

ROAST PORK

INGREDIENTS

SERVES 12
PREPARATION TIME:
3 HOURS,
PLUS 2 HOURS
MARINATING TIME

¹/₂ cup soy sauce
¹/₂ cup dry sherry
2 cloves of garlic, chopped
1 tablespoon dry mustard
1 teaspoon ground ginger
1 teaspoon dried thyme, crushed
1 (4- to 5-pound) pork loin roast, boned, rolled, tied

DIRECTIONS

- Combine the soy sauce, wine, garlic, dry mustard, ginger and thyme in a shallow dish. Add the roast, coating well. Marinate in the refrigerator for 2 to 12 hours, turning occasionally.
- Drain the roast, reserving the marinade. Place in a shallow roasting pan.
- Roast at 325 degrees for 2¹/₂ to 3 hours or to 175 degrees on the meat thermometer, basting with the reserved marinade during the last hour of roasting time.

Ripe Tomato Relish

Serve Ripe Tomato Relish, a popular item at the Georgia Grille, with grilled meats, seafood or vegetables. Drain a mixture of 8 cups chopped and seeded tomatoes and ³/₄ teaspoon salt in a colander. Bring the tomatoes, 1¹/₂ tablespoons puréed garlic, ¹/₂ cup chopped green bell pepper, ¹/₂ cup chopped red bell pepper, 2 sliced jalapeños, 1 teaspoon ground cloves, 1 teaspoon allspice, 1 teaspoon cinnamon, 1 teaspoon nutmeg, 1¹/₂ cups white vinegar and 1³/₄ cups sugar to a boil; reduce heat. Simmer until of the desired consistency, stirring occasionally. Store in the refrigerator.

MARINATED PORK TENDERLOIN

FOR THE PORK TENDERLOIN

> [SERVES 6
> PREPARATION TIME:
> 1 1/2 HOURS,
> PLUS 6 HOURS
> MARINATING TIME]

1/4 cup soy sauce
1/4 cup bourbon
1 tablespoon brown sugar
1 (2 1/2- to 3-pound) pork tenderloin

FOR THE SAUCE

1/3 cup sour cream or low-fat sour cream
1/3 cup mayonnaise or low-fat mayonnaise
2 or 3 green onions, chopped
1 tablespoon dry mustard

TO PREPARE THE PORK TENDERLOIN

- Combine the soy sauce, bourbon and brown sugar in a shallow baking dish; mix well. Add the pork tenderloin. Marinate in the refrigerator for 6 to 12 hours, turning 2 or more times; drain, reserving the marinade.
- Bake the tenderloin at 350 degrees for 1 hour, basting with the reserved marinade. Cut into 3/4-inch slices.

TO PREPARE THE SAUCE

- Combine the sour cream, mayonnaise, green onions and dry mustard in a bowl; mix well. Serve with the pork tenderloin.

Helpful Hint
———
For an easy cleanup, use plastic food storage bags to marinate meat or fish.

PORK LOIN WITH PLUM SAUCE

FOR THE PLUM SAUCE

SERVES 12
PREPARATION TIME:
3 1/2 HOURS

1 cup chopped onion
3 tablespoons butter or margarine
1 cup plum preserves
1/2 cup packed brown sugar
2/3 cup water
3 tablespoons lemon juice
1/3 cup soy sauce

FOR THE PORK LOIN

1 (6-pound) pork loin roast
Onion salt and garlic salt to taste

TO PREPARE THE PLUM SAUCE

• Sauté the onion in the butter in a saucepan until tender. Add the preserves, brown sugar, water, lemon juice and soy sauce; mix well.

TO PREPARE THE PORK LOIN

• Sprinkle the pork generously with the onion salt and garlic salt. Place fat side up in a roasting pan.
• Bake at 325 degrees for 30 minutes per pound or until nearly cooked through. Remove the roast from the oven about 20 minutes before cooking is complete and discard the fat. Baste with half the plum sauce. Bake for the remaining 20 minutes or until cooked through. Serve with the remaining plum sauce.

Cranberry Chutney

Cranberry Chutney is delicious with poultry or pork. Combine 4 cups cranberries, 1 cup packed brown sugar, 1 1/2 cups sugar, 1 cup water, 1 cup golden raisins, 1 sliced peeled apple, 1 sliced peeled pear, 1/2 cup sliced celery, the grated rind of 1 lemon, 6 whole cloves, 2 cinnamon sticks, 1/2 teaspoon cayenne and 1/2 teaspoon salt in a saucepan. Cook over medium heat for 30 minutes or until thickened to the desired consistency, stirring occasionally. Stir in 1/2 cup walnuts and simmer for 5 minutes longer.

ROSEMARY PORK TENDERLOIN

INGREDIENTS

2 teaspoons dried rosemary, crumbled
2 large cloves of garlic, minced
1 tablespoon Dijon mustard
2 teaspoons salt
4 teaspoons freshly ground pepper
2 (12-ounce) pork tenderloins
1 1/2 tablespoons olive oil

[
SERVES 6
PREPARATION TIME:
1 HOUR
]

DIRECTIONS

• Mix the rosemary, garlic, mustard, salt and pepper in a small bowl. Rub the mixture evenly over the pork; place in a shallow dish. Let stand at room temperature for 15 minutes or in the refrigerator for up to 2 hours.
• Brown the pork on all sides in heated olive oil in a skillet. Place in a baking pan.
• Bake at 400 degrees for 20 minutes or until cooked through.

Italian Spinach

Prepare Italian Spinach by sautéing 2 cloves of crushed garlic in 1/4 cup olive oil for 5 to 6 minutes; discard garlic. Stir in 20 ounces drained cooked spinach and sauté for 2 minutes; season with salt and pepper. Break 1 egg into the spinach mixture; scramble until the white is set. Fold in 6 tablespoons freshly grated Parmesan or Romano cheese. May sprinkle with feta cheese.

GRILLED SMOKED PORK CHOPS WITH SPINACH, CHEESE GRITS AND BLACK-EYED PEA SALSA

DANIEL O'LEARY, BUCKHEAD DINER

SERVES 4
PREPARATION TIME:
45 MINUTES

FOR THE PORK CHOPS

4 bone-in smoked pork loin chops, thick cut

FOR THE BLACK-EYED PEA SALSA

1/2 cup cooked black-eyed peas
2 tablespoons chopped red bell pepper
2 tablespoons chopped yellow bell pepper
2 tablespoons chopped green bell pepper
1 large shallot, minced
1 clove of garlic, minced
1 tablespoon minced fresh cilantro
1 teaspoon minced jalapeño
Juice of 2 limes
Salt to taste

FOR THE CHEESE GRITS

4 cups chicken or ham stock
1 cup uncooked stone-ground grits
1 teaspoon salt
1/2 cup shredded white Cheddar cheese

FOR THE SPINACH

2 cups fresh spinach, blanched
1 tablespoon olive oil
Salt and pepper to taste

True Grit(s)

Most authorities agree the best grits are stone-ground. This means the corn is actually ground between stones in an old-fashioned mill. For best results and really creamy grits, soak the grits overnight and always double the cooking time, stirring often! Feel free to be creative in cooking and substitute the water with milk or any type of broth.

TO PREPARE THE PORK CHOPS

• Grill the pork chops on both sides until cooked through. Keep warm in the oven.

TO PREPARE THE BLACK-EYED PEA SALSA

• Combine the black-eyed peas, bell peppers, shallot, garlic, cilantro, jalapeño, lime juice and salt in a bowl; mix well.

TO PREPARE THE CHEESE GRITS

• Bring the chicken stock to a boil in a saucepan. Stir in the grits and salt.
• Simmer for 4 to 6 minutes or until the liquid is absorbed, stirring frequently. Stir in the cheese.

TO PREPARE THE SPINACH

• Sauté the spinach in heated olive oil in a small sauté pan until heated through. Season with salt and pepper.

TO ASSEMBLE

• Arrange the pork chops on individual serving plates. Serve with the spinach, cheese grits and black-eyed pea salsa.

Green Bean Salad

Green Bean Salad makes a nice complement to any pork dish. Mix 3 minced shallots and 2 tablespoons balsamic vinegar. Whisk in $1/4$ cup olive oil; stir in $2/3$ cup chopped fresh basil. Pour just enough of the mixture over 2 pounds steamed fresh green beans to coat. Add $2/3$ cup grated Romano cheese, salt and pepper, tossing to mix. Chill, covered, for up to 4 hours.

PECAN CRUST PORK CHOPS

INGREDIENTS

SERVES 4
PREPARATION TIME:
30 MINUTES,
PLUS 1 HOUR
MARINATING TIME

1/2 cup light soy sauce
1/4 cup lemon juice
2 tablespoons dark brown sugar
4 medium green onions, chopped
2 teaspoons prepared horseradish
1/4 teaspoon grated gingerroot
4 (8-ounce) pork chops
1/4 cup flour
1/2 cup finely chopped pecans
1/4 cup white or yellow cornmeal
1 teaspoon salt
1/2 teaspoon white pepper
1/4 cup olive oil

DIRECTIONS

- Combine the soy sauce, lemon juice, brown sugar, green onions, horseradish and ginger in a shallow dish. Add the pork chops, turning to coat well. Marinate, covered, in the refrigerator for 1 hour or longer; drain.
- Combine the flour, pecans, cornmeal, salt and white pepper in a shallow dish. Add the pork chops and coat well.
- Heat the olive oil in a large skillet until hot but not smoking. Brown the pork chops in the olive oil for 5 to 7 minutes on each side or until cooked through.

Dijon Cognac Sauce

Try this Dijon Cognac Sauce from The Peasant Restaurants. Whisk 1 cup Dijon mustard, 2 tablespoons vegetable oil, 2 tablespoons honey, 1 tablespoon Cognac and 2 tablespoons chopped fresh chives in a saucepan. Cook just until heated through.

PORK MEDALLIONS WITH MUSTARD CREAM SAUCE

INGREDIENTS

1 (1-pound) pork tenderloin,
 cut into 1/2-inch slices
1/3 cup flour
1/2 teaspoon salt
1/4 teaspoon pepper
3 tablespoons butter or margarine
3 green onions
1/3 cup dry white wine
1 cup whipping cream
1/4 cup Dijon mustard
Salt and pepper to taste

[SERVES 4
PREPARATION TIME:
45 MINUTES]

Helpful Hint

To prevent grease from
spattering, dry food well with
paper towels before browning
in a skillet.

DIRECTIONS

• Pound the pork slices 1/4 inch thick between layers of waxed paper.
 Coat with a mixture of the flour, 1/2 teaspoon salt and 1/4 teaspoon
 pepper; shake off the excess.
• Sauté 1/3 at a time in the butter in a skillet for 2 minutes on each side;
 remove to a warm platter.
• Slice the green onions, reserving the white and green portions
 separately. Sauté the white portion in the drippings in the skillet for
 1 minute or until tender. Stir in the white wine.
• Cook for 3 minutes or until the liquid is reduced to 2 tablespoons.
 Add the cream. Simmer for 5 minutes or until thickened to the desired
 consistency. Whisk in the mustard and season with salt and pepper
 to taste.
• Spoon the sauce over the pork. Sprinkle with the reserved green
 onion tops.

BARBECUE SAUCE

TRAVIS HOLEWINSKI, SOUTH CITY KITCHEN

INGREDIENTS

[
YIELDS
1 GALLON SAUCE
PREPARATION TIME:
30 MINUTES
]

1 tablespoon chopped garlic
1 tablespoon chopped shallot
1/4 cup chopped fresh ginger
4 cups balsamic vinegar
1 (1-pound) package brown sugar
3 cups Bulldog sauce (see note)
3 1/3 cups catsup

DIRECTIONS

- Cook the garlic, shallot and ginger in a covered skillet over very low heat until tender.
- Add the vinegar, brown sugar, Bulldog sauce and catsup; mix well. Simmer until of the desired consistency.
- *Note: Bulldog sauce is tonkatsu sauce and can be found in the gourmet section of most supermarkets.*

Helpful Hint

Try South City Kitchen's Barbecue Sauce for your next cookout. Tastes great on any meat or pork or try on grilled swordfish for a unique variation.

You Are What You Drink, They Say.

BY FERROL SAMS
ILLUSTRATION BY KAREN STRELECKI

Intent on an early morning errand, my passage between my wife and the television screen was arrested when I overheard Katie Couric being cute on that particular day.

"You say it tastes better," I heard her ask her guest, "if you drink it while it's still warm and fresh from the horse?"

If this is a beer commercial, I thought, there is a new depth of tastelessness here that even Calvin Klein has not approached, and I stopped to watch. They were discussing the gustatory and nutritional virtues of milking horses,

▶

apparently having established before my arrival that Genghis Khan had been an habitual consumer of the product.

The segment ended with Ms. Couric, her little eyes widened and her forehead so wrinkled I expected her makeup to flake, touching a milk-filled glass to her lips and pronouncing the contents tasty. I was not present when Bill Clinton neglected to inhale, but I would sign an affidavit that Katie Couric did not swallow.

Bryant Gumbel, offered a glass, made a repudiating sign of the cross with both forefingers, and still managed to remain both urbane and sophisticated as he shrank away protesting, "I don't even like cow's milk." Mr. Gumbel is not only a figure of majestic presence but also a man of some principle.

I wondered for a brief moment about the definition of "progress," which permitted me, reared in the rural South without electricity or radio, to watch in my dotage shenanigans such as this in New York City.

▶

GRADUATION TEA

Brie Tart, page 18

Spicy Spinach Pinwheels, page 32

Tarragon Chicken Salad Finger Sandwiches, page 68

Fresh Strawberries

Lemon Pound Cake, page 205

Peach Cobbler, page 207

Chocolate Meringues, page 252

Assorted Teas

CAKES & PIES

Then I recalled an encounter many years earlier, even farther from my beloved Southland, which also involved strange characters. On a horse-packing trip in the Teton Wilderness area there was a lone cowgirl named Nyla. She was a true albino. Her long thick plait of hair was white as snow, as were her eyebrows and eyelashes. She might have been arrestingly beautiful if one could have ignored her eyes. They were completely colorless, and the retinas shone pink through them when one could catch her in deep shade long enough for her to still their constant roaming and rapid blinking. These were protective movements that caused her also to wag her head ceaselessly from side to side.

More or less an outcast from the male wranglers, definitely one of God's oddlings, Nyla was shy and illiterate, but a genius at catching and saddling unruly horses. The guests would have cultivated her had she not kept herself as definitely distanced from us as she did her fellow horse handlers.

One of these hands was a taciturn, reserved young man named Ole Dave. He had obviously been told that part of his job was to be nice to the tenderfoots, the guests, but he believed in doing it with an absolute minimum of conversation. He also gave Nyla a wide berth, averting his gaze and changing position if she approached the campfire.

►

APPLE CAKE WITH RUM GLAZE

FOR THE RUM GLAZE

1/2 cup butter or margarine
1 cup packed brown sugar
3 tablespoons (or more) dark rum

[SERVES 12
PREPARATION TIME:
1 1/2 HOURS]

FOR THE CAKE

2 cups sugar
1 cup vegetable oil
4 eggs
3 cups flour
1 teaspoon baking powder
1 teaspoon baking soda
1 teaspoon nutmeg
1 teaspoon allspice
1 teaspoon cinnamon
1 teaspoon salt
1 tablespoon vanilla extract
3 cups chopped peeled Golden Delicious apples
1 cup chopped pecans

TO PREPARE THE RUM GLAZE

- Melt the butter in a saucepan. Add the brown sugar and rum. Cook until the sugar has dissolved and the mixture is heated through; do not boil.

TO PREPARE THE CAKE AND ASSEMBLE

- Combine the sugar and oil in a mixer bowl; mix well. Beat in the eggs 1 at a time.
- Mix the flour, baking powder, baking soda, nutmeg, allspice, cinnamon and salt together. Add to the egg mixture gradually, mixing well after each addition.
- Add the vanilla. Fold in the apples and pecans. Spoon into a greased tube pan.
- Bake at 350 degrees for 1 hour or until a cake tester comes out clean. Remove immediately to a cake plate. Pierce with a fork. Brush with the warm glaze.
- *Note: This cake is especially good with vanilla bean ice cream. The glaze will become slightly crunchy.*

CARROT CAKE

FOR THE CAKE

[
SERVES 16
PREPARATION TIME:
55 MINUTES
]

2 cups sugar
1 1/4 cups vegetable oil
2 1/2 cups grated carrots
4 eggs
2 cups flour
2 teaspoons baking powder
2 teaspoons baking soda
2 teaspoons cinnamon
Salt to taste
1/2 cup chopped walnuts

FOR THE FROSTING

1/2 cup butter or margarine, softened
8 ounces cream cheese, softened
2 teaspoons vanilla extract
1 (1-pound) package confectioners' sugar

TO PREPARE THE CAKE

• Combine the sugar and oil in a mixer bowl; beat until smooth. Add the carrots; mix well. Beat in the eggs 1 at a time.
• Sift the flour, baking powder, baking soda, cinnamon and salt together. Add to the carrot mixture; mix well.
• Stir in the walnuts. Spoon into 2 greased and floured 9-inch cake pans.
• Bake at 350 degrees for 25 to 30 minutes or until the layers test done. Cool in the pans for 5 minutes; remove to a wire rack to cool completely.

TO PREPARE THE FROSTING AND ASSEMBLE

• Cream the butter, cream cheese and vanilla in a mixer bowl until light. Add the confectioners' sugar gradually, beating until fluffy. Spread between the layers and over the top and side of the cake.

One of the guests was an ebullient, almost raucous, little matzo ball of a woman who mingled enthusiastically with the other guests and also the hired help, asking questions with nasal and staccato clatter. Her name was Molly Goldstein. She professed to be doing work on a postgraduate sociology thesis by interviewing primitive back-country westerners on their way of life. She was determined to force the IRS thereby to recognize her vacation as a business expense. She would have earned from my grandmother the sobriquet of "pushy."

One chill morning Ole Dave was squatting on his haunches, conspicuously apart from the social campfire, swilling huge sucking gulps of overly-sweetened coffee in early morning privacy, when Molly invaded his territory.

"Dave," I heard her say, "have you ever drunk any koumiss?" The following silence was punctuated first by a belch and then the laconic reply, "I don't reckon I have."

Molly gushed a little. "Genghis Khan is said to have drunk it all his life."

"Never heard of him, neither."

"He was a fabulous horseman and warrior who led the Tartar hordes through China."

Ole Dave considered this a moment. "Ain't got many of them in Wyoming, I don't believe. At least not this high up and this far back."

►

Molly pressed with persistent cheeriness, "People nowadays seem to be embarrassed to admit they drink koumiss. Are you sure you never have? Not even way back in the mountains?"

"Lady, I don't even know what it is."

"It's mare's milk," pronounced Molly.

Ole Dave exploded. "Hell, no, I ain't ever drunk it!"

Molly retreated a defensive step and said with a conciliatory tone. "I asked Nyla and she said she used to drink it when she was a little girl."

Ole Dave rose abruptly to his feet, dashed the dregs from his coffee cup on the ground and looked straight at Molly for the first and last time.

"Maybe that's what's wrong with her _____ eyes!" he proclaimed.

Ole Dave and Bryant Gumbel appear in my mind as men of equal presence and principle. ■

COCA-COLA® CAKE

FOR THE CAKE

1 cup sugar
1 cup flour
1/2 teaspoon baking powder
1/2 cup unsalted butter
2 tablespoons baking cocoa
1/2 cup Coca-Cola
1/4 cup buttermilk
1 egg, beaten
1 teaspoon vanilla extract

FOR THE FROSTING

1/4 cup unsalted butter
1 1/2 tablespoons baking cocoa
3/4 cup Coca-Cola
2 to 2 1/4 cups confectioners' sugar
1 teaspoon vanilla extract
1/2 cup broken pecans

[SERVES 8
PREPARATION TIME:
40 MINUTES]

TO PREPARE THE CAKE

- Mix the sugar, flour and baking powder in a bowl. Bring the butter, baking cocoa and Coca-Cola to a boil in a medium saucepan, stirring to blend well. Pour over the dry ingredients gradually, mixing well.
- Combine the buttermilk, egg and vanilla in a bowl; mix well. Add to the batter; mix well. Spoon into a greased and floured 8x8-inch cake pan.
- Bake at 350 degrees for 25 to 30 minutes or until a cake tester comes out clean.

TO PREPARE THE FROSTING AND ASSEMBLE

- Bring the butter, baking cocoa and Coca-Cola to a boil in a medium saucepan, stirring to blend well; remove from heat. Stir in the confectioners' sugar and vanilla.
- Pour the hot frosting over the warm cake; top with the pecans. Let stand until cool.

CHOCOLATE TORTE

PEGGY FOREMAN, EXECUTIVE CHEF, THE ROBINSON-HUMPHREY CO.

INGREDIENTS

[SERVES 6

PREPARATION TIME:

1 HOUR]

12 ounces semisweet chocolate

1 1/2 cups butter or margarine

6 egg yolks

2/3 cup sugar

2/3 cup packed light brown sugar

1 tablespoon vanilla extract

2/3 cup flour

1 1/2 cups ground or very finely chopped toasted pecans

6 egg whites

2 tablespoons sugar

6 ounces semisweet or bittersweet chocolate

4 ounces German's sweet chocolate

1 1/2 cups unsalted butter

1 tablespoon vanilla extract

Helpful Hint

Cooked frosting does not
freeze well.

DIRECTIONS

- Butter two 8-inch cake pans; line with baking parchment.
- Melt 12 ounces semisweet chocolate and 1 1/2 cups butter in a double boiler over hot water. Cool slightly.
- Combine the egg yolks, 2/3 cup sugar and brown sugar in a bowl; mix well. Stir in 1 tablespoon vanilla. Add the chocolate mixture. Fold in a mixture of the flour and pecans.
- Beat the eggs whites in a mixer bowl until frothy. Add 2 tablespoons sugar, beating constantly until stiff peaks form. Fold into the chocolate mixture. Spoon into the prepared pans.
- Bake at 350 degrees for 15 to 20 minutes or just until set but still moist; do not overbake. Cool in the pans for 5 minutes; remove to a wire rack to cool completely.
- Combine 6 ounces semisweet chocolate, German's sweet chocolate, 1 1/2 cups unsalted butter and 1 tablespoon vanilla in a double boiler. Cook over hot water until the chocolate and butter melt, stirring to mix well.
- Place 1 torte layer on a serving plate. Pour some of the warm glaze over the layer. Top with the remaining layer. Allow the remaining glaze to cool slightly. Spread over the top and side of the torte. Garnish with raspberries.
- *Note: This may be baked in 3 pans if you prefer; reduce the baking time for the thinner layers.*

Chocolate Pecan Torte with Strawberry Buttercream

[
SERVES 15
PREPARATION TIME:
1 1/2 HOURS, PLUS
CHILLING AND
STANDING TIME
]

FOR THE TORTE

3/4 cup butter or margarine, softened
2 cups sugar
8 eggs
2 tablespoons vanilla extract
1/4 teaspoon salt
12 ounces bittersweet or semisweet chocolate, melted
3 1/2 cups finely ground pecans

FOR THE BUTTERCREAM

1 1/4 cups butter, sliced, softened
2 cups confectioners' sugar, sifted
4 egg yolks
1/2 cup puréed fresh strawberries
3 tablespoons strawberry preserves

FOR THE GLAZE

3 ounces semisweet chocolate, coarsely chopped
6 tablespoons butter or margarine
1/2 cup water
3 tablespoons safflower oil
3/4 cup baking cocoa
1/2 cup plus 2 tablespoons sugar
15 whole strawberries

Helpful Hint

If muffins or cake layers stick to the bottoms of the pans, place the hot pans on a cold damp towel for about thirty seconds before removing.

TO PREPARE THE TORTE

- Line 4 greased 9-inch cake pans with baking parchment.
- Cream the butter in a mixer bowl until light. Add the sugar; beat until fluffy. Beat in the eggs 1 at a time. Add the vanilla and salt; mix well. Fold in the chocolate and then the pecans. Spoon into the prepared pans.
- Bake at 375 degrees for 22 minutes or until a cake tester comes out fudgy but not wet; tops may crack. Cool in the pans on a wire rack for 5 minutes. Loosen from the sides of the pans with a knife. Invert onto a rack; remove the parchment. Cool completely.

TO PREPARE THE BUTTERCREAM

- Cream the butter and confectioners' sugar in a mixer bowl until light and fluffy. Beat in the egg yolks. Add the strawberries and preserves; mix well.

TO PREPARE THE GLAZE

- Combine the chocolate, butter, water and safflower oil in a double boiler. Heat over simmering water until the chocolate and butter melt, stirring to mix well; remove from heat.
- Add the baking cocoa and sugar; mix until the sugar dissolves and the glaze is smooth. Chill until slightly thickened.
- Dip the strawberries into the glaze; let stand until set.

TO ASSEMBLE THE TORTE

- Place 1 torte layer bottom side up on a cake plate. Spread with 3/4 cup of the buttercream. Repeat with the remaining layers, ending with the top layer bottom side up; press lightly.
- Chill, covered, for 6 hours or longer. Trim the edges of the torte with a serrated knife if necessary.
- Pour the glaze over the top and side of the torte; arrange the glazed strawberries around the edge. Let stand at room temperature for 1 hour before serving.
- *Note: The torte and buttercream may be made up to 2 days in advance and stored in the refrigerator. Wrap the layers individually in plastic wrap to store; allow the buttercream to return to room temperature before spreading.*

TRIPLE CHOCOLATE ECSTASY

FOR THE CAKE

> 4 ounces semisweet chocolate
> 1/2 cup butter or margarine, softened
> 2 eggs
> 2 cups sugar
> 1 1/2 cups milk
> 1 teaspoon vanilla extract
> 1/2 teaspoon salt
> 1 1/2 cups flour
> 1 teaspoon baking powder
> 1 cup finely chopped pecans

FOR THE FILLING

> 4 ounces semisweet chocolate
> 1/4 cup butter or margarine
> 1/2 cup confectioners' sugar
> 1/3 cup milk

FOR THE FROSTING

> 2 cups whipping cream
> 1 cup confectioners' sugar
> 1 teaspoon vanilla extract
> 2/3 cup baking cocoa

[
SERVES 12
PREPARATION TIME:
1 1/2 HOURS,
PLUS 1 HOUR
CHILLING TIME
]

Helpful Hint
—
Dust cake pans with baking cocoa when baking a chocolate cake.

TO PREPARE THE CAKE

- Grease two 9-inch cake pans; line the bottoms with waxed paper and grease the paper.
- Melt the chocolate and butter in a 3-quart saucepan over low heat, stirring to blend well; remove from heat.
- Beat in the eggs with a wooden spoon. Stir in the sugar, milk, vanilla and salt. Add the flour and baking powder; stir until smooth. Stir in the pecans. Spoon into the prepared pans.
- Bake at 350 degrees for 30 to 35 minutes or until a cake tester inserted near the center comes out clean. Cool in the pans on a wire rack for 5 minutes. Invert the layers onto the rack; remove the waxed paper. Cool completely.

TO PREPARE THE FILLING

- Melt the chocolate and butter in a small saucepan over low heat; remove from heat. Stir in the confectioners' sugar and then the milk.
- Chill for 1 hour or until of spreading consistency.

TO PREPARE THE FROSTING AND ASSEMBLE

- Combine the cream, confectioners' sugar and vanilla in a large mixer bowl. Sift the baking cocoa over the top; stir to mix well. Chill for 30 minutes.
- Beat at high speed for 30 to 60 seconds or until stiff peaks form.
- Place 1 cake layer bottom side up on a cake plate. Spread with the filling. Place the second layer bottom side down over the filling. Spread the frosting over the top and side of the cake. Garnish with fruit slices or chocolate curls.

BOURBON POUND CAKE

TRES BIEN

INGREDIENTS

SERVES 16
PREPARATION TIME:
2 HOURS

1 cup butter or margarine, softened
3 cups sugar
6 eggs
1 cup sour cream
1/2 cup bourbon
1 teaspoon vanilla extract
3 cups flour
1/4 teaspoon baking soda
1/2 teaspoon salt

DIRECTIONS

- Cream the butter and sugar in a mixer bowl until light and fluffy.
  Add the eggs 1 at a time, beating for 30 seconds after each addition.
- Whisk the sour cream, bourbon and vanilla in a small bowl. Mix the
  flour, baking soda and salt together. Add the dry ingredients to the
  creamed mixture alternately with the sour cream mixture, beginning
  and ending with the dry ingredients and mixing well after each addition.
  Spoon into a greased and floured 10-inch tube pan.
- Bake at 325 degrees for 1 1/2 hours. Cool in the pan for 10 minutes;
  remove to a wire rack to cool completely.
- *Variation: Substitute your favorite liqueur for the bourbon in this cake.*

Helpful Hint

Shortening will be easy to
remove from the measuring
cup if eggs have been beaten
or measured in the cup
beforehand.

LEMON POUND CAKE

THE DESSERT PLACE

SERVES 16
PREPARATION TIME:
2 HOURS,
PLUS 30 MINUTES
STANDING TIME

INGREDIENTS

1 1/2 cups unsalted butter, softened
8 ounces cream cheese, softened
3 cups sugar
1/4 cup fresh lemon juice
1 tablespoon grated lemon rind
1 1/2 tablespoons vanilla extract
6 eggs
3 cups flour
1/4 teaspoon salt
1 3/4 cups confectioners' sugar
3 tablespoons milk
1 tablespoon fresh lemon juice

DIRECTIONS

- Cream the butter in a mixer bowl until light. Add the cream cheese; beat until smooth. Add the sugar; beat for 3 minutes or until fluffy. Add 1/4 cup lemon juice, lemon rind and vanilla; mix well.
- Beat in the eggs 2 at a time. Add the flour and salt; beat until creamy. Spoon into a greased and floured 10-inch tube pan.
- Bake at 350 degrees for 1 1/2 hours or until a cake tester near the center comes out clean. Cool in the pan on a wire rack for 15 minutes; remove to a wire rack to cool completely.
- Mix the confectioners' sugar, milk and 1 tablespoon lemon juice in a small bowl. Drizzle over the top and side of the cake. Let stand for 30 minutes or until the glaze sets.
- Note: This cake can be made 8 hours in advance. Let stand, covered, at room temperature until serving time.

Helpful Hint

You will get more juice if you roll lemons, grapefruit or oranges on the counter to soften them before cutting.

EASY BLUEBERRY COBBLER

INGREDIENTS

SERVES 8
PREPARATION TIME:
50 MINUTES

2 pints fresh blueberries
1 tablespoon lemon juice
1 cup flour
1 cup sugar
1 teaspoon baking powder
1 egg, beaten
6 tablespoons melted butter or margarine
1 tablespoon light brown sugar
1/4 teaspoon cinnamon

DIRECTIONS

• Sprinkle the blueberries with the lemon juice in a 6x10-inch baking dish.
• Mix the flour, sugar, baking powder and egg with a fork in a bowl until crumbly; mixture may be lumpy. Sprinkle over the blueberries; drizzle with the butter. Sprinkle the top with a mixture of brown sugar and cinnamon.
• Bake at 350 degrees for 35 to 40 minutes or just until golden brown; the sauce will thicken as the cobbler cools.
• Serve with vanilla ice cream, light cream or half-and-half.

PEACH COBBLER

THE EASY WAY OUT

INGREDIENTS

SERVES 6
PREPARATION TIME:
1 1/2 HOURS

1/2 cup sugar
Juice and grated rind of 1 lemon
1/4 teaspoon almond extract
2 cups sliced peeled Georgia peaches
1 cup sugar
3/4 cup flour
3/4 cup milk
2 teaspoons baking powder
1/2 cup butter or margarine

DIRECTIONS

- Combine 1/2 cup sugar, lemon juice, lemon rind and almond flavoring in a bowl; mix well. Sprinkle over the peaches in a bowl; set aside.
- Mix 1 cup sugar, flour, milk and baking powder in a bowl. Melt the butter in a 2-quart baking dish. Spoon the batter into the dish. Spread the peach mixture over the top; do not stir.
- Bake at 300 degrees for 1 hour.
- *Variation: This can be made with any fresh fruit. A combination of peaches and blackberries is especially good.*

Helpful Hint

Dip peaches in boiling water for one minute for easy peeling.

Pies and Prejudice
by Marilyn Dorn Staats

———

I am a Southerner who revisits the lessons of her youth through cooking. Give me a cup of Christian tea and an apricot fried pie, and I am back on Homestead Avenue in Atlanta, an 8-year-old child sitting at the kitchen table on a scorching August night in 1949.

Unlike the fried pies I am baking now as I stand in my Buckhead kitchen more than forty years later, the ones that night were the creations of Bernice Jones, the brown-skinned woman who had been our cook for as long as I could remember.

"Don't you be bothering me," she'd say whenever I ventured near to watch her prepare them for company dinner. But she would be handing me her rolling pin even as she threatened me away. My job, after I'd flattened the dough, was to cut out circles with Daddy's empty pipe tobacco can. Bernice wouldn't allow me to scoop on the apricots. They might be cool by now, but the pot was not. "I got no time to fool with burned children," she'd say.

"Company's coming."

The company on that hot August night was my Uncle Clarence, a bachelor and a part-time preacher. While Bernice was serving the dinner, Uncle Clarence, who had no children of his own, received a calling to share his Christian understanding of child-rearing with my parents: God gave polio to little girls who went swimming in the summer, Nancy Drew was a bad influence because she tore around town in a blue coupe, one couldn't be too careful about who one's child was allowed to associate with…

The dining room was heavy with sighs. Daddy had set his bedroom fan on the sideboard, but the air

APPLE PIE
THE DESSERT PLACE

FOR THE PIE SHELL

1 1/2 cups flour
1/2 teaspoon cinnamon
1/2 cup butter, chilled, chopped
1/4 cup chilled apple juice

FOR THE FILLING

1 cup sour cream
1/4 cup flour
1 egg
1/4 cup sugar
1 teaspoon vanilla extract
1/2 teaspoon cinnamon
1/2 teaspoon salt
6 apples, peeled, sliced

FOR THE TOPPING

2/3 cup flour
1/3 cup sugar
1/4 cup packed light brown sugar
1/2 teaspoon cinnamon
1/4 cup pecan pieces
3 tablespoons butter
3 tablespoons unsalted butter

[SERVES 8
PREPARATION TIME:
2 HOURS]

TO PREPARE THE PIE SHELL

- Combine the flour and cinnamon in a food processor container fitted with a metal blade. Add the butter; pulse 4 to 6 times to process to the consistency of coarse cornmeal. Add the apple juice gradually, processing constantly until the mixture forms a ball.
- Roll immediately into a circle on a lightly floured surface. Fit into a deep-dish pie plate. Chill in the refrigerator.

TO PREPARE THE FILLING

- Combine the sour cream, flour, egg, sugar, vanilla, cinnamon and salt in a bowl; mix well. Add the apples; toss lightly to coat well. Spoon into the pie shell.

TO PREPARE THE TOPPING AND BAKE THE PIE

- Combine the flour, sugar, brown sugar, cinnamon and pecans in a bowl. Add the butter; mix to the consistency of coarse cornmeal. Sprinkle over the top of the pie.
- Bake at 350 degrees for 1 hour to 1 hour and 10 minutes or until golden brown.
- *Note: This makes more than enough filling for 1 pie, so use only as much as needed to lightly coat the apples.*

BUTTERSCOTCH PIE

INGREDIENTS

1/2 cup melted butter or margarine, cooled
2 eggs, slightly beaten
1/2 cup sugar
1/2 cup packed dark brown sugar
1/2 cup flour
1 teaspoon vanilla extract
1 cup chopped pecans
1/2 cup chocolate chips
1/2 cup butterscotch chips
1 unbaked (9-inch) pie shell

[SERVES 10
PREPARATION TIME:
1 HOUR]

DIRECTIONS

- Combine the butter, eggs, sugar, brown sugar and flour in a bowl; mix well. Stir in the vanilla, pecans, chocolate chips and butterscotch chips. Spoon into the pie shell.
- Bake at 375 degrees for 35 minutes or until the filling is set and the crust is golden brown. Serve with vanilla bean ice cream.

we waited impatiently to receive, counting the seconds it took to pass down the table from Uncle Clarence's perspiring face to ours, was warm and sticky. Steam rose from my tea cup.

"Hot water, sweet milk, and two teaspoons of brown sugar," Uncle Clarence had announced earlier when he ordered Bernice to take away my glass of iced tea and asked the Lord to bless the cup of Christian tea he'd prepared himself in her kitchen. "Exactly like Lipton's, but without the adult stimulation."

I picked at my ham until Bernice finally came into the room to remove the dishes.

"Wonderful supper," Uncle Clarence said to her. And then he told her how much he was looking forward to her dessert. "There's not a white woman alive who can touch your apricot fried pies."

"Burned up," Bernice mumbled. She left the room, swinging the door emphatically behind her.

"Burned up?" Daddy asked Mother.

"Yes, dear." Mother fanned the collar of her dress and turned to Uncle Clarence. "I'm terribly sorry. I'm afraid we don't even have any ice cream to offer you."

Bernice stayed in the kitchen. She never saw us leave the table without our dessert. And now, as I place a fried pie on a plate of my best china and take a sip of my tea, I am thinking about poor Uncle Clarence. He is long gone to heaven. Did he ever get to have company dinner with us again? Surely he must have.

But he was not with us later that night in Bernice's kitchen, sitting around the table with the fan blowing over a bowl of ice. Would he have been as surprised as I was to discover Bernice hadn't burned the dessert after all?

Bernice Jones' Apricot Fried Pies

Pastry:

Two cupfuls self-rising flour

¹/₄ cupful shortening

³/₄ cupful buttermilk

Powdered sugar

Filling:

8 ounces dried apricots

²/₃ cupful sugar

1 teaspoon lemon juice.

Sift flour into a mixing bowl, add shortening and mix with your fingers until it's crumbly.

Stir in milk. Knead the mixture into a soft dough (about 1 minute). Refrigerate until filling is ready.

Cook the apricots in a small amount of water until they're tender. Drain the water. Add the sugar and lemon juice. Add enough water to cover the ingredients, and cook the filling over low heat for 45 minutes, or until thick enough to coat a spoon.

Mash and let cool.

Roll out the dough to a ¹/₄-inch thickness. Use a coffee can to cut five-inch circles.

Place two tablespoonfuls of cooled filling on one side of each circle. Fold the pastry over. Seal the edges with the tines of a floured fork. Pierce the tops of the pastries.

Deep-fry the pies until the pastry turns golden brown.

Drain on paper towels, then sprinkle them liberally with powdered sugar.

Serves five to six persons.

AUTUMN CRANBERRY PIE

INGREDIENTS

1 cup flour

³/4 cup melted butter or margarine

1 cup sugar

2 eggs, beaten

1 teaspoon almond extract

2 cups cranberries

¹/2 cup chopped walnuts

¹/2 cup sugar

SERVES 8
PREPARATION TIME:
1 HOUR

DIRECTIONS

- Combine the flour, butter, 1 cup sugar, eggs and almond flavoring in a bowl; mix well. Spoon into a greased 10-inch pie plate.
- Combine the cranberries with the walnuts and ¹/2 cup sugar in a bowl; mix well. Spoon into the prepared pie plate, spreading evenly.
- Bake at 375 degrees for 35 minutes. Do not overbake; crust should be like a very moist cookie.

APPLE WALNUT PIE

THE PEASANT RESTAURANTS

INGREDIENTS

SERVES 8
PREPARATION TIME:
1 3/4 HOURS, PLUS
CHILLING TIME

1 recipe (2-crust) pie pastry
1 egg white
6 large baking apples, peeled,
    cut into 8 wedges
1 cup sugar
1 teaspoon cinnamon
1/4 teaspoon freshly grated nutmeg
1/8 teaspoon salt
1/4 teaspoon lemon juice
1/2 cup walnut pieces
10 tablespoons unsalted butter
2/3 cup packed light brown sugar
1 cup walnut pieces

DIRECTIONS

- Fit 1 pie pastry into a 9-inch pie plate; pierce side and bottom with a fork. Brush with the egg white. Bake at 400 degrees for 12 minutes or until light brown. Remove to a wire rack to cool.
- Combine the apples, sugar, cinnamon, nutmeg, salt, lemon juice and walnut pieces in a bowl; mix well. Spread evenly over the baked layer. Top with the remaining pie pastry; flute the edge and cut vents. Place on a baking sheet.
- Bake at 400 degrees for 1 hour or until brown. Let stand until cool.
- Heat the butter in a saucepan until melted. Add the brown sugar; mix well. Cook until the brown sugar melts, stirring constantly.
- Stir in the walnuts. Let stand until cool and firm, stirring occasionally.
- Spread the topping evenly over the top of the pie. Chill in the refrigerator or freeze.
- Reheat the pie on a baking sheet in a 350-degree oven just before serving. Serve with cinnamon ice cream.

Helpful Hint

Carrot cake, brownies, and muffins can be converted to delicious lower-fat versions by substituting a fruit preserve for the oil or butter in the recipe.

MANDARIN ORANGE PIE

INGREDIENTS

[
SERVES 8
PREPARATION TIME:
30 MINUTES, PLUS
CHILLING TIME
]

1 1/2 cups graham cracker crumbs
1/2 cup chopped pecans
3 tablespoons melted butter or margarine
1 (14-ounce) can sweetened condensed milk
1/2 cup fresh lemon juice
2 cups whipping cream, whipped
2 (11-ounce) cans mandarin oranges
1 cup broken pecans

Helpful Hint

Use the leftover liquid from canned fruits and vegetables in frozen desserts, gelatin molds, soups, stews or sauces.

DIRECTIONS

- Mix the graham cracker crumbs, pecans and butter in a bowl. Press into a 9-inch pie plate.
- Combine the condensed milk and lemon juice in a bowl; mix until thickened. Fold in the whipped cream.
- Drain the mandarin oranges well on paper towels and chop. Fold into the filling mixture with the pecans. Spoon into the prepared pie plate.
- Chill for several hours.

FRENCH SILK PIE

INGREDIENTS

2 egg whites
1/8 teaspoon cream of tartar
Salt to taste
1/2 cup sugar
1/2 teaspoon vanilla extract
3/4 cup pecan pieces
4 ounces German's sweet chocolate
3 tablespoons water, coffee liqueur or crème de cacao
1 cup whipping cream, whipped
1 teaspoon vanilla extract

SERVES 8
PREPARATION TIME:
1 HOUR AND
20 MINUTES,
PLUS 2 HOURS
CHILLING TIME

DIRECTIONS

• Beat the egg whites with the cream of tartar and salt in a mixer bowl until frothy. Add the sugar gradually, beating constantly until stiff peaks form. Stir in 1/2 teaspoon vanilla and pecans. Spread evenly in a greased 9-inch pie plate.
• Bake at 325 degrees for 55 minutes. Cool on a wire rack.
• Melt the chocolate in the water in a saucepan over low heat. Let stand until cool. Fold in the whipped cream and 1 teaspoon vanilla. Spoon into the cooled pie shell.
• Chill, covered, for 2 hours or longer.

Helpful Hint

Make chocolate curls by sliding a vegetable peeler along a bar of chocolate.

RED PEAR PIE

INGREDIENTS

[
SERVES 10
PREPARATION TIME:
1 1/2 HOURS
]

1 cup sugar
3 tablespoons cornstarch
1 teaspoon cinnamon
4 red pears, peeled, sliced
1 cup fresh cranberries
3/4 cup chopped walnuts
3/4 cup golden raisins
2 all ready deep-dish pie pastries
3 tablespoons sugar

DIRECTIONS

- Mix 1 cup sugar, cornstarch and cinnamon in a bowl. Add the pears, cranberries, walnuts and raisins; toss to coat well. Spoon into a pie plate lined with 1 of the pastries.
- Top with the remaining pastry. Seal the edge and cut 3 vents in the top. Sprinkle with 3 tablespoons sugar.
- Bake at 350 degrees for 1 hour.

PINEAPPLE SOUR CREAM PIE

INGREDIENTS

3/4 cup sugar
1/4 cup flour
1/2 teaspoon salt
1 (20-ounce) can crushed pineapple
1 cup sour cream
1 tablespoon lemon juice
3 egg yolks, slightly beaten
1 baked (9-inch) deep-dish pie shell
3 egg whites
1/4 teaspoon cream of tartar
1/2 teaspoon vanilla extract
6 tablespoons sugar

SERVES 8
PREPARATION TIME:
30 MINUTES

DIRECTIONS

- Mix 3/4 cup sugar, flour and salt in a saucepan. Add the undrained pineapple, sour cream and lemon juice. Cook until thickened, stirring constantly. Cook for 2 minutes longer.
- Stir a small amount of the hot mixture into the egg yolks; stir the egg yolks into the hot mixture. Cook for 2 minutes, stirring constantly. Spoon into the pie shell.
- Beat the egg whites with the cream of tartar until soft peaks form. Add the vanilla and 6 tablespoons sugar gradually, beating constantly until stiff peaks form. Spread over the pie, sealing to the edge.
- Bake at 350 degrees for 12 to 15 minutes or until golden brown.

PUMPKIN ICE CREAM PIE

INGREDIENTS

> ¹/4 cup honey
> ³/4 cup canned pumpkin
> ¹/2 teaspoon cinnamon
> ¹/4 teaspoon ginger
> Nutmeg and ground cloves to taste
> ¹/4 teaspoon salt
> 1 quart vanilla ice cream, slightly softened
> 1 (9-inch) graham cracker pie shell
> ³/4 cup pecans

[
SERVES 8
PREPARATION TIME:
20 MINUTES, PLUS
FREEZING TIME
]

DIRECTIONS

- Combine the honey, pumpkin, spices and salt in a saucepan; mix well. Bring to a boil, stirring constantly. Cool completely.
- Add the ice cream; mix well. Spoon into the pie shell; sprinkle with the pecans. Freeze until firm.

Crumb Pie Shell
—

For a delicious Crumb Pie Shell, combine 1¹/2 cups fine graham cracker crumbs, ¹/4 cup sugar and ¹/2 cup melted butter or margarine and press firmly into a 9-inch pie plate. Chill until firm or bake at 350 degrees for 8 minutes before chilling. For variety, substitute chocolate wafers, gingersnaps, vanilla wafers or Lorna Doone cookies for the graham crackers; omit the sugar if using chocolate wafers. Add ¹/4 to ¹/2 cup chopped nuts if desired.

SHERRY PIE

INGREDIENTS

> 18 large marshmallows
> ¹/2 cup cream sherry
> 1 cup whipping cream
> 1 graham cracker or chocolate wafer pie shell
> 1 (1-ounce) square unsweetened chocolate, grated

[
SERVES 8
PREPARATION TIME:
30 MINUTES
]

DIRECTIONS

- Melt the marshmallows with the sherry in a double boiler over hot water, stirring to mix well. Cool or chill until partially set.
- Beat the cream in a mixer bowl until soft peaks form. Beat the marshmallow mixture with the same beaters. Fold the whipped cream into the marshmallow mixture.
- Spoon into the pie shell. Sprinkle with the grated chocolate. Chill until serving time.

The Right Table for the Job

BY RHETA GRIMSLEY JOHNSON
ILLUSTRATION BY BRIAN OTTO

This one will conjure up memories of those Sunday church dinners. Today I forked over too much money for a beat-up, wobbly, eating table destined to go in the yard for meals served dinner-on-the-ground style.

"Eating table" is one of those comfortable old Southern redundancies, like "church house," "book learning," "bed sheets." You can say it shorter but you don't have as much.

▶

It's not grand to look at, this table. It once was white. It once was green. It once was any color you can name, but now it's mostly a spatter-painted gray over pine or poplar or something cheap. Bits of flowery linoleum curl from the top like cowlicks. The florist I bought it from said he didn't know its history; he sure knew its worth.

All I knew was I had to have it. It's a lot like the tables in the church-yards of my childhood's South Georgia, the ones the women covered with newspaper and sheets to keep flies and gnats at bay until the preaching was over. Sometimes a table was just some boards nailed between trees, but now and again there was a crude, handmade job like this one.

Such tables had to be sturdy. Cooking light was not so much an unknown concept; it was a disgrace. A woman who didn't produce three hot, lard-laced meals for her man and children wasn't much of a woman. Better to be caught in bed with the sewing notions salesman than caught serving peanut butter sandwiches.

▶

DESSERT AFTER THE SYMPHONY

Minted Fruits with Ginger, page 231

———

Chocolate Mousse, page 237

———

Cold Lemon Soufflé with Raspberry Sauce, page 242

———

Frosted Brownies, page 248

———

Spiced Hazelnut and Chocolate Biscotti, page 246

———

Capaccino or Decafe Coffee

DESSERTS

Churchyard cooking was competitive cooking at its best. Not for the faint of heart, the timid of soul. Willing women knocked themselves out to serve the best potato salad among 30 or so bowls, the darndest chicken that ever swam in lard, the flakiest crust wrapped around a stewed apple.

You were talked about if you lost, if your offering was lame, or, God-forbid, store-bought. I remember my paternal grandmother's delight in snipping about another's potato salad on the ride home: "It had so much mayonnaise it looked like it had already been digested once."

Presentation was important, too. French chefs have no monopoly on understanding the value of making food pretty. Grandmother's peers knew the importance of paprika and proper pickle dishes and a bouquet of zinnias on the table, believe you me. And they used their best serving dishes for the picnics, not practical paper or tin.

On the bottom of each dish they stuck a strip of masking tape with their name on it, though in South Georgia everyone knew everyone else's bowls and business. It was like an artist signing a canvas, or a reporter's byline.

The setting, of course, was an important part of presentation, if only subconsciously. Every country church had a graveyard next door, and something about dining in such proximity to those who already

▶

ALMOND CAKES WITH CINNAMON PORT WINE PEARS

CHEF PAUL ALBRECHT, PANOS AND PAULS

[SERVES 4
PREPARATION TIME:
1 1/4 HOURS]

FOR THE CAKES

6 tablespoons almond paste, softened
6 tablespoons butter or margarine, softened
6 tablespoons sugar
2 eggs
3 tablespoons cake flour
1/4 teaspoon baking powder

FOR THE PEARS

2 cups port
2 tablespoons sugar
Grated rind of 1 lemon
Grated rind of 1 orange
1 cinnamon stick
1 vanilla bean
3 medium Bosc pears, peeled, sliced

TO PREPARE THE CAKES

- Grease four 3-inch nonstick baking cups. Cream the almond paste and butter in a mixer bowl for 2 minutes or until smooth. Add the sugar; beat until fluffy.
- Beat in the eggs 1 at a time. Fold in the flour and baking powder. Spoon into the prepared cups.
- Bake at 325 degrees for 20 minutes or until a cake tester comes out clean.
- Cool in the cups for several minutes; remove to a wire rack to cool completely.

TO PREPARE THE PEARS AND ASSEMBLE

- Combine the wine, sugar, lemon rind, orange rind, cinnamon and vanilla in a saucepan. Simmer for 5 minutes. Add the pears.
- Poach the pears until tender; remove from the wine sauce.
- Cook the wine sauce until reduced to a light syrup; discard the cinnamon stick and vanilla bean.
- Spoon the pear syrup onto the serving plates. Place 1 cake on each plate; top with the pears.

IRRESISTIBLE CREME BRULEE

INGREDIENTS

2 cups fresh raspberries
10 egg yolks
13 tablespoons sugar
4 cups whipping cream
1 1/2 teaspoons vanilla extract
2 to 3 tablespoons sugar

[
SERVES 8
PREPARATION TIME:
30 MINUTES, PLUS
CHILLING TIME
]

DIRECTIONS

• Place the raspberries in 8 individual ramekins. Beat the egg yolks with 13 tablespoons sugar in a mixer bowl until thick and pale yellow.

• Bring the cream and vanilla to a boil in a saucepan over medium heat, stirring constantly. Add to the egg yolk mixture; mix well. Return the mixture to the saucepan. Bring to a boil; reduce heat. Simmer until thickened, stirring constantly. Cool slightly.

• Strain the mixture over the raspberries. Chill in the refrigerator. Sprinkle the remaining 2 to 3 tablespoons sugar on top. Broil until the top is golden brown and caramelized. Serve immediately.

• *Variation: Substitute blackberries or blueberries for the raspberries in this recipe.*

have had their Last Supper did much for the appetite. Eat, drink (iced tea) and be merry, for tomorrow you may be wearing marble.

The adage "Hunger is the best garnish" came into play at these culinary extravaganzas, too. Sometimes the preacher talked so long that you could have eaten the hymnal with a squirt of mustard.

Revival preachers were best at the miracle of marathons, turning a fish-and-loaf verse or two into a day-long feast of words. Brother Botulism might drone on until everything the ladies had spread was suspect, but the congregational hunger always overcame the fear.

Thinking back, the meals were all the more remarkable because of the work surrounding food then. Nobody went to Food World or Kroger's for their staples. The vegetables came from the garden, the pot roast from the feed lot, the lard from the pig. Vegetables were cooked until pools of grease from the seasoning fatback floated on top. The only thing involving steam was the weather, hotter than blazes during official dinner-on-the-ground season.

I miss my grandmothers, both of whom were classic cornucopia cooks. I miss idling under the big shade trees and marveling at the variety and quality of food. I miss going back for seconds, thirds and playing hide-and-go-seek amongst the tombstones.

So I'll wrestle this purchase ▶

to my backyard and let the weather and time continue its refinishing job. And the next really hot day I'll throw a bed sheet over the eating table and invite some hungry folks over for pizza. ∎

CHOCOLATE WHITE CHOCOLATE CHEESECAKE

THE DESSERT PLACE

> SERVES 12
> PREPARATION TIME:
> 2¹/2 HOURS, PLUS
> 11 HOURS COOLING
> AND CHILLING TIME

FOR THE CRUST

2¹/2 cups chocolate wafer crumbs
¹/4 cup sugar
¹/2 cup melted unsalted butter

FOR THE FILLING

40 ounces cream cheese, softened
1¹/4 cups sugar
¹/4 cup flour
1 teaspoon vanilla extract
5 eggs
2 egg yolks
8 ounces white chocolate, broken
¹/4 cup half-and-half

FOR THE GLAZE

¹/4 cup light corn syrup
2 tablespoons butter or margarine
3 tablespoons water
1¹/3 cups semisweet chocolate chips

TO PREPARE THE CRUST

- Mix the cookie crumbs and sugar in a bowl. Add the butter; mix well. Press over the bottom and side of an 11-inch springform pan. Chill in the refrigerator.

TO PREPARE THE FILLING

- Beat the cream cheese in a mixer bowl until light. Add the sugar, flour and vanilla; beat at low speed until smooth. Beat in the eggs and egg yolks 1 at a time. Add the white chocolate; mix well. Stir in the half-and-half. Spoon into the prepared crust.
- Bake at 250 degrees for 1¹/4 to 1³/4 hours or until set. Cool on a wire rack for 2 hours. Chill for 8 hours or longer.

TO PREPARE THE GLAZE AND ASSEMBLE

- Combine the corn syrup, butter and water in a saucepan. Bring to a full boil over medium heat; remove from heat. Stir in the chocolate chips until melted. Whisk until of the desired consistency.
- Place the cheesecake on a serving plate; remove the side of the pan. Pour the glaze over the top and spread evenly. Garnish with white chocolate shavings and milk chocolate shavings.

KEY LIME CHEESECAKE

SHAUN SMITHSON, TRES BIEN

INGREDIENTS

> 2 cups graham cracker crumbs
> 1/2 cup packed brown sugar
> 2 tablespoons melted butter or margarine
> 32 ounces cream cheese, softened
> 1 2/3 cups sugar
> 5 tablespoons sour cream
> 4 eggs
> 1 egg yolk
> 5 tablespoons whipping cream
> 1 cup flour
> 1 tablespoon vanilla extract
> 1/4 cup Key lime juice

[
SERVES 12
PREPARATION TIME:
1 3/4 HOURS
]

Helpful Hint

Cover the outside of a springform pan with aluminum foil before baking in a boiling water bath.

DIRECTIONS

- Mix the graham cracker crumbs, brown sugar and butter in a bowl. Press over the bottom of a buttered 10-inch springform pan.
- Beat the cream cheese and sugar in a mixer bowl until light and fluffy; scrape the bowl. Add the sour cream; mix well.
- Beat in the eggs and egg yolk 1 at a time, scraping the side of the bowl after each addition. Add the cream, flour, vanilla and lime juice; mix well.
- Spoon the mixture into the prepared pan. Place the springform pan in a water bath in a large pan.
- Bake at 325 degrees for 1 hour and 20 minutes or until a tester comes out clean. Cool on a wire rack. Place on a serving plate; remove the side of the pan.

PUMPKIN CHEESECAKE

THE PEASANT RESTAURANTS

SERVES 12
PREPARATION TIME:
1 1/2 HOURS PLUS
STANDING AND
CHILLING TIME

INGREDIENTS

3 cups graham cracker crumbs
1 cup melted unsalted butter
1/4 cup sugar
1 tablespoon cinnamon
48 ounces cream cheese, softened
2 2/3 cups sugar
6 eggs
2 teaspoons vanilla extract
1 3/4 cups puréed canned pumpkin
1 tablespoon cinnamon
2 teaspoons nutmeg
1/2 teaspoon ginger
1/8 teaspoon ground cloves
1 cup whipping cream
1 tablespoon confectioners' sugar
1/2 teaspoon cinnamon

DIRECTIONS

- Line the bottom of a 10-inch x 3-inch deep cake pan with parchment paper. Combine the graham cracker crumbs, 1 cup butter, 1/4 cup sugar and 1 tablespoon cinnamon in a bowl; mix well. Pat into the bottom of the prepared pan.
- Beat the cream cheese in a mixer bowl until soft and smooth. Add 2 2/3 cups sugar, beating until creamy. Add the eggs and vanilla, stirring until blended. Stir in the pumpkin, 1 tablespoon cinnamon, nutmeg, ginger and cloves. Spoon into the prepared pan.
- Place pan inside a larger pan filled with 1 1/2" of boiling water. Bake at 275 degrees for 2 hours. Let stand in the oven with the door closed until cool. Chill until serving time.
- Beat the whipping cream in a mixer bowl until soft peaks form.
- Add the confectioners' sugar and 1/2 teaspoon cinnamon; mix well.
- Dip the cheesecake pan in hot water for 10 seconds. Place a cardboard circle on top of the pan; invert the pan and tap lightly.
- Invert right side up onto a serving platter.
- Top with the whipped cream.

APPLE CRISP

INGREDIENTS

SERVES 6
PREPARATION TIME:
45 MINUTES

3 medium apples, peeled, sliced or cut
  into quarters
3/4 cup packed brown sugar
1/2 cup flour
3/4 cup quick-cooking oats
1/2 cup butter or margarine, softened
1 teaspoon cinnamon
1/8 teaspoon freshly ground nutmeg

DIRECTIONS

- Arrange the apples in a greased 8x8-inch baking pan. Combine the brown sugar, flour, oats, butter, cinnamon and nutmeg in a bowl; mix by hand until crumbly. Sprinkle over the apples.
- Bake at 350 degrees for 35 minutes.
- Serve with vanilla ice cream.
- *Variation: Omit the spices and serve this with cinnamon ice cream.*

Helpful Hint

To make cinnamon ice cream, mix softened vanilla ice cream with cinnamon to taste and freeze until firm.

BOCCONE DOLCE (SWEET MOUTHFUL)

THE DESSERT PLACE

SERVES 10
PREPARATION TIME:
1 1/2 HOURS,
PLUS 4 HOURS
CHILLING TIME

INGREDIENTS

4 egg whites
1/4 teaspoon cream of tartar
Salt to taste
1 cup sugar
1 cup semisweet chocolate chips
3 tablespoons water
3 cups whipping cream
1/3 cup sugar
1 1/2 pints strawberries, sliced
1/2 pint strawberries

Helpful Hint

Fresh eggs separate more easily
when they are cold.

DIRECTIONS

- Beat the egg whites with the cream of tartar and salt in a mixer bowl until soft peaks form. Add 1 cup sugar gradually, beating constantly until stiff peaks form.
- Line 2 baking sheets with waxed paper; trace three 8-inch circles on the waxed paper. Spread the meringue evenly over the 3 circles; layers will be 1/4 inch thick.
- Bake at 250 degrees for 20 to 25 minutes or until pale golden brown but still pliable. Peel the waxed paper from the bottoms carefully. Cool on wire racks.
- Melt the chocolate with the 3 tablespoons water in a double boiler over hot water, stirring to mix well. Whip the cream in a bowl until soft peaks form; beat in 1/3 cup sugar until stiff peaks form.
- Place 1 meringue on a serving plate. Spread half the chocolate, a 3/4-inch layer of the whipped cream and half the sliced strawberries over the meringue. Repeat the layers. Top with the third meringue.
- Spread the remaining whipped cream over the top and side; top with the whole strawberries. Chill for 4 to 5 hours before serving.

LOW-FAT CREME CARAMEL

INGREDIENTS

SERVES 8
PREPARATION TIME:
1 1/4 HOURS

1/4 cup sugar
3/4 cup egg substitute
1/3 cup sugar
2 1/2 cups skim or low-fat milk
1 tablespoon vanilla extract

DIRECTIONS

- Spread 1/4 cup sugar evenly in a small saucepan. Heat over medium-low heat until the sugar melts, shaking the pan occasionally and tilting the pan from side to side. Cook until the sugar turns a dark caramel color. Stir the syrup with a spoon; remove from heat. Pour the syrup immediately into 8 custard cups; the syrup will become firm quickly.
- Combine the egg substitute and 1/3 cup sugar in a bowl; stir until the sugar is dissolved. Stir in the milk and vanilla. Pour approximately 1/3 cup of the mixture into each prepared custard cup. Place the cups in a large roasting pan. Add 1 inch hot water to the roasting pan.
- Bake at 350 degrees for 45 minutes. Remove the cups to a wire rack to cool; the custard will become firm as it cools.

CHOCOLATE BROWNIE CAKE WITH A CHOCOLATE AND COCONUT CRUST

INGREDIENTS

SERVES 15
PREPARATION TIME:
1 1/2 HOURS, PLUS
CHILLING TIME

2 1/2 cups fine chocolate wafer crumbs
1/2 cup melted unsalted butter, cooled
7 ounces sweetened flaked coconut,
  lightly toasted
3/4 cup packed light brown sugar
1/4 cup unsalted butter, softened
3 eggs
12 ounces semisweet chocolate, melted, cooled
2 teaspoons instant coffee powder
1 teaspoon hazelnut liqueur
1/4 cup flour
1 cup unsalted cashews or pecans, coarsely chopped
2 cups whipping cream, chilled
3 ounces bittersweet chocolate, shaved into curls

DIRECTIONS

- Mix the cookie crumbs with 1/4 cup of the melted butter in a bowl. Press over the bottom of a buttered and floured 10-inch springform pan. Mix the remaining melted butter with the coconut in a bowl. Press the coconut mixture 1 inch up the side of the pan.
- Cream the brown sugar and 1/4 cup softened butter in a mixer bowl until light and fluffy. Beat in the eggs 1 at a time. Add the melted chocolate, coffee powder and liqueur; mix well.
- Fold in the flour and cashews. Spoon into the prepared pan.
- Bake at 375 degrees for 30 minutes or until set. Cool in the pan on a wire rack.
- Chill the cake for 8 to 10 hours. Loosen the side of the pan with a thin knife; remove the side. Place on a serving plate.
- Beat the cream in a mixer bowl until soft peaks form. Spread over the top and side of the cake. Decorate with the chocolate curls.

CHOCOLATE CHARLOTTE

INGREDIENTS

SERVES 12
PREPARATION TIME:
30 MINUTES,
PLUS 26 HOURS
CHILLING TIME

2 cups semisweet chocolate chips
1/4 cup sugar
1/4 teaspoon salt
1/2 cup coffee liqueur
4 egg yolks
1 1/2 teaspoons vanilla extract
4 egg whites
1/4 cup sugar
1 cup whipping cream
36 large ladyfingers
1 cup whipping cream

DIRECTIONS

- Melt the chocolate chips in a double boiler over hot water. Add 1/4 cup sugar, salt and liqueur. Cook until slightly thickened, stirring constantly. Add the egg yolks. Cook for 2 minutes longer. Stir in the vanilla; remove from heat.
- Beat the egg whites in a mixer bowl until foamy. Add 1/4 cup sugar gradually, beating constantly until stiff peaks form. Fold into the chocolate mixture. Chill, covered, in the refrigerator.
- Whip 1 cup whipping cream in a mixer bowl until soft peaks form. Fold into the chilled mixture.
- Line the bottom and side of a springform pan with some of the ladyfingers. Layer half the chocolate mixture, the remaining ladyfingers and the remaining chocolate mixture in the prepared pan. Chill for 24 hours.
- Whip the remaining whipping cream in a mixer bowl until soft peaks form. Place the dessert on a serving plate; remove the side of the pan. Top with the whipped cream.

Helpful Hint

If chocolate is being melted alone, it should be done in a small, completely dry pan, because even a very small amount of water can cause the chocolate to solidify. If the chocolate is being melted with liquid, use two or more tablespoons of the liquid.

Summer Fruit Terrine

FOR THE FRUIT TERRINE

2 (¹/₂-ounce) envelopes unflavored gelatin
2 cups water
¹/₂ cup sugar
3 tablespoons kirsch
¹/₂ cup sliced strawberries
¹/₂ cup blueberries
¹/₂ cup raspberries
¹/₂ cup blackberries

[
SERVES 8
PREPARATION TIME:
1 HOUR, PLUS
CHILLING TIME
]

FOR THE LEMON SAUCE AND ASSEMBLY

³/₄ cup sugar
2 tablespoons cornstarch
¹/₂ teaspoon salt
2 cups water
2 tablespoons butter or margarine
2 tablespoons lemon juice
¹/₂ teaspoon grated lemon rind
¹/₂ teaspoon ground nutmeg

TO PREPARE THE FRUIT TERRINE

- Soften the gelatin in a small amount of cold water.
- Bring 2 cups water and sugar to a boil in a saucepan; remove from heat. Add the softened gelatin; mix to dissolve the gelatin. Let stand until cool. Stir in the kirsch.
- Arrange a layer of the strawberries in a 4¹/₂-cup terrine. Add just enough of the syrup to cover the strawberries. Chill until set.
- Repeat the layers with the remaining fruit and syrup until all ingredients are used, allowing each layer to chill until set before adding the next. Chill until completely firm.

TO PREPARE THE LEMON SAUCE AND ASSEMBLE

- Combine the sugar, cornstarch, salt and water in a saucepan. Bring to a boil. Cook for 5 minutes, stirring constantly. Remove from heat.
- Stir in the butter, lemon juice, lemon rind and nutmeg.
- Spoon the lemon sauce onto 8 dessert plates. Chill in the refrigerator. Cut the terrine into slices. Arrange on the prepared plates.
- *Variation: Substitute lime juice and lime rind for the lemon juice and lemon rind. Serve the terrine without the sauce.*

MINTED FRUITS WITH GINGER

INGREDIENTS

[SERVES 6
PREPARATION TIME:
1 HOUR AND
10 MINUTES,
PLUS 1 HOUR
CHILLING TIME]

1 cup sliced Georgia peaches
1 cup grape halves
1 cup sliced strawberries
1 cup sliced bananas
1/2 cup orange liqueur
1 tablespoon thinly sliced gingerroot
2 tablespoons chopped fresh mint leaves

DIRECTIONS

- Combine the peaches, grapes, strawberries and bananas in a bowl; toss to mix well. Add the orange liqueur, gingerroot and mint leaves; mix well.
- Chill for 1 hour or longer. Spoon into serving bowls.
- *Variation: Substitute any seasonal fresh fruit for the fruit used in this recipe. Remove the gingerroot before serving if desired.*

Helpful Hint

A quick dip in pineapple juice is all it takes to prevent fresh fruits such as apples, bananas or avocados from browning.

KIWIFRUIT FROZEN YOGURT

INGREDIENTS

3 kiwifruit, peeled, cut into quarters
2 tablespoons fructose or 6 tablespoons sugar
2 cups low-fat vanilla yogurt
1/4 teaspoon vanilla extract

[
SERVES 6
PREPARATION TIME:
35 MINUTES
]

DIRECTIONS

• Purée the kiwifruit in a food processor or blender. Combine with the fructose, yogurt and vanilla in a bowl; mix well.
• Spoon into the ice cream freezer container.
• Freeze using the manufacturer's instructions. Garnish each serving with fresh mint leaves.

LEMON BUTTERMILK ICE CREAM

INGREDIENTS

1 quart buttermilk
2 cups whipping cream
1 1/2 cups sugar
7 tablespoons fresh lemon juice
Grated zest of 1 lemon
Salt to taste

[
SERVES 8
PREPARATION TIME:
30 MINUTES
]

DIRECTIONS

• Combine the buttermilk, cream, sugar, lemon juice, lemon zest and salt in a bowl; mix well. Pour into the ice cream freezer container.
• Freeze using the manufacturer's instructions.

MANGO SORBET

INGREDIENTS

2 cups puréed mangoes
2 tablespoons simple syrup
2 tablespoons fresh lime juice

[
SERVES 4
PREPARATION TIME:
30 MINUTES
]

DIRECTIONS

- Strain the mango purée through a sieve into a bowl. Add the simple syrup and lime juice; mix well. Spoon into the ice cream freezer container.
- Freeze using the manufacturer's instructions.

TANGERINE ICE

INGREDIENTS

3/4 cup sugar
1/2 cup water
3 cups fresh tangerine juice
1 to 2 tablespoons fresh lemon juice

[
SERVES 4
PREPARATION TIME:
30 TO 45 MINUTES,
PLUS 1 HOUR
CHILLING TIME
]

DIRECTIONS

- Heat the sugar and water in a large saucepan over low heat until the sugar dissolves. Cool completely. Stir in the tangerine juice and lemon juice. Chill in the refrigerator for 1 hour.
- Pour into the ice cream freezer container. Freeze using the manufacturer's instructions. Garnish each serving with fresh mint leaves.

Simple Syrup

To make simple syrup, bring equal parts of water and sugar to a boil in a saucepan, stirring to dissolve the sugar completely. Remove from heat and cool.

The Swan House

Named for the swan motif found throughout the interior of the house, the classically designed Swan House was completed in 1928 for Mr. and Mrs. Edward Hamilton Inman, heirs to a cotton-merchandising fortune. The house, which is listed on the National Register of Historic Places and has become a well-known Atlanta landmark, was designed by Atlanta architect Philip Trammell Shutze (1890-1982), who designed many other landmark buildings and private homes in the city. In 1966, the Society purchased Swan House, most of its original furnishings, ranging from 18th-century antiques to 20th century objects, and 22 acres of surrounding woodland; later additions have increased the Society's property to 32 acres. In 1982, Shutze bequeathed to the Society his research library and his personal collection of decorative arts, rotating selections from which are on exhibit in three second-floor rooms at Swan House. Guided tours of Swan House focus on the architecture, landscaping, interior design, furnishings, and historical context of the house that reflect the lifestyles of prominent Atlantans of the 1930s.

SWAN HOUSE PEACH ICE CREAM

INGREDIENTS

1 quart Georgia peaches
2 cups sugar
4 cups whipping cream
1 tablespoon vanilla extract
1 cup sugar

[
SERVES 12
PREPARATION TIME:
45 MINUTES
]

DIRECTIONS

• Peel the peaches and mash in a bowl. Add 2 cups sugar; mix gently. Chill in the refrigerator.
• Combine the cream with the vanilla and 1 cup sugar in a bowl; mix well. Pour into the ice cream freezer container.
• Freeze until partially firm using the manufacturer's instructions. Fold in the peach mixture. Freeze until firm enough to pack.
• *Note: This recipe was adapted in 1928 by Mrs. S. R. Dull, cooking school instructor and former editor of the home economics page of the Atlanta Journal. Ice cream was a frequent dessert at the Swan House. The Inman family kept cows and always had fresh milk for cream and cobbler, and made ice cream on Sundays on the Boxwood Porch.*

RASPBERRY MOUSSE

INGREDIENTS

[
SERVES 6
PREPARATION TIME:
1 1/2 HOURS,
PLUS CHILLING TIME
]

1 1/2 cups fresh raspberries
6 ounces white baking chocolate, chopped
1/4 cup butter or margarine
1/2 cup sugar
3 egg whites, stiffly beaten
1 cup whipping cream
1/4 cup sugar

DIRECTIONS

- Purée the raspberries in a blender. Strain through a sieve to remove the seeds.
- Melt the white chocolate and butter with 1/2 cup sugar and the raspberry purée in a double boiler over hot water, stirring constantly until smooth. Chill for 1 hour or longer.
- Fold stiffly beaten egg whites into the chilled raspberry mixture.
- Beat the cream in a large bowl until soft peaks form. Add 1/4 cup sugar gradually, beating constantly. Fold the raspberry mixture into the whipped cream. Spoon into individual serving dishes. Garnish with grated chocolate or chocolate curls. Chill until serving time.
- *Variation: Substitute thawed frozen raspberries for the fresh raspberries.*

Helpful Hint

A pinch of salt added to whipping cream before whipping strengthens the fat cells and makes the cream thicken faster.

CHOCOLATE MOUSSE

INGREDIENTS

3/4 cup whipping cream
1 cup chocolate chips
2 eggs
3 tablespoons strong brewed coffee
1 tablespoon coffee liqueur
1/4 cup whipping cream, whipped

SERVES 6
PREPARATION TIME:
15 MINUTES,
PLUS 6 HOURS
CHILLING TIME

DIRECTIONS

• Place a film of water in the bottom of a saucepan to prevent the whipping cream from burning when heated. Add the 3/4 cup whipping cream. Heat until the whipping cream is scalded.
• Combine the chocolate chips, eggs, coffee and liqueur in a blender container. Add the scalded whipping cream. Blend the mixture for 2 minutes. Pour into mousse cups.
• Chill, covered with plastic wrap, for 6 hours. Spoon the whipped cream on the top of each before serving.

FROZEN LEMON TORTE

INGREDIENTS

SERVES 8

PREPARATION TIME:
30 MINUTES, PLUS
FREEZING TIME

1 (6-ounce) package thin lemon cookies
or thin brown-edge cookies

4 egg whites

3/4 cup sugar

4 egg yolks

1/4 cup sugar

1/2 cup fresh lemon juice

1 1/2 tablespoons grated lemon rind

1 1/2 cups whipping cream, whipped

1 (10-ounce) package frozen raspberries, thawed

DIRECTIONS

- Line the bottom and side of a 9-inch springform pan with some of the cookies.
- Beat the egg whites in a mixer bowl until stiff peaks form. Add 3/4 cup sugar gradually, beating constantly until peaks are very stiff and glossy.
- Beat the egg yolks with 1/4 cup sugar, lemon juice and lemon rind in a mixer bowl. Fold into the egg white mixture. Fold in the whipped cream.
- Spoon into the prepared pan; smooth the top. Freeze until firm.
- Place on a plate; remove the side of the pan.
- Purée the raspberries in a blender. Serve over the slices of torte. Serve with the remaining cookies.
- *Variation: Substitute 2 cups fresh raspberries for the frozen raspberries.*

TOFFEE ICE CREAM SQUARES

FOR THE ICE CREAM SQUARES

[
SERVES 12
PREPARATION TIME:
30 MINUTES, PLUS
FREEZING TIME
]

1 1/2 cups chocolate wafer crumbs
6 tablespoons melted butter or margarine
9 ounces chocolate toffee candy bars
1/2 gallon vanilla ice cream or frozen yogurt,
  softened

FOR THE SAUCE

1/4 cup butter or margarine
1 cup chocolate chips
1 cup confectioners' sugar
3/4 cup evaporated milk
1 teaspoon vanilla extract

TO PREPARE THE ICE CREAM SQUARES

• Mix the cookie crumbs and butter in a bowl. Press into a 9x13-inch
  dish. Chill until set.
• Crush the candy bars a few at a time in the food processor. Combine
  with the softened ice cream in a bowl; mix well. Spoon into the
  prepared dish.
• Freeze until firm. Cut into squares.

TO PREPARE THE SAUCE

• Melt the butter and chocolate chips in a heavy saucepan. Stir in the
  confectioners' sugar and evaporated milk. Cook for 8 minutes or until
  thickened, stirring constantly. Stir in the vanilla.
• Serve warm over the ice cream squares.

BOURBON AND PECAN ICE CREAM SAUCE

INGREDIENTS

1/2 cup melted butter or margarine
1 cup packed brown sugar
1 cup chopped pecans
1 tablespoon light corn syrup
1/4 cup bourbon

[
SERVES 8
PREPARATION TIME:
10 MINUTES
]

DIRECTIONS

- Combine the butter, brown sugar, pecans and corn syrup in a heavy skillet. Bring to a boil, stirring constantly; reduce heat.
- Cook for just 1 minute. Stir in the bourbon. Serve immediately over ice cream.

DECADENT CHOCOLATE SAUCE

INGREDIENTS

1 1/2 cups whipping cream
2/3 cup packed brown sugar
4 (1-ounce) squares semisweet chocolate
3 (1-ounce) squares unsweetened chocolate
1/4 cup butter or margarine
1/4 cup amaretto or Grand Marnier
  or 1 tablespoon vanilla extract

[
SERVES 24
PREPARATION TIME:
15 MINUTES
]

DIRECTIONS

- Combine the cream and brown sugar in a small saucepan. Bring to a boil over medium-high heat, whisking until the brown sugar dissolves. Reduce heat to low.
- Stir in the chocolate until melted and blended. Whisk in the butter and liqueur. Serve warm.

Helpful Hint

When a sauce curdles, remove the pan from heat and plunge it into a pan of cold water to stop the cooking process. Beat the sauce vigorously or pour into a blender and process until smooth.

RASPBERRY SAUCE

INGREDIENTS

2 cups fresh or unsweetened frozen raspberries
2 tablespoons sugar
1 tablespoon cornstarch
2 tablespoons water
3 tablespoons chambord or crème de cassis

[SERVES 12
PREPARATION TIME:
20 MINUTES]

DIRECTIONS

• Bring the raspberries and sugar to a boil in a small heavy saucepan over medium heat, stirring to mash the raspberries. Add a mixture of the cornstarch dissolved in the water.
• Cook for 30 to 45 seconds or until thickened and clear, stirring constantly. Strain through a fine mesh into a bowl.
• Stir in the liqueur. Serve chilled or at room temperature over chocolate or lemon desserts.

KAHLUA CREAM FOR FRESH FRUIT

INGREDIENTS

8 ounces cream cheese or Neufchâtel cheese, softened
¼ cup Kahlúa
2 tablespoons light cream
2 tablespoons toasted, chopped, blanched almonds

[SERVES 8
PREPARATION TIME:
5 MINUTES]

DIRECTIONS

• Beat the cream cheese in a mixer bowl until creamy. Add the liqueur and cream gradually, beating constantly until the mixture is smooth. Stir in the almonds.
• Serve with fresh strawberries, bananas, pineapple or apple wedges.

CHOCOLATE SOUFFLE FOR TWO

FOR THE MOCHA CREAM

[
SERVES 2
PREPARATION TIME:
45 MINUTES, PLUS
CHILLING TIME
]

1/2 cup whipping cream
1 tablespoon sugar
1 1/2 teaspoons baking cocoa
1/2 teaspoon instant coffee granules

FOR THE SOUFFLE

2 tablespoons butter or margarine
1 (1-ounce) square unsweetened baking chocolate
2 tablespoons flour
1/2 cup milk
1 tablespoon instant coffee granules
Salt to taste
2 egg yolks
1/4 cup sugar
1/2 teaspoon vanilla extract
2 egg whites, stiffly beaten

TO PREPARE THE MOCHA CREAM

- Combine the cream, sugar, baking cocoa and instant coffee in a bowl; mix well. Chill in the refrigerator until serving time.

TO PREPARE THE SOUFFLE

- Melt the butter and chocolate in a saucepan over medium heat. Stir in the flour until smooth. Cook for 1 minute, stirring constantly. Add the milk gradually, stirring constantly. Cook until thickened and bubbly, stirring constantly. Stir in the coffee until dissolved. Add the salt. Remove from heat.
- Beat the egg yolks and sugar in a mixer bowl until thick and pale yellow. Stir in the vanilla. Stir a small amount of the hot chocolate mixture into the egg yolk mixture. Add the remaining hot chocolate mixture very gradually, stirring constantly. Fold in the stiffly beaten egg whites. Spoon into buttered ramekins.
- Bake at 325 degrees for 30 to 35 minutes or until puffed and set. Top with the mocha cream and serve immediately.

Letter from Grandma
by Neil Shulman, M.D.
Author of Doc Hollywood

Grandma was the inspiration for me to write books and go into medicine. Why, when I was four years old grandma started calling me a doctor. She was also a matchmaker. She met my brother's future wife at a bus stop, just walked up to her and said, "What does your father do? What's your dress size? I've got a nice grandson whose mother is very proud of him. He's very neat. He brushes his teeth in the morning and makes his bed. Please give me your phone number." Grandma matched up over 35 couples with a zero divorce rate. But to really get a flavor of grandma, I'd like to share with you a letter she wrote me when I was in my first year of medical school at Emory.

Dear Neil:

I have read your letter to your mother, how beautiful you write. I know you are smart and have a good feeling for others. You're giving good advice. I think you will go far in your profession. Only stay well. I should live to see you in your gown and cap and getting your diploma. Now, dear grandson, as far as your diet is concerned, don't eat bread, chicken, or meat. Eat Jell-o every day. I gave corn flakes to the birds. They wouldn't eat it so I don't eat it. Send away to the Jell-o people for a recipe book. Take a couple of milk of magnesia pills about

COLD LEMON SOUFFLE WITH RASPBERRY SAUCE

FOR THE RASPBERRY SAUCE

> 2 (10-ounce) packages frozen raspberries, thawed
> 2 tablespoons Cointreau

FOR THE SOUFFLE

> 1 tablespoon unflavored gelatin
> 1/4 cup cold water
> 5 egg yolks
> 3/4 cup sugar
> 3/4 cup fresh lemon juice
> 2 teaspoons freshly grated lemon rind
> 5 egg whites, at room temperature
> 3/4 cup sugar
> 1 cup whipping cream, whipped

[SERVES 8
PREPARATION TIME:
1 HOUR,
PLUS 4 1/2 HOURS
CHILLING TIME]

TO PREPARE THE RASPBERRY SAUCE

- Purée the raspberries in a blender. Strain through a sieve into a bowl. Stir in the liqueur. Chill until serving time.

TO PREPARE THE SOUFFLE

- Soften the gelatin in the cold water.
- Combine the egg yolks, 3/4 cup sugar, lemon juice and lemon rind in the top of a double boiler; mix well. Cook over hot water for 8 minutes or until thickened, stirring constantly. Remove from heat. Add the softened gelatin, stirring until dissolved.
- Chill for 30 to 40 minutes.
- Beat the egg whites in a mixer bowl until soft peaks form. Add 3/4 cup sugar gradually, beating constantly until stiff peaks form. Fold the stiffly beaten egg whites and whipped cream into the egg yolk mixture until no white streaks remain. Spoon into a 2-quart soufflé dish.
- Chill for 4 hours or longer. Serve with the raspberry sauce.

WINFIELD'S FRUIT TART

THE PEASANT RESTAURANTS

INGREDIENTS

32 ounces cream cheese, softened
1 1/2 cups sugar
4 eggs
1 teaspoon vanilla extract
1/2 cup melted unsalted butter
14 sheets phyllo pastry
1/3 cup confectioners' sugar
Assorted fruits

SERVES 10
PREPARATION TIME:
1 3/4 HOURS

DIRECTIONS

- Beat the cream cheese in a mixer bowl until smooth. Add the sugar, beating until blended; scrape the bowl frequently. Add the eggs and vanilla. Beat at low speed just until mixed.
- Brush a tart ring with some of the melted butter. Place on a baking sheet. Arrange 1 sheet of the phyllo dough in the ring, covering half of the ring; brush with some of the melted butter. Arrange another sheet of the phyllo dough in the other half of the ring, with a 2-inch overlap in the center; brush with some of the melted butter.
- Repeat the process until there are 6 layers, 2 sheets per layer, each layer at right angles to the last. Spoon the cream cheese mixture into the center.
- Brush the remaining 2 sheets of the phyllo dough with the remaining melted butter. Arrange in the center of the pan, with edges overlapping 4 inches to cover the cream cheese mixture. Fold edges of phyllo dough loosely and gently over the top, forming a 3-inch border.
- Bake at 375 degrees for 1 hour. Remove to a wire rack. Cool to room temperature; do not chill.
- Dust the edges with the confectioners' sugar just before serving.
- Fill the center with assorted fruits.

once a week. It coats the stomach and helps the digestion. Eat cooked vegetables. Put a glass of table salt in your bath. Don't eat too much at one meal. You should better eat five small meals than three heavy meals. Put your feet up when you study. Make sure you sleep seven or eight hours a day. Don't eat ice, no ice cream. Hungry? Eat a baked apple with a little cream on top. Chew on a few raisins for when you are hungry, that will not make you fat. Use a cream to wash your face and that will keep you beautiful. Get a one-a-day vitamin or B-12 and don't love too much, you know what I mean. If you observe all this you will live to be 100 years of age. The reason I tell you this is because I love you.

Love, Grandmother

P.S. After grandma wrote me the letter, I wrote her back and asked if I could include the letter in my novel, Finally…I'm a Doctor. I didn't hear anything from her for six weeks. I was getting nervous and thought that maybe she was contacting a lawyer to negotiate royalties. However, one day I did come home and find a thick envelope by my front door. I opened it and inside was a letter from grandma saying that I had her permission to use the letter in my book and enclosed were 35 other letters. Would I include those as well?

TIRAMISU CLASSICO

INGREDIENTS

SERVES 12
PREPARATION TIME:
1 HOUR, PLUS 8 1/2
HOURS OR MORE
CHILLING TIME

1 3/4 cups whipping cream
6 egg yolks
1 1/4 cups sugar
8 ounces cream cheese, softened
1/4 cup sour cream
2 tablespoons whipping cream
3 (3-ounce) packages ladyfingers
4 teaspoons instant coffee granules
1 tablespoon brandy
2/3 cup hot water
3/4 cup whipping cream
2 tablespoons confectioners' sugar
1/2 teaspoon vanilla extract
2 teaspoons baking cocoa

DIRECTIONS

- Chill 1 3/4 cups cream in a metal bowl for 30 minutes.
- Combine the egg yolks and sugar in a double boiler. Beat until thick and pale yellow. Place over boiling water; reduce heat. Cook for 10 minutes, stirring constantly; remove from heat.
- Beat the cream cheese with the sour cream and 2 tablespoons cream in a small bowl. Add to the egg yolk mixture; beat until smooth. Let the mixture cool.
- Whip the chilled cream until soft peaks form. Fold into the egg yolk mixture; set aside.
- Line a greased springform pan with some of the ladyfingers. Brush the ladyfingers with a mixture of the coffee granules, brandy and hot water. Spread with half the custard mixture. Top with the remaining ladyfingers; brush with the remaining coffee mixture. Add the remaining custard.
- Combine 3/4 cup cream, confectioners' sugar and vanilla in a bowl; beat until soft peaks form. Spread over the tiramisu; sift the baking cocoa over the top.
- Chill for 8 to 10 hours. Place on a serving plate; remove the side of the pan. Cut to serve.

CHRISTMAS TRIFLE

FOR THE CUSTARD

3/4 cup sugar
2 tablespoons flour
2 tablespoons cornstarch
2 cups milk
6 egg yolks
6 tablespoons butter
1 teaspoon vanilla extract

[
SERVES 10
PREPARATION TIME:
40 MINUTES
]

FOR THE TRIFLE

5 (1/2-inch) slices pound cake
2 tablespoons sherry
3/4 cup raspberry jam
3/4 cup crumbled almond macaroons or
   similar flavored cookie
1 (10-ounce) package frozen raspberries, thawed
1 cup whipping cream
1/2 teaspoon vanilla extract
2 tablespoons confectioners' sugar

TO PREPARE THE CUSTARD

- Mix the sugar, flour and cornstarch in a saucepan. Whisk in the milk gradually. Cook until thickened, stirring constantly.
- Stir a small amount of the hot mixture into the egg yolks; stir the egg yolks into the hot mixture. Cook until thickened, stirring constantly; remove from heat.
- Stir in the butter and vanilla. Place a piece of plastic wrap directly on the surface of the custard; let stand until cool.

TO PREPARE THE TRIFLE

- Arrange the cake slices in a trifle bowl or glass bowl. Drizzle with the wine; spread evenly with the jam.
- Layer the crumbled macaroons, raspberries and cooled custard over the cake.
- Whip the cream with the vanilla and confectioners' sugar in a mixer bowl. Swirl over the top of the trifle. Garnish with slivered almonds and candied red cherries.

Helpful Hint
———
Press plastic wrap directly onto the surface of custards, puddings and white sauces after cooking to prevent the formation of a film.

SPICED HAZELNUT AND CHOCOLATE BISCOTTI

INGREDIENTS

SERVES 40
PREPARATION TIME:
2 1/4 HOURS

1 3/4 cups flour
1 cup sugar
1/3 cup baking cocoa
1 teaspoon baking soda
1 tablespoon cinnamon
1 teaspoon freshly grated nutmeg
1/2 teaspoon ground cloves
4 ounces bittersweet chocolate, coarsely chopped
1 cup coarsely chopped hazelnuts or almonds
1/4 cup dark-roasted coffee beans, coarsely ground
3 eggs
1 teaspoon vanilla extract
1 teaspoon hazelnut or almond extract

DIRECTIONS

- Sift the flour, sugar, baking cocoa, baking soda, cinnamon, nutmeg and cloves into a large bowl. Add the chocolate, hazelnuts and ground coffee; mix well.
- Beat the eggs with the flavorings in a small bowl. Add to the chocolate mixture; mix and knead until the mixture forms a stiff dough, adding 1 to 2 teaspoons water if necessary.
- Divide the dough into 2 portions. Dust each portion with flour and form into a 12-inch roll. Place on a baking sheet lined with lightly greased foil.
- Bake at 350 degrees for 50 minutes. Cool on a wire rack for 10 minutes. Reduce the oven temperature to 300 degrees.
- Place the rolls on a cutting board. Cut diagonally with a serrated knife into 1/2-inch slices. Place cut side down on a cookie sheet.
- Bake at 300 degrees for 40 minutes or until crisp, turning once halfway through the baking time. Cool on a wire rack. Store in an airtight container.

APRICOT SQUARES

INGREDIENTS

1 1/2 cups flour
1 teaspoon baking powder
1 1/2 cups rolled oats
1 cup packed light brown sugar
3/4 cup margarine
1 (9-ounce) jar apricot preserves

SERVES 40
PREPARATION TIME:
45 MINUTES

DIRECTIONS

- Sift the flour and baking powder into a bowl. Stir in the oats and brown sugar. Cut in the margarine until crumbly. Press 2/3 of the mixture into a greased 9x13-inch baking pan.
- Spread the apricot preserves over the prepared layer; top with the remaining oat mixture.
- Bake at 325 degrees for 25 minutes or until golden brown. Cool on a wire rack. Cut into squares. Store in the refrigerator.

CHOCOLATE SCOTCHEROOS

INGREDIENTS

1 cup light corn syrup
1 cup sugar
1 cup peanut butter
6 cups crisp rice cereal
1 cup semisweet chocolate chips
1 cup butterscotch chips

SERVES 30
PREPARATION TIME:
45 MINUTES

DIRECTIONS

- Bring the corn syrup and sugar to a boil in a 3-quart saucepan; remove from heat. Stir in the peanut butter and cereal. Press into a greased 9x13-inch dish. Let stand until firm.
- Melt the chocolate chips and butterscotch chips in a double boiler over hot water, stirring to blend well. Spread over the peanut butter mixture.
- Chill for 5 minutes or until firm. Cut into bars.

FROSTED BROWNIES

FOR THE BROWNIES

4 eggs
2 cups sugar
1 cup flour
1 tablespoon vanilla extract
1 cup unsalted butter
4 (1-ounce) squares unsweetened chocolate
2 cups chopped pecans

FOR THE FROSTING

2 (1-ounce) squares unsweetened chocolate
2 tablespoons butter or margarine
1/4 cup water
2 cups confectioners' sugar
2 teaspoons vanilla extract

SERVES 30
PREPARATION TIME:
1 HOUR, PLUS
STANDING OR
CHILLING TIME

TO PREPARE THE BROWNIES

• Beat the eggs and sugar in a mixer bowl. Add the flour and vanilla; mix well.
• Melt the butter and chocolate in a heavy saucepan, stirring to blend well. Add to the batter; mix well. Fold in the pecans. Spoon into a greased 9x13-inch baking pan.
• Bake at 350 degrees for 30 minutes.

TO PREPARE THE FROSTING AND ASSEMBLE

• Melt the chocolate and butter with the water in a saucepan, whisking until smooth. Add the confectioners' sugar and vanilla. Whisk for 1 minute.
• Pour the frosting over the top of the hot brownies.
• Let stand for 8 hours or chill in the refrigerator until set. Cut into bars.

WHITE CHOCOLATE AND PECAN BROWNIES

INGREDIENTS

[SERVES 30
PREPARATION TIME:
1 HOUR]

3 ounces unsweetened chocolate, broken into
   small pieces
3/4 cup unsalted butter, slightly softened
3/4 cup sugar
3/4 cup packed brown sugar
3 eggs
3/4 cup flour
6 ounces white chocolate, cut into 1/2-inch pieces
1/2 cup chopped pecans
2 tablespoons confectioners' sugar

DIRECTIONS

- Butter and flour a 9x13-inch baking pan. Line the bottom with foil;
  butter and flour the foil, shaking off the excess.
- Melt the unsweetened chocolate in a double boiler over simmering
  water, stirring until smooth. Set aside.
- Cream the butter in a mixer bowl until light. Add the sugar and brown
  sugar, beating until fluffy. Add the melted chocolate, mixing at low speed.
- Add the eggs 1 at a time, mixing just until moistened after each
  addition. Blend in the flour. Fold in the white chocolate and pecans.
  Spoon into the prepared pan.
- Bake on the center rack at 350 degrees for 20 to 25 minutes or until
  a wooden pick comes out clean. Cool on a wire rack.
- Invert onto a work surface; remove the foil. Invert onto a serving plate;
  sprinkle with the confectioners' sugar. Cut into bars.

Helpful Hint

Keep toasted or chopped nuts
in the freezer to have on
hand for recipes or to use as
toppings for ice cream when
unexpected guests arrive.

CARAMEL BARS

INGREDIENTS

[SERVES 16
PREPARATION TIME:
45 MINUTES]

1/2 cup butter or margarine
1 cup packed brown sugar
3/4 cup flour
1 teaspoon baking powder
1 egg, beaten
1 teaspoon vanilla extract
1 cup chopped pecans
2 tablespoons confectioners' sugar

Helpful Hint

Add a small slice of soft bread to a package of hardened brown sugar, close the bag tightly and in a few hours the sugar will be soft again.

DIRECTIONS

- Melt the butter with the brown sugar in a double boiler over hot water, stirring to blend well. Cool to room temperature.
- Add the flour, baking powder, egg, vanilla and pecans; mix well. Spread in a greased 9x9-inch baking pan.
- Bake at 350 degrees for 25 to 30 minutes or until golden brown. Cool on a wire rack. Sprinkle with the confectioners' sugar. Cut into 1x2-inch bars.

ICED CHOCOLATE AND COCONUT BARS

INGREDIENTS

1/2 cup butter or margarine, softened
1/4 cup sugar
5 tablespoons baking cocoa
1 egg
1 teaspoon vanilla extract
2 cups fine graham cracker crumbs
1 cup flaked coconut
1/2 cup chopped walnuts
2 tablespoons vanilla instant pudding mix
3 tablespoons milk
1/4 cup butter or margarine
2 cups confectioners' sugar
4 (1-ounce) squares semisweet chocolate
2 tablespoons butter or margarine

[
SERVES 48
PREPARATION TIME:
1 HOUR
]

Helpful Hint

Measure ingredients accurately. Use a glass measure for liquids. Use metal or plastic measuring cups for solids or dry ingredients; fill to overflowing and level off with a knife or spatula.

DIRECTIONS

• Combine 1/2 cup butter, sugar, baking cocoa, egg and vanilla in a double boiler. Cook over hot water until thickened or until the consistency of a thin custard, stirring constantly.

• Mix the graham cracker crumbs, coconut and walnuts in a bowl. Add to the double boiler; mix well. Press evenly into a 9x9-inch baking pan.

• Combine the pudding mix and milk in a bowl; mix well. Cream 1/4 cup butter in a small bowl until smooth. Add to the pudding mixture; mix well. Blend in the confectioners' sugar. Spread over the chocolate mixture. Chill for 15 minutes or longer.

• Melt the semisweet chocolate with 2 tablespoons butter in a double boiler over hot water or microwave in a glass bowl. Spread or drizzle over the pudding layer. Cut into small bars.

• Chill until serving time. Store in the refrigerator or freezer.

CHOCOLATE MERINGUES

INGREDIENTS

3 cups packed confectioners' sugar
7 tablespoons baking cocoa
2 tablespoons flour
3 egg whites
2 cups finely chopped pecans

SERVES 50
PREPARATION TIME:
45 MINUTES

DIRECTIONS

- Mix the confectioners' sugar, baking cocoa and flour in a medium mixer bowl. Add the egg whites; beat at high speed for 1 minute or until stiff. Stir in the pecans.
- Drop by 1/2 teaspoonfuls 2 inches apart on cookie sheets lined with baking parchment. Press lightly with the back of a spoon.
- Bake at 350 degrees for 15 minutes. Cool on the cookie sheets for 15 minutes. Remove from the baking parchment.

Helpful Hint

Use foil for baking if you do not have baking parchment.

CHOCOLATE CARAMEL CHEWS

INGREDIENTS

28 caramels
3 tablespoons margarine
2 tablespoons water
1 (3-ounce) can chow mein noodles
1 cup peanuts
1 cup semisweet chocolate chips
2 tablespoons water

SERVES 30
PREPARATION TIME:
30 MINUTES

DIRECTIONS

- Melt the caramels with the margarine and 2 tablespoons water in a double boiler over hot water or a saucepan over low heat, stirring occasionally to blend well. Stir in the noodles and peanuts. Drop by rounded teaspoonfuls onto a greased tray.
- Melt the chocolate chips with 2 tablespoons water in a double boiler over hot water. Spoon onto the caramel chews. Chill or let stand at room temperature until set.

CHOCOLATE CHIP AND NUT COOKIES

INGREDIENTS

1 cup butter or margarine, softened
1/4 cup sugar
1 1/4 cups packed dark brown sugar
2 eggs
2 1/4 cups flour
1 teaspoon baking soda
1/2 teaspoon salt
2 teaspoons vanilla extract
2 cups semisweet chocolate chips
1 cup chopped pecans
1 cup chopped macadamia nuts
1/2 cup flaked coconut

Helpful Hint

When baking cookies, always
drop the dough onto cool
cookie sheets.

DIRECTIONS

- Cream the butter in a mixer bowl until light. Add the sugar and
  brown sugar gradually, beating constantly until fluffy. Beat in the eggs
  1 at a time.
- Add the flour, baking soda and salt gradually, mixing well after each
  addition. Add the vanilla, chocolate chips, pecans, macadamia nuts
  and coconut; mix well. Drop by rounded teaspoonfuls onto a greased
  cookie sheet.
- Bake at 375 degrees for 9 to 11 minutes or until golden brown.
  Remove to a wire rack to cool.

WHITE CHOCOLATE ALMOND BARS

INGREDIENTS

4 ounces white chocolate
1 cup butter or margarine
1 1/2 cups sugar
4 eggs
1 1/3 cups flour
1 teaspoon baking powder
1/2 teaspoon salt
2 teaspoons almond extract
1 cup chopped almonds
2 tablespoons confectioners' sugar

[
SERVES 48
PREPARATION TIME:
45 MINUTES
]

DIRECTIONS

• Grease and flour the bottom of a 9x13-inch baking pan.
• Melt the white chocolate in a medium saucepan over low heat, stirring constantly. Add the butter. Cook until the butter melts, whisking constantly; remove from heat.
• Stir in the sugar. Whisk in the eggs 1 at a time. Add the flour, baking powder, salt and almond flavoring; mix well. Mix in the almonds. Spread in the prepared baking pan.
• Bake at 350 degrees for 30 to 35 minutes or until the top is golden brown and the center is set. Cool on a wire rack. Sprinkle with the confectioners' sugar. Cut into bars.

CINNAMON BARS

SERVES 48
PREPARATION TIME:
45 MINUTES

INGREDIENTS

$^1/_2$ cup butter, softened
$^1/_2$ cup margarine, softened
1 cup sugar
1 egg yolk
2 cups sifted flour
1 $^1/_2$ tablespoons cinnamon
1 teaspoon salt
1 egg white
$^1/_2$ cup chopped walnuts or pecans

DIRECTIONS

• Cream the butter, margarine and sugar in a mixer bowl until light and fluffy. Beat in the egg yolk.
• Sift the flour, cinnamon and salt together. Fold gently into the creamed mixture. Spread in a greased 9x13-inch baking pan.
• Beat the egg white in a mixer bowl until stiff peaks form. Spread over the batter; sprinkle with the walnuts.
• Bake at 300 degrees for 25 to 30 minutes or until golden brown. Cool in the pan on a wire rack. Cut into bars.

GINGER COOKIES

INGREDIENTS

[SERVES 40
PREPARATION TIME:
1 1/4 HOURS]

3/4 cup margarine, softened
1 cup sugar
2 egg whites
1/4 cup molasses
2 cups flour
2 teaspoons baking soda
1 teaspoon cinnamon
1 teaspoon ginger
1 tablespoon sugar

DIRECTIONS

- Cream the margarine and 1 cup sugar in a mixer bowl until light and fluffy. Beat in the egg whites and molasses. Stir in a sifted mixture of the flour, baking soda, cinnamon and ginger.
- Chill the dough in the refrigerator. Shape into small balls; roll in 1 tablespoon sugar. Place on an ungreased cookie sheet.
- Bake at 350 degrees for 15 minutes. Remove to a wire rack to cool.

Helpful Hint

Baked cookies or dough may be frozen for nine to twelve months.

PEANUT BUTTER CHOCOLATE DROPS

INGREDIENTS

[SERVES 84
PREPARATION TIME:
1 HOUR, PLUS
1 HOUR
CHILLING TIME]

1 (28-ounce) jar peanut butter
3/4 cup butter or margarine, softened
1 (1-pound) package confectioners' sugar
Salt to taste
3 cups crisp rice cereal
1 (24-ounce) package chocolate bark, melted

DIRECTIONS

- Combine the peanut butter, butter, confectioners' sugar and salt in a mixer bowl; beat until smooth. Stir in the cereal. Shape into small balls; place on a tray. Chill for 1 hour to several days.
- Dip the chilled balls into the melted chocolate bark. Place on a tray lined with waxed paper. Let stand until cool.

"You don't like grits? Grit your teeth and eat them anyway."

BY CELESTINE SIBLEY
ILLUSTRATION BY SALLY WERN COMPORT

He said he hates grits. Flesh of my flesh, bone of my bone, beloved grandson, he hates grits! He tried to be tactful. But at 12, he hasn't learned to conceal a major shortcoming like that. He simply didn't eat the grits, didn't even stir them around a bit, streaking them gently with butter. The nice little white bowl of God's gift to the hungry was just as I put it before him, untasted, unsullied by fork or spoon.

"What's the matter" I cried, putting

▶

an anxious palm against his forehead. "You sick? You got a fever? What's the matter?"

His little brother spoke up.

"David hates grits," he said.

"That can't be true," I cried. "He is a fine upstanding citizen of Atlanta, born here. His mother was born here. His great-grandmother was born in Pearson, Ga. He comes from a long line of grits people."

His brother and little sister, pleased to catch him at such a disadvantage, ate their grits hungrily and beamed at me smugly.

"What's so good about grits?" David asked glumly. (Without grits his supper was going to be mighty skimpy.)

Why, grits, I said, are among nature's finest gifts to mankind. Cheap and filling and delicious, they have nourished generations of our family, seeing us through hurricanes and fires and depressions and even the dread days of the Reconstruction when our poor kin in South Georgia had a little corn to grind and were, therefore, assured of survival. In time of illness or sadness a pot of ▶

grits staying hot on the back of the stove is wondrously comforting.

"Well, I do like cheese grits, I guess," David offered bravely.

It was a good try. But cheese grits is sort of a make-do, the kind of thing you offer Yankees, a cover-up for the real thing.

I gave him another sausage and brooded. It's really not the child's fault that he has such a benighted attitude toward the mainstay of our family. After all, on his father's side —I shouldn't be telling this— there was a grandmother who lived in Iowa. Blood will tell.

It was wrong so close to Christmas to load the child with guilt, so we hid our trepidation under horseplay. The other children and I staged a snake dance through the cabin, chanting as we gamboled, "G-R-I-T-S! G-R-I-T-S!"

He tried to laugh it off but he knew he had put a serious blot on the family escutcheon. He grinned sheepishly and mentioned cheese grits again and we jeered and organized a cheering squad with 5-year-old Betsy leading us: "We like grits! We like grits!"

But when supper was over and bedtime came, we debated our problem with suitable gravity. How will he grow up strong and healthy without grits? How will he cope in moments of travail? Suppose he grows up and has children and a depression hits this land? How will he feed them?

▶

BREAKFAST PIE

INGREDIENTS

8 ounces mild sausage
1 1/2 cups creamed cottage cheese
1 cup shredded Cheddar cheese
3 ounces cream cheese, softened
1 cup shredded mozzarella cheese
2 eggs
1 cup baking mix
1/4 cup chopped green onions
2 eggs, beaten
1/4 cup whole milk or low-fat milk
1 tablespoon sesame seeds, toasted

[
SERVES 6
PREPARATION TIME:
1 1/4 HOURS
]

DIRECTIONS

- Brown the sausage in a skillet, stirring until crumbly; drain.
- Combine the sausage, cottage cheese, Cheddar cheese, cream cheese, mozzarella cheese and 2 eggs in a bowl; mix well.
- Combine the baking mix and green onions in a bowl; mix well. Add the 2 beaten eggs and whole milk, stirring just until moistened.
- Spoon 1/2 of the batter into a greased 9-inch pie plate. Spread with the sausage mixture; top with the remaining batter. Sprinkle with the sesame seeds.
- Bake at 350 degrees for 30 to 40 minutes or until set. Let stand for 5 minutes before serving.
- *Note: May be prepared in advance and frozen. Thaw in the refrigerator and bake the day of serving.*

BREAKFAST SOUFFLE

INGREDIENTS

1 pound mild pork sausage
1 cup shredded Cheddar cheese
4 eggs, slightly beaten
2 cups evaporated milk
1/2 teaspoon salt
1/2 teaspoon pepper
Chopped fresh parsley to taste

[SERVES 15
PREPARATION TIME:
50 MINUTES]

DIRECTIONS

- Brown the sausage in a skillet, stirring until crumbly; drain. Spread evenly in a greased 9x13-inch baking dish. Sprinkle with the cheese.
- Pour mixture of remaining ingredients over the prepared layers.
- Bake at 400 degrees for 25 minutes or until set and light brown.
- Let stand for 5 minutes before slicing.

CRUSTLESS HAM AND GRITS PIE

INGREDIENTS

1/3 cup quick-cooking grits
1 cup water
1 cup evaporated milk
3/4 cup shredded Cheddar cheese
3/4 cup chopped cooked lean ham
3 eggs, beaten
1 tablespoon chopped fresh parsley
1/2 teaspoon dry mustard
1/2 teaspoon hot pepper sauce
1/4 teaspoon salt

[SERVES 6
PREPARATION TIME:
1 HOUR]

DIRECTIONS

- Cook the grits in water using package directions, omitting the salt.
- Mix the grits, evaporated milk, cheese, ham, eggs and seasonings in a bowl. Spoon into a greased 9-inch pie plate.
- Bake at 350 degrees for 35 minutes. Let stand for 10 minutes.

You can apply a patch to most wounds and we did our best with our dear wounded David. Betsy and John Steven and I bought and wrapped and placed under the Christmas tree in his name three big boxes of grits. Sometimes you have to give people you love things that are good for them instead of things that they want. ■

Reprinted with permission from *The Atlanta Journal* and *The Atlanta Constitution*. Reproduction does not imply endorsement.

MORNING CASSEROLE

FOR THE CHEESE SAUCE

SERVES 8
PREPARATION TIME:
1 HOUR, PLUS
12 HOURS
CHILLING TIME

2 tablespoons butter or margarine
2¹/2 tablespoons flour
2 cups whole milk or low-fat milk
1 cup shredded sharp Cheddar cheese
¹/4 teaspoon salt
¹/8 teaspoon cracked black pepper

FOR THE CASSEROLE

1 pound bacon
¹/4 cup chopped green onions
3 tablespoons butter or margarine
12 eggs, beaten
1 (4-ounce) can sliced mushrooms, drained
¹/8 teaspoon salt
¹/8 teaspoon cracked black pepper

TO PREPARE THE CHEESE SAUCE

- Melt the butter in a saucepan. Stir in the flour. Cook until bubbly, stirring constantly. Cook for 1 to 2 minutes, stirring constantly. Remove from heat. Stir in the whole milk.
- Cook until thickened, stirring frequently. Stir in the cheese, salt and pepper.
- Cook until the cheese melts, stirring constantly.

TO PREPARE THE CASSEROLE

- Fry the bacon in a skillet until crisp; drain and crumble.
- Sauté the green onions in the butter in a skillet. Add the eggs; mix well.
- Cook until soft-scrambled, stirring frequently. Stir in the mushrooms, salt and pepper. Fold in the cheese sauce and bacon. Spoon into a lightly greased 9x13-inch baking dish.
- Chill, covered with plastic wrap, for 12 hours.
- Bake at 350 degrees for 30 minutes. Cool slightly before serving.

Parmesan Cheese Sticks

Serve Parmesan Cheese Sticks for Sunday brunch. Unroll one 17-ounce package puff pastry; brush with 2 beaten egg whites. Sprinkle with ¹/3 cup freshly grated Parmesan cheese, salt, paprika and chopped fresh herbs to taste. Cut the pastry into ¹/2-inch strips. Bake in a 350-degree oven for 15 to 20 minutes or until light brown. May freeze and reheat before serving.

SHRIMP HASH

INGREDIENTS

4 cups shrimp, peeled, deveined, chopped
3 cups finely chopped cooked potatoes
1 cup grated or finely chopped onion
Salt and pepper to taste
3 tablespoons butter or margarine
2 tablespoons vegetable oil
1/2 cup whipping cream

[
SERVES 6
PREPARATION TIME:
40 MINUTES
]

DIRECTIONS

- Combine the shrimp, potatoes and onion in a bowl. Add the salt and pepper, tossing to mix.
- Heat the butter and oil in a large skillet until the butter melts. Spread the hash evenly in the skillet; press with a spatula. Pour the cream over the prepared layer.
- Cook, covered, over medium heat for 10 minutes or until the bottom is light brown. Increase heat to high.
- Cook, uncovered, for 5 minutes. Invert the hash onto a warm serving platter. Serve immediately.

VEGGIE CHEESE OMELET

INGREDIENTS

1 cup chopped fennel
1/2 cup chopped red onion
1/2 cup chopped red bell pepper
1 tablespoon olive oil
1 to 2 tablespoons water
1/4 cup chopped green onions
2 eggs, slightly beaten
1/3 cup half-and-half
Salt and pepper to taste
1 tablespoon olive oil
1/3 cup shredded smoked Gouda cheese
1 tablespoon chopped fresh chives
1/4 cup chopped seeded tomato
1 tablespoon sour cream

[
SERVES 2
PREPARATION TIME:
20 MINUTES
]

DIRECTIONS

- Sauté the fennel, red onion and red pepper in 1 tablespoon olive oil in a skillet until tender. Add the water as needed for the desired consistency; reduce heat.
- Simmer, covered, for 5 minutes, stirring occasionally. Remove from heat. Stir in the green onions.
- Whisk the eggs and half-and-half in a bowl. Stir in the salt and pepper.
- Heat 1 tablespoon olive oil in a skillet over medium heat. Add the egg mixture.
- Cook until almost set. Spread the cheese and desired amount of the fennel mixture over 1 side of the omelet. Fold the remaining half over the filling.
- Cook for 1 minute. Turn the omelet. Cook for 1 minute. Sprinkle with the chives and tomato; top with sour cream.
- *Variation: May add crisp-fried crumbled bacon to the fennel mixture. For a lighter fare, substitute milk for the half-and-half and yogurt for the sour cream.*

Old-Fashioned Buttermilk Biscuits

Old-Fashioned Buttermilk Biscuits make a great accompaniment to any meal. Combine 2 cups flour, 1 tablespoon baking powder, 1/2 teaspoon salt and 1/2 teaspoon baking soda. Cut in 1/2 cup shortening until crumbly. Stir in 2/3 cup buttermilk until dough forms a cohesive mass. Knead on lightly floured surface 12 to 14 times. Roll dough 1/2 to 3/4 inch thick; cut with 2-inch biscuit cutter. Arrange biscuits with sides touching on ungreased baking sheet; brush tops with 2 tablespoons melted butter. Bake at 425 degrees for 15 to 20 minutes.

CHICKEN PECAN QUICHE

FOR THE PASTRY

1 cup flour
4 ounces sharp Cheddar cheese, shredded
3/4 cup chopped pecans
1/2 teaspoon salt
1/4 teaspoon paprika
1/3 cup vegetable oil

SERVES 6
PREPARATION TIME:
1 1/2 HOURS

FOR THE QUICHE

3 eggs, beaten
1/2 cup chicken broth
1 cup sour cream
1/4 cup mayonnaise
2 cups chopped cooked chicken
3 drops of hot pepper sauce
1/2 cup shredded Cheddar cheese
1/4 cup minced onion
1/4 teaspoon dried dillweed
1/4 cup pecan halves

TO PREPARE THE PASTRY

- Combine the flour, cheese, pecans, salt and paprika in a bowl; mix well. Stir in the oil. Reserve 1/4 of the mixture.
- Press the remaining mixture over the bottom and side of a 9-inch quiche pan; prick with a fork.
- Bake at 350 degrees for 10 minutes. Let stand until cool.

TO PREPARE THE QUICHE

- Combine the eggs, chicken broth, sour cream and mayonnaise in a bowl; mix well. Stir in the chicken, hot pepper sauce, cheese, onion and dillweed. Spoon into the baked crust; sprinkle with the reserved flour mixture and pecan halves.
- Bake at 350 degrees for 45 minutes or until set.

Roasted Corn and Chile Relish

For a spicy relish, combine 1 1/2 cups canned corn niblets, 2 roasted and chopped poblano peppers, 1/2 chopped red bell pepper, 1/2 cup chopped green onions, 1/2 cup chopped red onion, 1/4 cup chopped fresh cilantro, 3 1/2 tablespoons fresh lime juice, 1 1/2 tablespoons olive oil and 3 cloves of minced garlic. Season with salt and pepper. Serve this relish with grilled fish or chicken or as a dip with chips.

Tokyo,
September 18, 1990
by Valerie Jackson

Talk about a bad hair day! I'll never forget it. It was the night the International Olympic Committee (I.O.C.) would announce the host of the 1996 Summer Olympic Games. My husband, and then mayor, Maynard Jackson hurried me with assurances that my hair looked "just fine." Knowing better, I resorted to my "if in doubt, wear a hat" mode. Fortunately, I had brought along a plain black crown-like head wrap that I secured with a favorite pin of pearls. Maynard cautiously asked if perhaps the hat was a "bit much." I said "No. This is going to be a good luck hat tonight! I am dressing to win!" As he laughed in agreement, I urged him to go on ahead.

Even though I arrived downstairs nearly 45 minutes early, having passed two security checkpoints, every seat in the hugh ballroom seemed taken. I could not even make it to the front of the room where Maynard, Andy Young and Billy Payne nervously sat with the rest of the ACOG group, waiting to see who would host the most significant Olympic games in 100 years. There were rumors that for sentimental reasons Athens, Greece, the birthplace of the modern Olympics, would be the winner. I confess, I was afraid that sentimentality would sway the I.O.C. vote in

CRUSTLESS QUICHE

INGREDIENTS

3 slices bacon
1/2 cup baking mix
2 eggs, slightly beaten
1 cup whole milk or low-fat milk
3 tablespoons melted butter or margarine
1/4 teaspoon pepper
1/2 cup chopped cooked ham
1/2 cup shredded Monterey Jack cheese
1/2 cup shredded Cheddar cheese
Paprika to taste

SERVES 6
PREPARATION TIME:
50 MINUTES

DIRECTIONS

• Fry the bacon in a skillet until crisp; drain and crumble.
• Combine the baking mix, eggs, whole milk, butter and pepper in a bowl; mix well. Stir in the bacon, ham and cheeses. Spoon into a 9-inch pie plate; sprinkle with the paprika.
• Bake at 375 degrees for 30 minutes or until light brown.
• *Variation: Add 1/2 cup drained, thawed frozen spinach and 1/2 cup sautéed mushrooms.*

QUICHE BENNINGTON

INGREDIENTS

[SERVES 6
PREPARATION TIME:
1 HOUR]

1 unbaked (9-inch) pie shell
1 1/2 cups half-and-half
3 eggs, slightly beaten
1/8 teaspoon nutmeg
1/4 teaspoon salt
1/8 teaspoon coarsely ground pepper
1/8 teaspoon dried oregano
1/8 teaspoon dried tarragon
1/8 teaspoon dried basil
1 cup 1/4-inch pieces Polish sausage
1 cup shredded Swiss cheese
1 cup chopped red onion

DIRECTIONS

- Bake the pie shell at 425 degrees for 9 to 11 minutes or until light brown. Let stand until cool.
- Combine the half-and-half, eggs, nutmeg, salt, pepper, oregano, tarragon and basil in a bowl; mix well. Stir in the sausage, cheese and red onion. Pour into the pie shell.
- Bake at 350 degrees for 30 to 40 minutes or until set and light brown.
- *Note: As quiche cools, it will become firmer.*

favor of Athens in spite of the fact that Atlanta's infrastructure, housing and security measures all surpassed those of Athens (not to mention our Southern hospitality!).

After five rounds of secret voting, Juan Samaranch, President of the I.O.C., came to the podium to announce the winner. Silence permeated the ballroom. Would it be Atlanta or Athens? That second between the first syllable "Ah"—and the rest of the name seemed more like a full minute! Finally the rest of the name came through— "At—lanta!" With it came my scream and tears. The moment was so full of emotion, energy, relief, confirmation and exhilaration that it has been seldom equalled. So much effort and time by so many finally had been rewarded.

Upon reflection, I daresay that Maynard's tremendous drive to obtain the Olympics—he was the only mayor of the final six bid cities to attend every major Olympic gathering— in addition to the stressful demands as mayor may have impacted his health. Less than a year after winning the games he was hospitalized for by-pass surgery. The successful surgery was the beginning of an excellent recovery and a new lifestyle with respect to our eating habits. I had to learn how to convert his favorite recipes to low-fat versions, including his favorite Lasagna. Replacing ground beef with

▶

ground turkey and using cheeses that are fat-free or "lite" can still produce tasty meals, especially if a little extra love and spices are added.

Valerie Richardson Jackson is Co-Chair of The Children's Olympic Ticket Fund, a non-profit foundation that will provide free tickets to physically, mentally, and financially challenged children.

Turkey-Wise Lasagna

Try Valerie Richardson Jackson's husband's favorite lasagna recipe in the low-fat version. Combine 1½ to 2 pounds ground cooked turkey with 48 ounces low-fat spaghetti sauce, 1 teaspoon Mrs. Dash seasoning, ¼ teaspoon garlic powder, 1 teaspoon sugar, 1 tablespoon chopped parsley, salt and pepper. Simmer for 30 minutes. Combine light ricotta cheese, 1 beaten egg and ½ cup grated Parmesan cheese in a bowl. Spoon 1 cup turkey sauce into a 9x13-inch baking pan. Layer one (12-ounce) package cooked lasagna noodles, remaining turkey sauce, ricotta cheese mixture and mozzarella cheese ⅓ at a time in prepared pan, ending with mozzarella cheese. Bake at 350 to 375 degrees for 30 minutes. Let stand for 10 to 15 minutes before serving.

TOMATO PROVENCAL

INGREDIENTS

5 medium tomatoes, peeled, seeded, chopped
1 large clove of garlic, crushed
2 cups chopped onions
¼ cup olive oil
¼ teaspoon salt
½ teaspoon pepper
½ teaspoon dried oregano
¼ teaspoon cayenne
1 tablespoon tomato paste
1 egg, beaten
3 egg yolks, beaten
¼ cup chopped fresh parsley
1 baked (8-inch) pie shell
¼ cup grated Parmesan cheese
2 medium tomatoes, sliced
1 tablespoon olive oil

SERVES 6
PREPARATION TIME:
1 ¾ HOURS

DIRECTIONS

- Combine chopped tomatoes, garlic, onions and ¼ cup olive oil in a saucepan; mix well.
- Cook for 10 minutes or until thickened, stirring frequently. Stir in the salt, pepper, oregano, cayenne and tomato paste.
- Let stand until lukewarm. Add the egg, egg yolks and parsley; mix well. Spoon into the pie shell; sprinkle with the cheese.
- Top with the sliced tomatoes; drizzle with 1 tablespoon olive oil.
- Bake at 375 degrees for 45 minutes. Let stand for 5 minutes before serving.
- *Variation: Spread 8 mashed oil-pack anchovies over the bottom of the pie shell before adding the filling.*

VIDALIA STRATA

INGREDIENTS

[SERVES 6
PREPARATION TIME:
1 1/2 HOURS,
PLUS 6 HOURS
CHILLING TIME]

8 slices white bread, crusts trimmed
1 3/4 cups thinly sliced Vidalia onions
8 ounces sharp Cheddar cheese, shredded
4 eggs, beaten
2 1/4 cups skim milk
1 teaspoon salt
1/4 teaspoon dry mustard
1/4 teaspoon Worcestershire sauce

DIRECTIONS

• Layer the bread, onions and cheese 1/2 at a time in a greased 9x9-inch baking dish.
• Combine the eggs, skim milk, salt, dry mustard and Worcestershire sauce in a bowl; mix well. Pour over the prepared layers.
• Chill, covered, for 6 to 24 hours.
• Bake at 350 degrees for 50 to 60 minutes or until set. Let stand for 10 minutes before serving.
• *Variation: Layer 1 cup chopped cooked ham over the onions. Increase the spiciness by adding 1/8 teaspoon cayenne.*

World's Sweetest Onion

Vidalia Onions have developed an international reputation as the "world's sweetest onion." Their mild flavor is due to the unique combination of soils and climate found in the 20-county production area.

HEAVENLY CHEESE GRITS

INGREDIENTS

4 cups boiling water
1 cup quick-cooking grits
1 1/2 teaspoons salt
6 tablespoons butter or margarine
1 1/2 teaspoons Worcestershire sauce
1 1/2 teaspoons hot pepper sauce
1 1/4 cups shredded sharp Cheddar cheese
1 tablespoon sherry
1 egg, beaten

DIRECTIONS

- Combine the boiling water, grits and salt in a saucepan; mix well.
- Cook, covered, over low heat for 5 minutes or until most of the water is absorbed. Stir in the butter, Worcestershire sauce, hot sauce, 1 cup of the cheese and sherry. Fold in the egg until mixed.
- Spoon into a greased 2 1/2-quart baking dish; sprinkle with the remaining cheese.
- Bake at 300 degrees for 1 hour or until bubbly.
- *Note: May prepare 1 day in advance and refrigerate. Bring to room temperature and bake just before serving.*

Helpful Hint

Whatever you do, do not throw away leftover grits. (Must be bad luck or something.) Shape cold grits into patties or slice, dredge in flour and fry in hot oil. Makes a great breakfast or lunch accompaniment. Or just add a little milk to the cold grits and reheat.

ROSEMARY MUSHROOM GRITS

INGREDIENTS

SERVES 8
PREPARATION TIME:
1 1/2 HOURS, PLUS
CHILLING TIME

3 1/2 cups beef broth
3/4 cup grits
1 clove of garlic, minced
3/4 cup grated Parmigiano-Reggiano cheese
2 1/2 tablespoons butter or margarine
1 teaspoon freshly ground pepper
1 clove of garlic, minced
1 tablespoon olive oil
1 sprig of rosemary, chopped
2 cups fresh shiitake mushrooms
2 tablespoons chopped fresh parsley
Salt and pepper to taste

DIRECTIONS

- Bring the broth to a boil in a saucepan. Stir in the grits and 1 clove of garlic; reduce heat.
- Cook, covered, for 20 minutes or until thickened, stirring occasionally. Remove from heat. Stir in the cheese, butter and pepper.
- Cook over low heat until the cheese and butter melt, stirring frequently.
- Sauté 1 clove of garlic in the olive oil in a skillet until tender but not brown. Stir in the rosemary and mushrooms.
- Cook over medium heat for 8 to 10 minutes or until brown, stirring frequently. Remove from heat. Stir in the parsley, salt and pepper. Let stand until cool.
- Spoon 1/2 of the grits mixture into a large baking dish. Spread with the mushroom mixture; top with the remaining grits mixture.
- Chill, covered, for several hours to overnight. Cut into squares or desired shapes.
- *Variation: If you prefer to serve the grits squares hot, arrange on a baking sheet. Broil until light brown.*

No Stone Unturned

Those who perceive themselves as connoisseurs de grits will have nothing to do with the mass-produced kind, insisting instead on the genuine stone-ground variety. Stone-ground grits taste better, and they are better for you nutritionally. This is because the corn in stone-ground grits is milled much more slowly and retains the heart of the kernel, where most of the nutritional value is located. If you have doubts as to what you are buying, a quick look will tell: mass produced grits look like sand, and stone-ground grits look grainy with speckles of bran and bits of kernel.

SPICY GRITS CASSEROLE

INGREDIENTS

SERVES 8
PREPARATION TIME:
1 HOUR AND
20 MINUTES

6 cups water
1 teaspoon salt
1 1/2 cups quick-cooking grits
2 cups shredded sharp Cheddar cheese
1/4 cup chopped jalapeño
2 dashes of hot pepper sauce
3 eggs, beaten
1 teaspoon pepper
1/2 cup margarine

DIRECTIONS

- Bring the water and salt to a boil in a saucepan. Stir in the grits.
- Cook using package directions. Stir in the cheese.
- Cook over low heat until melted, stirring constantly. Remove from heat. Stir in the jalapeño, hot pepper sauce, eggs, pepper and margarine. Spoon into a greased 3-quart baking dish.
- Bake at 350 degrees for 1 hour.

Presidential Grits

If we continue to show a penchant for electing Southerners as our president, there will likely continue to be grits in the White House. While Bill Clinton and Jimmy Carter are the most recent of the grits gang on Pennsylvania Avenue, rumor has it that F.D.R. had a special grits bowl at his Warm Springs, Georgia, retreat and that Ulysses S. Grant ate grits in the White House after he defeated the Confederacy.

CREME FRAICHE BISCUITS WITH CHEVRE AND COUNTRY HAM BUTTER

CHEF BRUCE BARTZ, THE GEORGIAN CLUB

[
SERVES 10
PREPARATION TIME:
30 MINUTES
]

FOR THE BUTTER

1/3 cup chopped Smithfield ham
1/2 cup butter or margarine, softened
3 1/2 ounces chèvre (goat cheese), crumbled

FOR THE BISCUITS

3 1/2 cups flour
4 teaspoons baking powder
1 teaspoon kosher salt
1 cup shortening
3/4 cup crème fraîche
1/4 cup buttermilk

TO PREPARE THE BUTTER

• Fry the ham in a nonstick skillet using package directions.
• Cream the butter in a mixer bowl until smooth. Stir in the cheese and ham.

TO PREPARE THE BISCUITS

• Sift the flour, baking powder and salt together.
• Cream the shortening in a mixer bowl until light and fluffy. Add the dry ingredients. Beat until smooth, scraping the bowl occasionally. Whisk in the crème fraîche and buttermilk just until blended. Drop by spoonfuls onto a baking sheet.
• Bake at 350 degrees for 12 minutes.
• Serve hot with the butter.

Crème Fraîche

To make *crème fraîche* whisk 1 cup of heavy cream and 1 cup of sour cream together in a bowl. Cover and let stand in a warm place overnight or until thickened. Stir well, cover and refrigerate for at least 4 hours. The tart flavor will continue to develop as it sits in the refrigerator. *Crème fraîche* will keep for up to 2 weeks. Makes 2 cups. Use as a topping on fresh berries or to add body to soups and cream sauces.

Banana Nut Bran Muffins

INGREDIENTS

SERVES 12
PREPARATION TIME:
40 MINUTES

3 tablespoons vegetable oil
1/4 cup molasses
1/4 cup packed brown sugar
1 egg
4 medium very ripe bananas, mashed
1 cup whole wheat flour
1/2 cup all-purpose flour
1/2 cup bran flakes
1/4 cup wheat germ
1 tablespoon baking soda
1/2 teaspoon salt
1/2 cup chopped pecans

DIRECTIONS

- Combine the oil, molasses, brown sugar, egg and bananas in a mixer bowl or food processor container. Beat until smooth, scraping the bowl occasionally. Stir in the flours, cereal, wheat germ, baking soda and salt just until moistened. Stir in the pecans.
- Fill greased or paper-lined muffin cups 2/3 full.
- Bake at 375 degrees for 20 to 25 minutes or until the muffins test done.
- *Variation: Substitute oatbran for bran flakes.*
- *Note: Omitting the egg makes these muffins low-fat and cholesterol-free without sacrificing the flavor or texture.*

Helpful Hint

Most muffin recipes may be baked in miniature muffin cups. Count on three miniature muffins for every two-inch muffin. Reduce baking time 5 minutes.

LOW-FAT MUFFINS

TRES BIEN

INGREDIENTS

SERVES 12
PREPARATION TIME:
30 MINUTES

2 1/2 cups flour
2/3 cup sugar
1 teaspoon baking soda
1/2 teaspoon salt
3/4 teaspoon cinnamon
1 1/2 cups mashed mangoes
1 cup buttermilk
1/3 cup melted margarine
2 teaspoons vanilla extract
1 egg, beaten
1 egg white
1 1/2 tablespoons sugar

DIRECTIONS

- Combine the flour, 2/3 cup sugar, baking soda, salt and cinnamon in a bowl; mix well. Fold in the mangoes. Make a well in the center of the flour mixture.
- Combine the buttermilk, margarine, vanilla, egg and egg white in a bowl; mix well. Pour into the well, stirring just until moistened.
- Spoon the batter into paper-lined muffins cups or muffin cups sprayed with nonstick cooking spray. Sprinkle with 1 1/2 tablespoons sugar.
- Bake at 350 degrees for 20 minutes or until light brown.
- *Note: Any ripe, non-citrus fruit may be used. Try mashed or finely chopped bananas or whole blueberries.*

MORNING GLORY MUFFINS

INGREDIENTS

2 cups flour
1/2 teaspoon salt
2 teaspoons baking soda
2 teaspoons cinnamon
3 eggs, slightly beaten
1 cup vegetable oil
1 1/4 cups sugar
2 teaspoons vanilla extract
2 cups grated carrots
1 Granny Smith apple, peeled, chopped
1/2 cup raisins
1/2 cup shredded coconut
1/2 cup chopped pecans

DIRECTIONS

- Mix the flour, salt, baking soda and cinnamon together.
- Combine the eggs, oil, sugar, vanilla, carrots, apple, raisins, coconut and pecans in a bowl; mix well. Stir in the dry ingredients just until moistened.
- Fill greased and floured or paper-lined muffin cups 2/3 full.
- Bake at 350 degrees for 15 to 20 minutes or until the muffins test done.

BANANA BREAD

INGREDIENTS

1/2 cup butter or margarine, softened
1 cup sugar
1 teaspoon vanilla extract
2 eggs
1 cup mashed bananas
1/2 cup quick-cooking oats
1 1/2 cups flour
1 teaspoon baking soda
1/4 teaspoon salt
1/2 cup chopped pecans
3/4 cup fresh blueberries

[
SERVES 12
PREPARATION TIME:
1 HOUR AND
10 MINUTES
]

DIRECTIONS

- Beat the butter in a mixer bowl until smooth. Add the sugar and vanilla gradually, beating until light and fluffy. Add the eggs 1 at a time, beating well after each addition. Stir in the bananas.
- Combine the oats, flour, baking soda and salt in a bowl; mix well. Stir in the pecans and blueberries gently. Add to the banana mixture, stirring just until moistened.
- Spoon the batter into a 5x9-inch loaf pan sprayed with nonstick cooking spray.
- Bake at 350 degrees for 50 to 55 minutes or until the loaf tests done. Cool in the pan for 10 minutes. Remove to a wire rack to cool completely.
- *Variation: Substitute chopped walnuts for the pecans.*

CRAZY MONKEY BREAD

INGREDIENTS

SERVES 24
PREPARATION TIME:
1 HOUR AND
20 MINUTES

1 cup sugar
1 1/2 cups flour
1 teaspoon baking soda
1 teaspoon salt
1 teaspoon cinnamon
1 egg, slightly beaten
1/4 cup melted butter or margarine
1 medium banana, mashed
1 1/2 cups chopped peeled fresh fruit
1 cup chopped pecans

DIRECTIONS

- Combine the sugar, flour, baking soda, salt and cinnamon in a bowl; mix well. Add the egg and butter, stirring just until moistened. Fold in the banana, fresh fruit and pecans.
- Spoon into two 5x9-inch loaf pans sprayed with nonstick cooking spray.
- Bake at 350 degrees for 50 minutes or until the loaves test done.
- Cool in the pans for 15 minutes. Remove to a wire rack to cool completely.
- *Note: Any combination of ripe, non-citrus fresh fruit may be used. Try one of these combinations: 1 Granny Smith apple and 2 pears; 1 banana and 2 to 3 plums; 1 peach, 1 apple and 1 pear. Extremely juicy fruit should be drained.*

Helpful Hint

Bread will remain fresh longer if stored at room temperature or frozen. Do not store bread in the refrigerator.

ORANGE BREAD

INGREDIENTS

Rind of 2 medium navel oranges,
  white pith removed
1 1/2 cups sugar
2 tablespoons water
2 cups flour
2 teaspoons baking powder
1 teaspoon salt
3/4 cup whole milk or low-fat milk
1 egg
2 tablespoons vegetable oil

SERVES 12
PREPARATION TIME:
1 HOUR AND
20 MINUTES

DIRECTIONS

- Place the orange rind in a steamer basket over boiling water in
  a saucepan.
- Steam, covered, for 10 minutes or until tender. Remove from heat.
  Let stand until cool. Chop the rind.
- Combine the rind, 1 cup of the sugar and water in a saucepan; mix well.
- Cook over low heat until the sugar melts and coats the rind, stirring
  frequently.
- Combine the remaining sugar, flour, baking powder and salt in a bowl;
  mix well. Stir in the orange rind. Add a mixture of the whole milk,
  egg and oil gradually, mixing well after each addition.
- Spoon into a 5x9-inch loaf pan sprayed with nonstick cooking spray.
- Bake at 350 degrees for 1 hour or until the loaf tests done. Remove
  to a wire rack to cool.
- Note: Serve this flavorful bread with broiled oranges.

Helpful Hint

Remove hot bread immediately
from the pan to prevent
the bottom and sides from
becoming soggy.

Peanut Buttermilk Bread

INGREDIENTS

SERVES 12
PREPARATION TIME:
50 MINUTES

1 2/3 cups unbleached flour
1 teaspoon baking soda
1/2 teaspoon salt
3/4 cup packed brown sugar
1/3 cup creamy or crunchy peanut butter
1 egg, slightly beaten
1 cup buttermilk

DIRECTIONS

- Combine the flour, baking soda, salt and brown sugar in a bowl; mix well. Stir in the peanut butter, egg and buttermilk.
- Spoon the batter into a 5x9-inch loaf pan.
- Bake at 325 degrees for 40 to 45 minutes or until the loaf tests done. Invert onto a wire rack.
- *Variation: Add 1/2 cup raisins or chocolate chips.*
- *Note: The flavor of the bread is best when served warm.*

PUMPKIN BREAD

INGREDIENTS

SERVES 12
PREPARATION TIME:
1 HOUR AND
20 MINUTES

1 2/3 cups flour
3/4 teaspoon salt
1/4 teaspoon baking powder
1 teaspoon baking soda
1/2 teaspoon cinnamon
1/2 teaspoon ground cloves
1/2 teaspoon allspice
1 1/2 cups sugar
1 cup puréed canned pumpkin
1/3 cup water
2 eggs, beaten
1/2 cup vegetable oil

DIRECTIONS

- Grease the bottom and sides of a 5x9-inch loaf pan. Line the bottom with waxed paper; grease the waxed paper.
- Sift the flour, salt, baking powder, baking soda, cinnamon, cloves and allspice together.
- Combine the sugar, pumpkin, water, eggs and oil in a bowl; mix well. Add the flour mixture gradually, mixing well after each addition. Spoon the batter into the prepared loaf pan.
- Bake at 350 degrees for 1 hour or until the loaf tests done.
- Remove to a wire rack to cool.
- *Variation: Reduce the fat and cholesterol by substituting 4 egg whites or the equivalent amount of egg substitute for the whole eggs.*

APPLE PANCAKE TATIN

INGREDIENTS

1 tablespoon butter
1/4 cup sugar
3 tablespoons water
1 Golden Delicious apple, peeled,
  cut into 8 wedges
1/2 cup pancake or crepe batter
1 tablespoon confectioners' sugar

SERVES 1
PREPARATION TIME:
30 MINUTES

DIRECTIONS

- Combine the butter, sugar and water in a 6-inch ovenproof sauté pan.
- Sauté over medium heat for 5 minutes or until thickened, stirring constantly.
- Arrange the apple cut side down in spoke fashion over the sugar mixture.
- Cook until the sugar begins to caramelize. Pour the pancake batter evenly over the apples.
- Cook until bubbles appear on the surface of the batter.
- Bake at 400 degrees for 15 minutes or until light brown. Invert onto a serving plate; sprinkle with the confectioners' sugar.
- *Note: This recipe may be doubled and baked in an 8-inch sauté pan or in two 6-inch sauté pans.*

GERMAN PANCAKE WITH PEACH COMPOTE

FOR THE PEACH COMPOTE

2 Georgia peaches, peeled, chopped
2 tablespoons melted butter or margarine
2 tablespoons brown sugar
1 teaspoon cinnamon

[
SERVES 4
PREPARATION TIME:
40 MINUTES
]

FOR THE PANCAKE

2 tablespoons butter or margarine
1/2 cup flour
1/2 cup whole milk or low-fat milk
2 eggs, slightly beaten
1/4 teaspoon salt

TO PREPARE THE PEACH COMPOTE

• Sauté the peaches in a mixture of the butter, brown sugar and cinnamon in a skillet until tender.

TO PREPARE THE PANCAKE

• Heat the butter in a round baking dish in a 425-degree oven until melted.
• Combine the flour, whole milk, eggs and salt in a bowl; mix well. Pour over the butter.
• Bake for 20 to 25 minutes or until the edge is brown.
• Invert the pancake onto a serving platter. Spoon the peach compote into the center. Cut into wedges.
• *Note: The center of the pancake will sink after being removed from the oven.*

SOUR CREAM BLUEBERRY PANCAKES

INGREDIENTS

[
SERVES 10
PREPARATION TIME:
15 MINUTES
]

1 1/2 cups blueberries
1 tablespoon sugar
2 cups flour
1 teaspoon baking powder
1/2 teaspoon baking soda
1 teaspoon salt
1/4 teaspoon cinnamon
1 1/2 cups milk
1/2 cup sour cream
1/4 cup vegetable oil
2 egg yolks, slightly beaten
1 teaspoon vanilla extract
2 egg whites, stiffly beaten

DIRECTIONS

- Toss the blueberries with the sugar in a bowl.
- Sift the flour, baking powder, baking soda, salt and cinnamon into a bowl.
- Combine the milk, sour cream, oil, egg yolks and vanilla in a bowl; mix well. Add to the flour mixture, stirring just until moistened. Fold in the egg whites and blueberries. Spoon the batter onto a hot greased griddle in the desired amounts.
- Bake on medium heat until golden brown on both sides.
- *Variation: For low-fat pancakes, substitute skim milk for whole milk and nonfat yogurt for sour cream, decrease the oil to 2 tablespoons and use egg substitute for egg yolks.*

CORNMEAL WAFFLES WITH PEACH SAUCE

FOR THE PEACH SAUCE

SERVES 3
PREPARATION TIME:
30 MINUTES

*8 small Georgia peaches, peeled,
    cut into thick slices*
3/4 cup water
2/3 cup sugar
1/2 teaspoon cinnamon
1/2 teaspoon ground cloves
1/8 teaspoon salt
2 tablespoons fresh lemon juice

FOR THE WAFFLES

3 cups self-rising cornmeal
3 cups self-rising flour
1/2 cup sugar
1/8 teaspoon salt
6 eggs, slightly beaten
3 cups whole milk or low-fat milk
1/2 cup melted butter or margarine

TO PREPARE THE PEACH SAUCE

• Combine the peaches, water, sugar, cinnamon, cloves, salt and lemon
  juice in a saucepan; mix well.
• Cook over medium heat until the peaches are tender, stirring frequently.

TO PREPARE THE WAFFLES

• Combine the cornmeal, flour, sugar and salt in a bowl; mix well.
  Add a mixture of the eggs, whole milk and butter, stirring just until
  moistened.
• Pour a portion of the batter onto a hot greased waffle iron. Bake
  using manufacturer's instructions. Repeat the process using the
  remaining batter.
• Serve hot with the warm peach sauce.
• *Variation: Substitute apples or pears for the peaches. Serve a variety of
  sauces with the waffles.*

CREAM CHEESE SCONES WITH RAISINS

TRES BIEN

INGREDIENTS

3³/4 cups flour
6 tablespoons sugar
2 tablespoons baking powder
1 teaspoon salt
16 ounces cream cheese, cut into small pieces
1 cup raisins
1 egg, beaten
1 cup milk
¹/2 cup whipping cream

DIRECTIONS

- Spray a baking sheet with nonstick cooking spray.
- Sift the flour, sugar, baking powder and salt together.
- Combine the flour mixture and cream cheese in a food processor container. Process with a steel blade for 2 to 3 seconds or until mixed.
- Combine the cream cheese mixture, raisins, 1 tablespoon of the beaten egg, milk and cream in a large bowl; mix well.
- Drop the batter 1 inch apart on the prepared baking sheet, using 2 tablespoons of batter for each scone. Brush the scones with the remaining beaten egg.
- Bake at 400 degrees for 12 to 17 minutes or until light brown. Remove to a wire rack to cool.

Apple Butter

INGREDIENTS

3 1/2 pounds apples, cut into quarters
2 cups water, cider or cider vinegar
1/2 cup packed brown sugar per cup of pulp

[
YIELDS 4 CUPS
PREPARATION TIME:
2 1/2 HOURS
]

DIRECTIONS

- Combine the apples and water in a heavy saucepan; mix well.
- Cook, covered, over medium heat until the apples are tender, stirring occasionally. Remove from heat.
- Press the apples through a food mill into a bowl, discarding the peel, seeds and excess fruit. Measure the pulp. Combine the pulp with the recommended amount of brown sugar in a saucepan; mix well.
- Cook over medium heat until the brown sugar dissolves, stirring constantly. Cook for 1 1/2 hours longer or until the mixture is thickened and dark, stirring occasionally.
- *Note: To test readiness of the apple butter, place a spoonful on a plate and if no liquid appears around the butter it is ready.*

Helpful Hint
—
Before measuring honey or syrup, grease the measuring cup with vegetable oil and rinse in hot water.

Apple Nut Syrup

INGREDIENTS

3 tablespoons chopped pecans
3 tablespoons butter or margarine
1 cup maple syrup
1/2 teaspoon cinnamon
1/8 teaspoon salt
1 1/3 cups thinly sliced tart apples

[
YIELDS 2 CUPS
PREPARATION TIME:
15 MINUTES
]

DIRECTIONS

- Sauté the pecans in the butter in a saucepan until light brown. Remove the pecans to a bowl.
- Stir the maple syrup, cinnamon and salt into the pan drippings. Add the apples; mix well.
- Simmer, covered, for 10 minutes, stirring occasionally. Simmer, uncovered, for 3 minutes, stirring occasionally. Remove from heat. Stir in the pecans.
- Serve on waffles, pancakes, French toast or ice cream.

SPECIAL COFFEE

INGREDIENTS

2 cups sugar-free hot chocolate mix
2 cups light nondairy creamer
1 cup decaffeinated instant coffee granules
1 1/2 cups aspertame
1 teaspoon cinnamon
1/2 teaspoon nutmeg

DIRECTIONS

- Combine the hot chocolate mix, creamer, coffee granules, aspertame, cinnamon and nutmeg in a bowl; mix well.
- Store in an airtight container.
- Combine 3 to 4 teaspoons of the coffee mixture with 1 cup boiling water for each serving.
- Note: This is a great sugar-free decaffeinated drink. Give jars of this mixture for Christmas gifts, hostess gifts and housewarming gifts.

MISS PRISS PUNCH

INGREDIENTS

1 (16-ounce) can orange juice, chilled
1 (6-ounce) can pineapple juice, chilled
1 (32-ounce) jar cranberry juice, chilled
2 oranges, sliced
1 lemon, sliced
1 (50-ounce) bottle ginger ale, chilled

DIRECTIONS

- Combine the orange juice, pineapple juice, cranberry juice, orange slices and lemon slices in a large container; mix well.
- Chill, covered, for several hours.
- Pour the fruit mixture into a punch bowl. Add the ginger ale; mix well.

WINE GUIDE

The pairing of good food with fine wine is one of the great pleasures of life. The rule that you drink white wine only with fish and fowl and red wine with meat no longer applies—just let your own taste and personal preference be the guide. Remember to serve light wines with lighter foods and full-bodied wines with rich foods so the food and wine will complement rather than over-power each other.

The best wine to cook with is the one you will be serving at the table. The real secret is to cook with a good wine, as the alcohol evaporates during the cooking process, leaving only the actual flavor of the wine. A fine wine with rich body and aroma will insure a distinct and delicate flavor. When used in cooking, the wine should accent and enhance the natural flavor of the food while adding its own inviting fragrance and flavor.

SEMIDRY WHITE WINES

These wines have a fresh fruity taste and are best served young. Serve with: Dove, quail or shellfish in cream sauce; Roast turkey, duck or goose; Seafood, pasta or salad; Fish in a herbed butter sauce.

- Johannisberg Riesling – *(Yo-hann-is-burg Rees-ling)*   • Frascati – *(Fras-cah-tee)*
- Gewurztraminer – *(Ge-vert-tram-me-ner)*   • Bernkasteler – *(Barn-kahst-ler)*
- Sylvaner Riesling – *(Sil-vah-nur Rees-ling)*   • Fendant – *(Fahn-dawn)*   • Dienheimer – *(Deen-heim-er)*
- Krauznacher – *(Kroytz-nock)*

DRY WHITE WINES

These wines have a crisp, refreshing taste and are best served young. Serve with: Chicken, turkey and cold meats; Roast young gamebirds and waterfowl; Shellfish; Fried or grilled fish; Ham and veal.

- Vouvray – *(Voo-vray)*   • Chablis – *(Shab-lee)*   • Chardonnay – *(Shar-doh-nay)*
- Pinot Blanc – *(Pee-no Blawn)*   • Chenin Blanc – *(Shay-nan Blawn)*   • Pouilly Fuisse *(Pwee-yee-Fwee-say)*
- Orvieto Secco – *(Orv-yay-toe Sek-o)*   • Piesporter Trocken – *(Peez-porter)*   • Meursault – *(Mere-so)*
- Hermitage Blanc – *(Air-me-tahz Blawn)*   • Pinot Grigio – *(Pee-no Gree-jo)*   • Verdicchio – *(Ver-deek-ee-o)*
- Sancerre – *(Sahn-sehr)*   • Sauvigon Blanc – *(So-vin-yawn Blawn)*   • Soave – *(So-ah-veh)*

LIGHT RED WINES

These wines have a light taste and are best served young. Serve with: Grilled chicken; Fowl with highly seasoned stuffings; Soups and stews; Creole foods; Veal or lamb.

- Beaujolais – *(Bo-sho-lay)*   • Bardolino – *(Bar-do-leen-o)*   • Valpolicella – *(Val-po-lee-chel-la)*
- Moulin-A-Vent Beaujolais – *(Moo-lon-ah-vahn)*   • Barbera – *(Bar-bear-ah)*   • Lambrusco – *(Lom-bruce-co)*
- Lirac – *(Lee-rack)*   • Nuits-Saint Georges "Villages" – *(Nwee San Zhorzh)*   • Gamay Beaujolais – *(Ga-mai Bo-sho-lay)*   • Santa Maddalena – *(Santa Mad-lay-nah)*   • Merlo di Ticino – *(Mair-lo dee Tee-chee-no)*

HEARTY RED WINES

These wines have a heavier taste, improve with age, and are best opened thirty minutes before serving. Serve with: Game including duck, goose, venison and hare; Pot roast; Red meats including beef, lamb and veal; Hearty foods; Cheese & egg dishes, pastas and highly seasoned foods.

- Barbaresco – *(Bar-bah-rez-coe)*   • Barolo – *(Bah-ro-lo)*   • Burgundy – *(Ber-gun-dee)*
- Zinfandel – *(Zin-fan-dell)*   • Chianti Riserva – *(Key-ahn-tee Ree-sairv-ah)*   • Bordeaux – *(Bore-doe)*
- Côte Rotie – *(Coat Ro-tee)*   • Hermitage – *(Air-me-tahz)*   • Taurasi – *(Tah-rah-see)*   • Merlot – *(Mair-lo)*
- Syrah – *(Sir-rah)*   • Chateauneuf-Du-Pape – *(Shot-toe-nuff dew Pop)*   • Petite Sirah – *(Puh-teet Seer-rah)*
- Côte de Beaune – *(Coat duh Bone)*   • Cabernet Sauvignon – *(Cab-air-nay So-vin-yawn)*

Appetizer Wines

Sherry, vermouth and flavored wines are considered appetizer wines. Appetizer wines can be served with or without food at room temperature or chilled to around 50 degrees. They are usually served in a 2 1/2 to 4 ounce glass.

Red Dinner Wines

Red dinner wines are usually served at cool room temperature, around 65 degrees, in 6 to 9 ounce glasses.

Rose Wines

Roses are served chilled about 50 degrees in 6 to 9 ounce glasses with ham, chicken, picnic foods, shellfish and cold beef.

White Dinner Wines

White dinner wines are served chilled to about 50 degrees in 6 to 9 ounce glasses. They compliment light foods.

Dessert Wines

Port, Tokay, Muscatel, Catawba, Sweet Sauterne, Aurora and Sherry are dessert wines. Dessert wines are served at cool room temperature, around 65 degrees in 2 1/2 to 4 ounce glasses.

Sparkling Wines

Champagne, Sparkling White Zinfandel, Sparkling Burgundy, Sparkling Rose and Cold Duck are sparkling wines. Sparkling wines are served chilled to 45 degrees with all foods for all occasions.

TERMS & DEFINITIONS

BAKE

To cook covered or uncovered in an oven or oven-type appliance. For meats cooked uncovered, it's called roasting.

BASTE

To moisten foods during cooking with pan drippings or special sauce to add flavor and prevent drying.

BEAT

To make mixture smooth by adding air with a brisk whipping or stirring motion using spoon or electric mixer.

BLANCH

To plunge food into a large quantity of rapidly boiling water for one minute or less to set color and preserve nutrients. Following boiling water food is drained and quickly plunged into ice water, so that cooking is arrested at once.

BLEND

To thoroughly mix two or more ingredients until smooth and uniform.

BOIL

To cook in liquid at boiling temperature (212 degrees at sea level) where bubbles rise to the surface and break. For a full rolling boil, bubbles form rapidly throughout the mixture.

EQUIVALENT MEASURES

dash	=	less than $1/8$ tsp
1 tsp	=	60 drops
1 Tbs	=	3 tsp
2 Tbs	=	1 fl oz
4 Tbs	=	$1/4$ cup
1 cup	=	$1/2$ pt or 8 fl oz
2 cups	=	1 pt
1 pt	=	16 oz
1 qt	=	2 pts
2 qts	=	$1/2$ gal
4 qts	=	1 gal
1 lb	=	16 oz
1 lb	=	2 cups liquid
1 lb	=	$3 3/4$ cups dry

BRAISE

To cook slowly with a small amount of liquid in tightly covered pan on top of range or in oven.

BROIL

To cook by direct heat, usually in broiler or over coals.

CANDIED

To cook in sugar or syrup when applied to sweet potatoes and carrots. For fruit or fruit peel, to cook in heavy syrup till transparent and well coated.

CHILL

To place in refrigerator to reduce temperature.

CHOP

To cut in pieces about the size of peas with knife, chopper, or blender.

COOL

To remove from heat and let stand at room temperature.

CREAM

To beat with spoon or electric mixer till mixture is soft and smooth. When applied to blending shortening and sugar, mixture is beaten till light and fluffy.

CUT IN

To mix shortening with dry ingredients using pastry blender or knives.

DEGLAZE

To heat stock, wine, or other liquid in the pan in which meat has been cooked, mixing with pan juices and sediment to form a gravy or sauce base.

DICE

To cut food in small cubes of uniform size and shape.

DISSOLVE

To disperse a dry substance in a liquid to form a solution.

GLAZE

A mixture applied to food which hardens or becomes firm and adds flavor and a glossy appearance.

GRATE

To rub on a grater that separates the food into very fine particles.

MARINATE

To allow food to stand in a liquid to tenderize or to add flavor.

MINCE

To cut or finely chop food into very small pieces.

MIX

To combine ingredients, usually by stirring, till evenly distributed.

POACH

To cook in hot liquid, being careful that food holds its shape while cooking.

PRECOOK

To cook food partially or completely before final cooking or reheating.

ROAST

To cook uncovered without water added, usually in an oven.

SAUTE

To brown or cook in a small amount of hot shortening.

SCALD

To bring to a temperature just below boiling point where tiny bubbles form at the edge of the pan.

SCALLOP

To bake food, usually in a casserole, with sauce or other liquid. Crumbs are often sprinkled atop.

STEAM

To cook in steam with or without pressure. A small amount of boiling water is used, more water being added during steaming process if necessary.

STIR

To mix ingredients with a circular motion until well blended or of uniform consistency.

TOSS

To mix ingredients lightly.

TRUSS

To secure fowl or other meat with skewers to hold its shape during cooking.

WHIP

To beat rapidly to incorporate air and produce expansion, as in heavy cream or egg whites.

ABOUT THE AUTHORS

DR. JOHNNETTA B. COLE

Dr. Johnnetta B. Cole is the president of Spelman College in Atlanta. She published *Conversations* in 1993 and is the author of two textbooks. Dr. Cole is the 1994 recipient of the Martin Luther King Distinguished Service Award given by the Georgia State Holiday Commission and has served on the advisory board of the Department of Education's Fund for the Improvement of Post Secondary Education.

CARMEN DEEDY

Carmen Deedy is a mesmerizing storyteller who has charmed children and adults alike throughout the United States and Canada with her stories. She contributes regular commentary to National Public Radio's "Weekend All Things Considered." She is the author of *Agatha's Feather Bed: Not Just Another Wild Goose Story* and *Treeman*. She lives with her husband and children in Decatur, Georgia.

WILLIAM DIEHL

William Diehl, a longtime reporter and columnist for the *Atlanta Constitution*, also served as editor of *Atlanta* magazine. He is a New York native, a graduate of University of Missouri, and now makes his home on St. Simons Island, Georgia. Mr. Diehl's first novel, *Sharky's Machine*, was made into a movie.

RHETA GRIMSLEY JOHNSON

Rheta Grimsley Johnson is a columnist with the *Atlanta Journal* and the *Atlanta Constitution*. She was born in South Georgia, but grew up in Montgomery, Alabama during the height of the 1960s civil rights movement. She has won numerous awards for her columns. She was the 1983 winner of the American Society of Newspaper Editor's Distinguished Writing Award for Commentary; the 1984 winner of the Ernie Pyle Journalism Award, and winner in 1983, 1984, and 1985 of the Scripps Howard Writer of the Year Award. She was inducted into the Scripps Howard Editorial Hall of Fame in 1985 and in 1986 she won the National Headliner Award for commentary.

LEWIS GRIZZARD

Known as an "American by birth and a Southerner by the grace of God," Coweta County, Georgia native Lewis Grizzard was a columnist for the *Atlanta Journal* and the *Atlanta Constitution* until his death in March 1994. Syndicated from coast to coast, Mr. Grizzard's column voiced the amusing side of everyday life.

He also authored many books, was a frequent guest on the *Tonight Show* and recorded several albums and tapes addressing topics such as the battle of the sexes and political incorrectness.

VALERIE RICHARDSON JACKSON

Valerie Richardson Jackson is co-chair of the Children's Olympic Ticket Fund, which was established by the Atlanta Committee for the Olympic Games to purchase tickets to 1996 Olympic events for mentally, physically and economically challenged children. Mrs. Jackson formerly hosted the award-winning weekly Public Affairs program, "Primetime," for Georgia Public Television and currently hosts the Department of Education series, "Perspectives on Education." When her husband served as Mayor of Atlanta, she was special advisor to the Mayor's Office of Economic Development. She has worked with numerous civic boards and is a sustaining member of the Junior League of Atlanta, Inc.

TERRY KAY

Terry Kay is the author of the Emmy Award-winning screenplay, *Run Down the Rabbit*, and the novels *The Year the Light Came On*, *After Eli*, *Dark Thirty*, *Shadow Song*, and *To Dance With the White Dog*, which won the Southeastern Library Association's Outstanding Author Award and was adapted for a Hallmark Hall of Fame television presentation.

EUGENIA PRICE

Known all over the world for both her nonfiction and historical novels based on the lives of people living in the Southeast, Eugenia Price is the author of books that have been translated into 17 languages. Ms. Price grew up in West Virginia and lived and worked as a radio writer in Chicago for many years before discovering St. Simons Island, Georgia in 1960. Ms. Price now lives on St. Simons Island and is an avid Braves fan.

FERROL SAMS

Ferrol Sams has been heralded by the *New York Times* as a "storyteller sure of his audience... gifted with perfect timing." Sams was born and raised in Fayetteville, Georgia. He, his wife, and two of their four children practice medicine there.

DR. NEIL SHULMAN

Dr. Neil Shulman is the real "Doc Hollywood" and associate producer of the hit movie *Doc Hollywood*, starring Michael J. Fox. He also initiated the development of the CBS movie of

the week, *Dreams of Gold*, starring Cliff Robertson, and is associate producer of *The Backyard Tribe*, a major motion picture in production by Walt Disney Studios. An associate professor at Emory Medical School, he is the co-editor and publisher of *Health Access News*, a researcher in hypertension, and a consultant to the Georgia Department of Human Resources in establishing rural and inner city community health clinics.

CELESTINE SIBLEY

Celestine Sibley is an award-winning journalist and columnist for the *Atlanta Journal* and the *Atlanta Constitution*. One of the South's most beloved writers, Ms. Sibley is the author of 15 books and innumerable articles in which she often discusses Southern family traditions. She lives in Atlanta.

ANNE RIVERS SIDDONS

Anne Rivers Siddons began her career writing for *Atlanta* magazine in the 1960s. With her first four novels earning her a reputation as one of the South's foremost storytellers, her next novel, *Peachtree Road*, landed her on the *New York Times* bestseller list. Her other books include *Outer Banks*, *Colony*, *Hilltowns*, and *Downtown*.

MARILYN DORN STAATS

Marilyn Dorn Staats, a lifelong resident of Atlanta, is the author of *Looking for Atlanta* and a former editor of *Purple Cow* and *Goodlife* magazines. She has published articles in *Veranda*, *Atlanta Magazine*, and *Southern Magazine*. Ms. Staats is a sustaining member of the Junior League of Atlanta, Inc.

MICHAEL LEE WEST

Michael Lee West was compared to Flannery O'Connor for her wry humor and humanity when she published her debut novel, *Crazy Ladies*. The Louisiana native's second novel is entitled: *She Flew the Coop: A Novel Concerning Life, Death, Sex and Recipes in Limoges, Louisiana*.

STUART WOODS

A former Atlantan, Stuart Woods is the Edgar Award-winning, bestselling author of 12 novels, two of which, *Chiefs* and *Grass Roots*, have been made into highly regarded television miniseries. He has been hailed by the *Chicago Tribune* as "a no-nonsense, slam-bang storyteller...who doesn't disappoint." Woods now lives in Key West, Florida, and Sante Fe, New Mexico.

ABOUT THE JUNIOR LEAGUE OF ATLANTA, INC.

The Junior League of Atlanta ... A history of service.

On October 2, 1916, the city of Atlanta was still in its adolescence; still very much the small town despite such sophisticated airs as the automobiles that had all but replaced the horse and carriage. Department stores were still locally owned; bank presidents knew their customers by name; and the sight of a woman smoking a cigarette in public warranted lengthy notice in the newspapers.

World War I had been raging in Europe for two years and its economic impact hit Atlanta like a freight train, scattering unmarketable cotton and depression through the city in its wake.

As the country prepared to do battle for freedom, a group of young women armed themselves to serve their community on the home front. Led by Miss Isoline Campbell, these young women formed The Junior League of Atlanta, an organization then as now devoted to improving the quality of life for the citizens of Atlanta.

The League's first successful fund-raising effort was undertaken when it was less than a month old. The first League enterprise, The Domestic Science Institute, became the site of the first Red Cross military hospital kitchen in the South. It was the Junior League of Atlanta that pioneered furnishing free school books and lunches to needy children in the community. This effort, the first in the country, was taken over by the Public School System and continues to this day.

The reality is this. Through the years, the Junior League of Atlanta has shown a keen ability to identify the needs of the day and marshal the resources to meet them.

A few examples.

The need for a Council on Battered Women would have shocked the people in turn of the century Atlanta—or anywhere, for that matter. But this League project, which began in 1984, has been tremendously important in both its service to victims and its public education and prevention efforts.

The Family Literacy Project, the League's 75th Anniversary gift to Atlanta in 1991, focuses on improving one of the most important skills for any society—literacy. By reducing illiteracy among young parents, this project helps them get back into the workforce or school. By working with their children, the project helps even the youngest Atlantans get a good head start on the road to success.

The Atlanta Children's Shelter, established in 1986, was the first of its kind in the country simply because it served homeless children during the day. Most such shelters are only open at night, which makes it difficult for homeless men and women with children to look for work during the day. This shelter, a prototype for shelters nationwide, provides loving daycare that actually helps families put their lives back together.

The Domestic Science Institute, the Atlanta Speech School, Young Audiences, and LAWS (Laws Applied to Women's Status) were all established by the Junior League.

Grady Memorial Hospital, the Egleston Children's Hospital at Emory University, the Scottish Rite Children's Medical Center and the Ronald McDonald House are all served by League volunteers.

The High Museum, The Atlanta Symphony, the Atlanta Public Library and the Atlanta History Center are all the beneficiaries of League programs.

The list of past and current Atlanta League projects is long. The common thread has been need; the common response, service.

Today, the Junior League of Atlanta is the largest in the world. It is composed of over 5,000 women of many diverse backgrounds who share the belief that a personal commitment to voluntarism is essential to the betterment of the community as a whole.

All proceeds from League fundraising efforts, including those of this book, are returned to the community.

A few of the current programs developed and implemented by League volunteers include the following.

Atlanta History Center promotes the study of Atlanta history and the preservation of sources of information about that history. Volunteers serve as tour guides for the museum and historic houses such as the Tullie Smith House and the Swan House.

Atlanta Speech School volunteers assist teachers and staff with lesson planning, tutorials, art enrichment and other special projects at the teacher's discretion. This school was established by the Junior League of Atlanta in 1938 and has served generations of children and in recent years, seniors.

Dorcas House, a woman-centered program facility of the Atlanta Union Mission, provides food, shelter, clothing and personal development or rehabilitation for homeless and needy women.

Egleston At Home serves Egleston Children's Hospital at Emory University by hand-making hard to find pediatric items like gowns for premature babies, special vests for the gastro-intestinal ward and hand puppets for the children to decorate.

Egleston Day and Night assists doctors and nurses with patient care and the patients and their families with much-needed entertainment and support.

The Atlanta Children's Shelter, the first daytime shelter for homeless children whose parents are either seeking or have recently found employment, provides loving day care for children and vital support to the parents.

The Council on Battered Women aids battered women and their children through crisis counseling, children's in-shelter programs, and public awareness efforts.

The Family Literacy Project, the League's 75th anniversary gift to the city, focuses on reducing illiteracy—and thus improving employability—among young parents and their children in the Atlanta area.

The High Museum of Art program serves the community through art and art education. Volunteers work as docents, in hospital art therapy projects and in outreach programs in the Atlanta community.

The Native Plant Conservation Program, a part of the Atlanta Botanical Garden, helps the public to understand the importance of conservation. League volunteers serve as docents, in the preparation of educational materials, and in active recovery programs targeting endangered plants.

The Nearly New Shop, an important part of Atlanta for over 45 years, raises funds for targeted community agencies while it provides the public with a source of quality used clothing and goods for men, women and children.

The Scottish Rite Children's Medical Center provides comprehensive health care for infants, children and adolescents. League volunteers assist doctors, nurses and parents with patient care.

For more information about the Junior League of Atlanta, please contact us at 3154 Northside Parkway, N.W. Atlanta, Georgia, 30327.

CREDITS & ACKNOWLEDGEMENTS

True Grits could never have been realized without the dedication and shared vision of countless individuals. Our deepest gratitude goes to all those listed here and to anyone we may have inadvertently failed to mention. We thank you for your generous contributions of time, talent, energy, and resources.

SPECIAL THANKS

The Junior League of Atlanta expresses thanks and grateful appreciation to the following:

Alston & Bird
Benjamin T. White
Janet E. Witt
Jim Wolfson
Atlanta Convention & Visitors Bureau
Atlanta Journal and Atlanta Constitution
David Berney
Beverly Bremer
Faith Brunson
Buckhead Fine Wines
Buckhead Life Restaurant Group
Tracy Carnes, The Ritz-Carlton® Buckhead
Mark Conner
Ellen Corley
James David Dean
Robin DeFoe
Favorite Recipes Press
Roger Conner
Mary Cummings
Helen Hayes
Linda Jones
Dave Kempf
George McAllister
John Moulton
Debbie Van Mol
Mary Wilson
Vicky Meadows Favorite
Kay Goldstein
Susan Hancock, Rich's
David Scott Hinchman
Gerry Klaskala
David LeBoutillier
Lenox Square
The Lovett Schools
Cheryl & Philips Johnson
C. Randolph Jones, The Randolph Partnership
Oxford Books
Florine DeVeer
Roni Pastore
Lillian Yeilding
Pearson's Wine of Atlanta
Phipps Plaza
Chris Poole
John & Charles Robinson (Blue Seal Onions®)
Ron Scharbo
André Touzet
Trenton Tunnell

ILLUSTRATORS

Diane Borowski
Lindy Burnett
Sally Wern Comport
Cheryl Cooper
Don Morris
Brian Otto
Nip Rogers
Karen Strelecki
Elizabeth Traynor

PROFESSIONAL CREDITS

Mike Melia, Art Director
Rebecca D'Attilio, Designer
Audrey Bienz, Project Coordinator
Rhonda Rayburn, Account Executive
Barbara Teeslink,
   Typesetting/Production
Dianna Thorington, Writer
Kent Barton, Illustrator
   (*True Grits* logo)
Steve Pelosi, Photographer
Chris Cobb, Photographer's Assistant
Tracy Haas, Account Representative
Terry Colby, Food Stylist
Andrea Frank, Food Stylist's
   Assistant
Beverly Beard, Prop Stylist
Kiki Pollard, Illustrator's
   Representative

PHOTO CREDITS

Beverly Bremer Silver Shop
Bittersweet Antiques, Ltd.
City Art Works
Deering Antiques
   (formerly Heirloom Wicker)
Garson Goodman
Nottingham Antiques
Pier One
The Stalls: Judy Bartel, Forget Me
   Not, Mary Baldwin Antiques,
   Cowboy, Once Upon a Time, Mary
   Barry, Nancy Brittain Antiques.
Williams Sonoma
Fragile
Alfresco at Interiors Market, Bennett
   Street
Smith Hanes

CHEF CONTRIBUTORS TO TRUE GRITS

Art Institute of Atlanta
Atlanta Catering Company
Aunt Sara's Bakery (Sara McGaha)
Bacchanalia (Chef Clifford)
Brasserie LaCoze Restaurant
Benton & Associates Caterers
Bistango
Buckhead Diner (Daniel O'Leary)
Canoe (Gerry Klaskala)
Chef's Grill (Michael Gravely)
Cherokee Town and Country Club
   (Mark Erickson)
Chops (Tom Minchella)

City Grill (Roger M. Kaplan)
Ciboulette Restaurant
Terry Colby
The Dessert Place
To Dine For (Robin Churchill)
Doubletree Hotel
Linda Easterlin Caterers
The Easy Way Out
Events Catering (Caroline Wilkerson)
Gary & Forsythia (Gary Ronin)
Georgia Grille (Karen Hilliard)
Georgian Club (Bruce Bartz)
Horseradish Grill (Scott Peacock)
Huntcliff Summit (Chris D. Kerr)
Lindy's (Linda Beigh & Patrick Foster)
Luna Si (Chef Luna)
Mary Mac's Tea Room
   (Marge Klepinger)
Pano's & Paul's (Paul Albrecht)
Piedmont Driving Club
   (Ex Chef Pierre DuPont)
The Peasant Restaurants
Pricci (John Carver)
Ritz-Carlton–Buckhead
   (Gunter Seeger; Mauro Canaglia;
   David Robins)
Robinson Humphrey, Inc.
   (Ex Chef Peggy Foreman)
South City Kitchen
   (Travis Holewinski)
Tom Tom
   (Tom Catheral & Richard Jones)
Tres Bien
Vickery's (Jerry Nagler)
Vinings Club (Jack Shoop)

RECIPE CONTRIBUTORS

Holly L. Abel
Elizabeth Turner Ables
Cynthia Hinrichs Acree
Susan Holland Adams
Anne Jentzen Addison
Kristina Alexander
Terry Alexander
Susanne Pichard Alford
Patti Lander Allaman
Alexandra M. Allen
Cathy Hesselman Allen
Jennifer Johnson Allen
Nancy Dameron Almquist
Elizabeth K. Ambler
Ginger Haddow Amoni
Debbie McParland Andrews
Karen Apple
Jane Lauderdale Armstrong
Deborah London Arnold
Kelly Legare Augenstein
Judy Farrington Aust
Angela Averett-Rock
Deborah Roach Avery
Mimi Jenkins Baird
Ann Girand Baker
Virginia Rosemond Baldwin
Susan Anne Baldwin
Jinx Baldwin
Sandra Haynie Baldwin
Rosemary K. Barber
Ann Skobba Barrett
Shelley Sharp Bass
Johannah Bauknight

Mary Crain Beard
Ellen Marshall Beard
Judi D. Beck
Allyson Parr Beckley
Dianne L. Zeiller Beidel
Mary Ann Bender
L. Cameron Bennett
Barbara Elebash Benson
Suzanne W. Bergmann
Beth Beskin
Betsy Alexander Best
Erin Conner Blair
Anne Burckhardt Block
Susan Westmoreland Bloomfield
Anna Bauer Bonaparte
Marie C. Bond
Susan Botha
Laura Hailey Bowen
Claire Olliff Bowen
Laura Walker Bozzolo
Kitty D. Bray
Jill Chestnut Brennan
Lisa Ward Bridges
Margaret Ann Briggs
Laura Brightwell
Virginia G. Brooks
Cynthia Briscoe Brown
Maribeth Ryman Brown
Bettina Schiebler Brown
Paige Lammerts Brown
Frank W. Brown
Tami Lewis Brown
Janet Brooks Brunson
Nina Sledge Burke
Eleanor H. Burke
Leslie Maloney Burns
Carol Preller Bush
Sara E. Cahillane
Nancy Owen Caldwell
Margaret Leonard Camac
Diane Winkler Campbell
Mary Jane Simmons Candler
Linda Pretz Candler
Jenny Gordy Cannon
Laura Briscoe Carey
Myrna Iddings Carlock
Catherine Pennell Carney
Julie Riley Carr
William Pitts Carr
Tara Schultz Carvin
Dr. J. K. Champion
Lynda Chapman
Ellen Harris Chastain
Susan Fawcett Chewning
Bonnie Childers
Helen W. Christiansen
Dalin Clark
Margaret McEver Cobb
Pamela B. Coffey
Frances Coile
Laurie McBrayer Coleman
Jamie G. Collier
Bonnie Bailey Collings
Frances Oehmig Collins
Ansley Merritt Conner
Stiles Young Conrad
Elizabeth Raines Cook
Carolynn Cooper
Angela Tarkenton Cordle
Jan M. Costas
Sara Stewart Cotton
Michelle A. Couch
Marlys Lenz Cox
Claire Collier Cronk
Ashley Crosier
Lucy Sparkman Crosswell
Catherine Davis Culberson
Carol C. Culp
Louise Vaughan Cunningham
Hana Cunningham
Laura Smith Currie
Jan Busbee Curtis
Carol Huey Danaher

Nancy Zax Darden
Mary B. Davenport
Theresa Maiuri Dean
Gail Robinson Dearing
Mary Frances Dennis
Missy Haydel Diaz
Michelle J. DiPauli
Amanda Templeton DiResta
Trish Dooley
Elizabeth S. Downey
Lee Yeilding Downey
Lianne Akin Driver
Mary M. Drye
Ann Clodfelter DuPre
Harriett Dwyer
Nan Storey Easterlin
Judy Ebert
Page Moore Edenfield
Jo Ann Pate Edwards
Jane G. Elias
Janet M. Elliot
Linda S. Elliot
Jean Elliott
Deborah Hicks Ellis
Paula Fry Elmore
Barbara Erickson
Amy Ginn Eubanks
Kim Dice Evans
Susan McLeod Farrow
Nancy S. Faux
Stephanie Guice Feininger
Barbara Feinour
Lee Ann S. Fennessy
Michele Ebbeskotte Fields
Joanne L. FitzGerald
Renee Massey Fitzpatrick
Maribeth Fletcher
Jane Shatten Flowerree
Katherine Whitesides Fristoe
Griffin D. Fry
Sandy Coleman Furrh
Elizabeth F. Wineland Gamble
Alesa Garner
Terrell Garrard
Virginia Garrett
Laura Jane Gash
Lucinda A. Gibson
Sabina Miller Gilbert
Donna Schneidewind Gilli
Jean Candler Glenn
Sarah Reese Glover
Kelly Ann Goggin
Shirley Timewell Golden
Claire Lindsey Graham
Deborah Dever Gray
Leslie Ann Greely
Allyson Edwards Greene
Lynda Harris (Grove) Griffin
Mary V. Grigsby
Cynthia Smith Grinnell
Marlene Turner Grisham
Jane Elias Grumman
Monica Kirwan Gummig
Betsy O'Brien Hackman
Peggy Wardle Hagood
Mary Stewart Hagy
Cathy Young Hall
Ruth Chapman Hancock
Mary Ann Layden Hardman
Norma M. Hardy
Susie R. Harman
Darcy Carter Harper
Linda Spofford Harris
Dana L. Harrison
Merrel Callaway Hattink
Betsy Clayton Heaberg
Carolyn King Hearn
Jane Warren Hedgepeth
Virginia Hendrick
Anne Taylor Hendry
Barbara Henkel
Gay Henry
Peggy E. Herndon

Kendle Jenkins Hessinger
Ann Smith Hewatt
Lori Koch Heys
Kathy Johnstone Hibbitts
Stacie Wigley Hill
Melissa Davis Hinchman
Carol Wallace Hinrichs
Sue Taylor Hinton
Kimberly C. Hodgson
Wilburta Trout Holden
Lane Holt
Glenda B. Hope
Teri Mack Hopkins
Jane G. Houghton
Kat Howard
Judith Turton Hoyt
Russell Carden Huber
Erin D. Hunsinger
Susanna Hyatt
Faith Carter Inglis
Janice C. Irvine
Maribeth Moore Jameson
John W. R. Jenkins
Emily Farber Rubin Jennewein
Shannon W. Johnson
Beverly K. Johnson
Victoria Ridinger Jones
Trish Sheehan Jones
Susan Bowen Joyner
Gay Mitchell Kattel
Kelli Hennessy Keb
Jane Ray Kell
Carol C. Kelley
Beth S. Kempe
Margaret Taylor Kendrick
Jacqueline Thiesen Kennedy
Holly Jensen Kerr
Sal Kibler
Jenny Lee Kirby
Kathleen Parson Klatt
Clair Krizov
Ann Bierbower Lally
Cathy Wilson LaMon
Anne MacDaniel Landis
Margaret Stitt Lantz
Mitzi Harris Lau
Lisa Patterson Lawrence
Karen Lanier League
Alice Gumbert Lebkuecher
Susan J. Leithead
Betty Hollifield Leonard
Caroline E. Lesesne
Reet O. Lewis
Joanna Alfieris Link
Julie M. Little
Debbi Baldwin Little
Millie Avery Lochridge
Susie D. Lochridge
Lisa Wray Longino
Sherry Lundeen
Annis Paschal Lyles
Katrina V. Mabon
Nancy Rogers MacDonald
Bonnie Bell MacNaughton
Virginia Herbst Maffitt
Joanne Letts Magbee
Suzanne McMillin Maiden
Melissa Malmberg
Jennifer Manning
Melissa R. Marsh
Cary Cox Martin
Susan Garrett Mason
L. Gardiner Mason
Janet Bell Matlock
Bonnie Bell Mausz
Melinda D. Maxwell
Megan E. McArn
Anne Hodges McClatchey
Kimberly Schlundt McCollam
Sara Williams McDaniel
Liz Moore McDermott
Dorothy Allison McDougall
Jane Whitney McGreevy

Robin Brower McKenzie
Judy McLaurine
Ann Joye McLeod
Dianna G. McShane
Anne DemÉrÈMeeker
Lisa M. Menendez
Donna C. Merck
Elizabeth O. Merritt
Beth Armknecht Miller
Cathey Jones Millichap
Anne Edgerton Mills
Carolyn Rose Milner
Jana Baxley Minter
Elizabeth Millsap Mixon
Arue Norris Moore
Ellen Peters Morrison
Penny Morriss
Tanya Oakley Murphy
Beth Lyon Murray
Septima Porcher Murray
Coleman Mobley Nalley
Frances Erickson Naugle
Laurine Gray Nazworth
Betsy Ziegler Neesley
Elizabeth Dale Nellums
Nan Newman
Becky Jo Dilcher Nickles
Katherine Rich Niehaus
Betty Yopp Nunnally
Elizabeth O'Brien
Mary Catherine O'Kelley
Emily Haltom Olsen
Renata Summerford Parker
Nancy Parker Parson
Pamela Poole Payne
Kelley Bogle Peace
Elizabeth Anderson Perkins
Sue Oswald Peterson
Lawrie Canale Peyton
Ginny Phillippi
Mary Upshaw Pike
Pat Fitzhugh Plomgren
Carey Mills Poole
Barbara L. Propst
Nina M. Radakovich
Deborah Collins Ragen
Beth Bickley Reagan
Holly Holder Reese
Sarah Anne Reese
Betsy Coleman Rehmert
Mary Anne Wagstaff Richardson
Virginia Beverly Ring
Donna M. Ritchie
Phyllis Royster Rivers
Mike Roe
Dana L. Rogers
Ashley Sutherland Rogers
Michelle Ellenburg Rolader
Cathy Craig Rollins
Michaella Collins Roman
Mary Scott Rooker
Beaumont Rooker
Stefanini S. Rosemond
Barbara Rosse
Laura Mims Routt
Nancy J. Rowen
Julie Carter Rowland
Elizabeth Cassels Rubenoff
Lynn Mount Rudder
Ellen Martin Sanders
Julie Sand Sanders
Mary Cisco Satcher
Sandee Murphree Schaefer
Kellie Taylor Schonberg
Eileen E. Schroder
Claire Peterson Schwall
Mary Bondurant Scurry
Marilyn Denise Selles
Mary Brooks Morgan Sewell
Helen Schley Sharpley
Helen Thompson Sharpley
Arlene Baldwin Shatten
Sylvia Tabor Shealy

Kimberly Osias Sheldon
Karen E. Shepherd
Teresa Penley Sheppard
Emily C. Shiels
Tad F. Shineman
Brenda Ewan Shute
Allison Miller Sinkler
Judy Slavinski
Early C. Smith
Susan Lorenzo Smith
Margaret Vance Snoke
Margaret Kelly Sonnier
Elizabeth Morgan Spiegel
Lorraine G. Staats
Libby Hughes Stamps
Nancy Dalton Steele
Reba Willis Stewart
Lucy Holman Stone
Linda S. Stovall
Janet Lea Street
Leslie Lanier Stumpff
Sandy Sturdivant
Maria C. Suarez
Leslie Stewart Sullivan
Sandra Lynne Sumner
Erika Anderson Swartzwelder
Catherine Cardoso Sweat
Madelon E. Sweat
Mary Frances Taormina
Jane Taylor
Amy Taylor
Susan Tabas Tepper
Berkeley Lupton Teston
Kevin Allen Teston
Lynn Thatcher
Deborah L. Thompson
Beth Wilson Thomsen
Meg Lines Thrash
Allen M. Thrasher
Maida Yates Tipping
Sarah Robinson Topfl
Beth Bishop Touzet
Martha Trammell
Kris Pappas Trotman
Nancy Santon Turner
Margaret E. Turner
Kim B. Turner
Beth Tye
Laurie Tyler
Jean Barry Underwood
Angela C. Valen
Elizabeth Adams Vann
Kelley M. Ventulett
Anne Trumpf Wallis
Wendy L. Warner
Teresa Smith Waters
Melissa Reaves Weatherly
Clare Magbee Weaver
Kathy Weiss
Pamela Miller Welsch
Cricket Werkheiser
Nannette Manning West
Kristin Danbury Whatley
Barbara Palmer White
Peyton Potter White
Pat Kaplan Wiedemann
Sharon Williams
Meredith Little Williams
Jane H. Willson
Victoria Abbott Willson
Diane Louise Wilson
Cathy Young Wilson
Camille M. Wingate
Elizabeth A. Witman
Kathleen Marie Wood
Catherine Eagles Woodward
Ann Michele Worrall
Lynne Griffin Yancey
Mary Mitchell Yates
Lee Klie Yeilding
Janie Louise Yntema
Joyce Rosemond Young
Martie Edmunds Zakas

NUTRITIONAL PROFILE

ABBREVIATIONS FOR NUTRITIONAL PROFILE

Cal — Calories	
Prot — Protein	
Carbo — Carbohydrates	
Fiber — Dietary Fiber	
T Fat — Total Fat	
Chol — Cholesterol	
Sod — Sodium	
g — grams	
mg — milligrams	

Nutritional information for these recipes is computed from information derived from many sources, including materials supplied by the United States Department of Agriculture, computer databanks, and journals in which the information is assumed to be in the public domain. However, many specialty items, new products, and processed foods may not be available from these sources or may vary from the average values used in these profiles. More information on new and/or specific products may be obtained by reading the nutrient labels. Unless otherwise specified, the nutritional profile of these recipes is based on all measurements being level.

- *Artificial sweeteners* vary in use and strength so should be used "to taste," using the recipe ingredients as a guideline. Sweeteners using aspartame (NutraSweet and Equal) should not be used as a sweetener in recipes involving prolonged heating, which reduces the sweet taste. For further information on the use of these sweeteners, refer to package.

- *Alcoholic ingredients* have been analyzed for the basic ingredients, although cooking causes the evaporation of alcohol, thus decreasing caloric content.

- *Buttermilk, sour cream,* and *yogurt* are the types available commercially.

- *Cake mixes* which are prepared using package directions include 3 eggs and 1/2 cup oil.

- *Chicken,* cooked for boning and chopping, has been roasted; this method yields the lowest caloric values.

- *Cottage cheese* is cream-style with 4.2% creaming mixture. Dry curd cottage cheese has no creaming mixture.

- *Eggs* are all large. To avoid raw eggs that may carry salmonella, as in eggnog or 6-week muffin batter, use an equivalent amount of commercial egg substitute.

- *Flour* is unsifted all-purpose flour.

- *Garnishes,* serving suggestions, and other optional additions and variations are not included in the profile.

- *Margarine* and *butter* are regular, not whipped or presoftened.

- *Milk* is whole milk, 3.5% butterfat. Lowfat milk is 1% butterfat. Evaporated milk is whole milk with 60% of the water removed.

- *Oil* is any type of vegetable cooking oil. *Shortening* is hydrogenated vegetable shortening.

- *Salt* and other ingredients to taste as noted in the ingredients have not been included in the nutritional profile.

- If a choice of ingredients has been given, the nutritional profile reflects the first option. If a choice of amounts has been given, the nutritional profile reflects the greater amount.

PG #	RECIPE TITLE (APPROX PER SERVING)	CAL	PROT (G)	CARBO (G)	T FAT (G)	% CAL FROM FAT	CHOL (MG)	FIBER (G)	SOD (MG)
13	WHITE BEAN DIP	27	2	5	<1	6	<1	2	113
16	ASIAN CHICKEN FINGERS	209	24	22	3	12	64	1	296
30	ULTIMATE SALSA	28	<1	2	2	65	0	1	153
38	FRESH FRUIT SOUP	128	5	18	5	31	16	4	58
38	PEACH AND RASPBERRY SOUP	293	5	38	3	13	19	5	39
43	ESPRESSO BLACK BEAN CHILI WITH GRITS	413	14	67	11	23	0	15	1153
45	TORTILLA SOUP+	441	37	31	19	39	78	5	1906
46	HEARTY VEGETABLE SOUP	207	10	41	3	10	4	10	904
48	WILD MUSHROOM SOUP	249	7	30	12	39	14	6	445
52	ALMOND SALAD WITH ORANGE VINAIGRETTE*	371	4	18	34	78	0	4	55
54	WHITE BEAN SALAD*	138	7	18	5	30	0	2	53
56	CALYPSO SALAD	217	6	26	11	43	0	5	457
57	ORIENTAL COLESLAW*	225	4	16	17	65	0	2	207
58	LENTIL AND MUSHROOM SALAD*	218	11	23	10	41	0	5	679
60	RED PEPPER AND TOMATO COUSCOUS SALAD	173	5	27	6	28	0	2	149
64	GREEN SALAD WITH LEMON DRESSING*	189	3	6	19	83	0	2	466
66	SPINACH AND STRAWBERRY SALAD*	466	6	42	34	61	0	5	53
69	CHICKEN SALAD WITH WILD RICE*	530	29	21	38	64	60	2	607
78	GREEN BEANS WITH PEPPERS AND LEEKS	104	3	13	5	38	0	4	368
81	FRUITED CARROTS	233	2	42	7	24	16	7	115
85	SPICY CORN STIR-FRY	145	3	22	7	38	16	4	104
88	SUGAR SNAP PEAS WITH LEMON AND BASIL	93	5	13	3	25	0	5	273
89	STUFFED YELLOW PEPPERS	284	6	51	8	23	0	2	43
90	SCALLOPED POTATOES WITH GARDEN TOMATOES	317	9	42	14	38	29	5	542
94	ACORN SQUASH WITH APPLE STUFFING	427	5	69	19	36	23	12	105
95	SWEET POTATO SOUFFLE	278	4	44	10	33	80	3	98
101	GRILLED VEGETABLE KABOBS#	86	4	19	1	7	0	5	644
102	VEGETABLE PAELLA	527	22	93	7	12	2	5	1874
109	ANGLE HAIR PASTA WITH MUSSELS AND TOMATOES	681	32	95	12	16	40	4	278
111	PASTA WITH ITALIAN SAUSAGE AND VEGETABLES	524	22	66	20	33	38	7	649
114	FETTUCCINI WITH SCALLOPS	317	20	43	6	18	23	2	430
116	SEAFOOD PASTA CAKES	450	21	58	14	29	181	2	257
118	SOUTHWESTERN SPAGHETTI	557	22	68	26	39	30	5	595
121	PAELLA VALENCIANA	672	45	63	23	31	110	4	729
123	WILD RICE WITH OYSTERS	293	18	34	10	30	79	1	865
125	HEARTY MUSHROOM RISOTTO	232	8	33	5	20	4	1	504
128	CREAMY POLENTA WITH MINT AND CHERVIL	290	10	36	12	37	38	2	205

Pg #	Recipe Title (Approx Per Serving)	Cal	Prot (g)	Carbo (g)	T Fat (g)	% Cal from Fat	Chol (mg)	Fiber (g)	Sod (mg)
132	Grilled Sea Bass with Pink-Eyed Ragout	377	37	22	16	37	74	8	373
134	Spanish-Style Orange Roughy	126	18	5	4	28	24	1	264
140	Grilled Swordfish#	440	46	0	27	57	91	0	209
151	Grilled Shrimp with Black Bean Salad	407	30	56	9	20	158	12	1165
164	Duck Breasts with Port and Grapefruit Sauce	388	35	11	15	35	155	<1	302
172	Beef with Apricots and Leeks	402	30	40	12	27	80	3	336
184	Roast Pork#	245	36	2	9	33	92	<1	738
186	Pork Loin with Plum Sauce	402	43	27	13	30	118	<1	563
198	Coca-Cola Cake	463	3	74	19	35	73	1	41
204	Bourbon Pound Cake	407	5	56	17	36	117	1	229
206	Easy Blueberry Cobbler	285	3	49	10	30	50	2	142
207	Peach Cobbler	441	3	71	17	35	48	1	289
215	Pineapple Sour Cream Pie	393	5	58	16	37	92	1	324
220	Almond Cakes with Cinnamon Port Wine Pears	661	7	72	27	35	153	7	258
227	Low-Fat Creme Caramel	108	5	19	1	8	2	0	81
230	Summer Fruit Terrine	190	2	37	3	14	8	1	167
231	Minted Fruits with Ginger	164	1	30	1	3	0	3	3
232	Kiwifruit Frozen Yogurt	113	4	22	1	9	4	1	56
233	Mango Sorbet	121	1	32	<1	3	0	3	4
233	Tangerine Ice	227	1	57	<1	1	0	<1	2
240	Raspberry Sauce	36	<1	7	<1	3	0	1	<1
242	Cold Lemon Souffle with Raspberry Sauce	384	6	59	14	33	173	3	53
246	Spiced Hazelnut and Chocolate Biscotti	79	2	12	3	37	16	1	26
247	Apricot Squares	92	1	14	4	35	0	<1	53
247	Chocolate Scotcheroos	185	3	29	8	35	<1	1	127
256	Ginger Cookies	80	1	12	3	39	0	<1	85
274	Banana Nut Bran Muffins	202	4	32	8	33	18	3	317
275	Low-Fat Muffins	232	4	41	6	23	18	2	249
278	Crazy Monkey Bread	129	2	19	6	38	14	1	146
279	Orange Bread	211	3	42	3	14	20	1	246
280	Peanut Buttermilk Bread	155	5	25	4	25	18	<1	222
281	Pumpkin Bread	260	3	40	10	35	35	1	221
282	Apple Pancake Tatin	587	6	101	19	28	77	3	562
288	Special Coffee	29	<1	6	<1	<1	1	<1	16
288	Miss Priss Punch	47	<1	12	<1	1	0	<1	4

+ Nutritional profile does not include oil for frying.
* Nutritional profile includes entire amount of dressing.
# Nutritional profile includes entire amount of marinade.

INDEX